~ THE LONG PATROL ~

This book is dedicated to
BOB HALL and HILARY BLYTHE
whose faith and encouragement
have always been music to my ears.

The Long Patrol

The British in Germany Since 1945

Roy Bainton

MAINSTREAM
PUBLISHING

EDINBURGH AND LONDON

First published in Great Britain in 2003 by
MAINSTREAM PUBLISHING (EDINBURGH) LTD
7 Albany Street
Edinburgh EH1 3UG

ISBN 1 84018 715 8

A catalogue record for this book is available from the British Library

Typeset in Apollo and Cochin

Printed in Great Britain by
Creative Print & Design Wales

Acknowledgements: The Long Patrollers

To all of the following who served at various times in BAOR, without whose detailed recollections this book would not exist, I offer my sincere thanks for your contributions.

1945–60
Ronald Loveday, M.V. Bayes, Terry Barber, Harry Jackson, Dennis Pell, Albert Winstanley, Jed Cressy, John Appleby, Geoff Gilbert, J.G. Rooth, J.E. Booth, Alec Kingsmill, Gordon Cox, Allen Parker, Gerald Gurney, Ted Levy, Stan Roberts, Peter Daniels, George Walker, Gerda Walker, Norman Baldwin, R. Doney, John Saville, Hugh Martin, Betty R. Radley, Adrian Cooper, Margaret Shelley, Mrs H. Roberts, Rosalee Meehan, Bob McLaughlin, Andrew Burns, Iain Leggatt, Major Reg Jones

1960–70
Jimmy King, Phil 'Tommo' Thompson, Brian Morris, T. Clark BEM, Hilary Plews, Susan Cullen, Brian Airey, Iain Leggatt, Don Rowley, Charlie Landsborough, George Enderby

1970–89
Carole Gladman, Janine Soyer, Cheryl Ciccone, Dr Hugh Thomas, Shirley Houston, Marguerite Frost, Rosemary Blackwood, Lieutenant Colonel Robin Greenham, Martin McIntyre, Nigel Dunkley MBE, Mike Robinson

IN GERMANY
Carolyn Battey, Media Operations, Herford; Mike Whitehurst, Information Officer, Herford; Warrant Officer Will Betts, Herford;

Colin Gordon, Liaison, Herford; Major Martin Waters, Sennelager; Lieutenant-Colonel Martin Bacon, Sennelager; Simon Tanner, Sennelager; Erich Kessler, Bielefeld; Madeline Donelly, Gütersloh; Warrant Officer Dave Walkley, Gütersloh; Stephan Grimm, Gütersloh; Erwin Gotthald, Berlin; Lieutenant Colonel Robin Greenham, Berlin; Nigel Dunkley MBE, Berlin; Gunter Steinmeyer, Berlin; BFBS, Germany; *Soldier* magazine; Sixth Sense; The Museum of The Allied Forces, Berlin; The Checkpoint Charlie Museum, Berlin; and special thanks to the MOD for their help.

AND SPECIAL THANKS TO:
My agent, Malcolm Imrie, for his faith and support in this project; to my wife, Wendy, for suffering yet another year of penury; to Bill Campbell at Mainstream; my son, Dr Martin Bainton for his support; Jane Aisbitt; Graeme Blaikie and Will Mackie at Mainstream; my daughter Sarah and her partner, Ivan Ball, for their continuing encouragement; Peter Jackson, Mark Chamberlain and the members of The Over The Hill Club for always buying my books; and Peter Moody, for making life easier.

Contents

DIVIDED BERLIN 1945-1989

In 1949, the repercussions of the Berlin Airlift created further political tension between the eastern and western blocs. The three western zones – British, American and French – were fused together to become the Federal Republic of Germany (FDR) or West Germany. In the east, the Soviets formed the German Democratic Republic (GDR), which would become known as East Germany. West Berlin kept its zones and East Berlin became the capital of East Germany, whilst Bonn became the capital of West Germany. In 1951 Walter Ulbricht became leader of the GDR until 1971, when he was replaced by Erich Honecker. Dissatisfaction in the East had led to a mass revolt among the population in 1953 that was quickly subdued by Soviet troops. In 1955, the GDR joined the Warsaw Pact, whilst West Germany joined the North Atlantic Treaty Organisation (NATO). In 1961, an estimated four million crossed from the East to the West, which prompted the Soviets to build the Berlin Wall. Following mass demonstrators in Berlin on 1989, the wall was finally breached, and by July 1990 Germany was reunited.

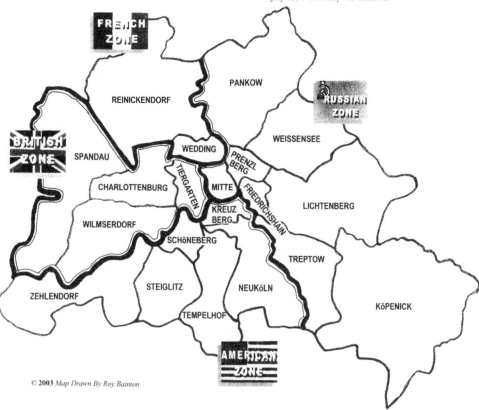

© 2003 Map Drawn By Roy Bainton

A Brief Guide to Army Organisation

Army Group This is usually commanded by a **field marshal** and consists of several armies grouped together with as many as a million soldiers involved.

Army Commanded by a **general** or a **lieutenant-general**, this consists of various **corps** usually numbering up to 450,000 men.

Corps Consist of a number of **divisions** numbering anywhere between 75,000 and 150,000 men. Corps are under the command of either a lieutenant-general or a **major-general**.

Division This is made up of a number of **brigades** commanded by a major-general. A division can number up to 20,000 soldiers.

Brigade This is formed from **regiments** or **battalions** commanded by a **brigadier** or a **brigadier-general**, and can number up to 8,000 men.

Regiment In the British Army a **regiment** is an administrative body which organises all the operations of the services and arms, with the exception of infantry, which operates under the title 'battalion'.

Battalions are mainly formed from infantry; they are a formation of around 600 to 1,000 soldiers under the command of a **lieutenant-colonel**. The battalion consists of various **companies**.

Company (or squadron) This is a group of soldiers, usually numbering up to 150 men. It is commanded by a **major** or a **captain** and is broken down into smaller units known as **platoons**.

Platoons usually consist of up to 30 men and are sometimes referred to as **troops**. A platoon is commanded by a **junior officer**.

Section This is the Army's smallest fighting formation of up to ten soldiers, commanded by an **NCO** (non-commissioned officer). (The Americans refer to this grouping as a 'squad'.)

After the Second World War, Germany was divided into four zones of control: British, American, French and Russian. The western zones were fused to become West Germany in 1949. The immediate post-war period was accompanied by the mass movement of millions of refugees and displaced persons. Following economic recovery in the West as a result of the Marshall Plan, in 1957 the European Economic Comunity (EEC) was formed. In the East, Soviet reparations drained the economy, the result being that recovery did not get under way until the death of Stalin in 1953.

BALTIC SEA

NETHERLANDS

○ Hamburg

○ Bremen

BRITISH ZONE

○ Berlin

POLAND

BELGIUM

○ Köln (Cologne)

○ Hannover

RUSSIAN ZONE

○ Dresden

FRANCE

○ Frankfurt

CZECHOSLOVAKIA

DIVIDED GERMANY

FRENCH ZONE

○ Stuttgart

AMERICAN ZONE

○ Munich

SWITZERLAND

AUSTRIA

ITALY

© 2003 *Map Drawn By Roy Bainton*

Army Ranks

There are a great number of ranks in the Army depending on which department – Infantry, Armour or Artillery – soldiers are serving in, so this again is a very basic overview of the chain of command. For instance, the rank of private goes under a number of titles; if he's serving with the Royal Electrical and Mechanical Engineers (REME), he's known as 'craftsman'; in the Royal Signals he'll be 'signalman'; in the Guards a 'guardsman'; and in the Special Air Service (SAS) he'd be a 'trooper'.

The following, from the top down, gives an elementary view of ranks. The British Army has also taken on the US Army's 'star system' for Generals, and these are noted below.

Field marshal (5 stars)
General (4 stars)
Lieutenant-general (3 Stars)
Major-general 2 stars)
Brigadier (1 star)
Colonel
Lieutenant-colonel
Major
Captain
Lieutenant
Second-lieutenant (both lieutenants and second-lieutenants are also referred to as subalterns)
Regimental sergeant-major (RSM) is a warrant officer class I
Company sergeant-major (CSM) is a warrant officer class II
Colour-sergeant
Sergeant
Corporal
Lance-corporal
Private

Glossary & List of Abbreviations

Battle Group Mixed force with tanks, armoured vehicles and infantry
Bundeswehr Germany's post-war armed forces
Lumpie A slang Army term for a female soldier
Redcap Military Police (noted for their red headgear)
Singlies Unmarried soldiers
Squaddie A general slang term for soldiers usually at the rank of private
Stag Sentry duty
Tour (or **Tour of Duty**) Denotes a period of service in a particular location
Towel Head Slang term for an Arab
WRAC Women's Royal Army Corps
AAC Army Air Corps
BAOR British Army of the Rhine
BFBS British Forces Broadcasting Service
BFES British Forces Education Service
BFPO British Forces Post Office
ENSA Entertainments National Service Association
FDR *Federal Deutsches Republic* – the Federal Republic of Germany (known as West Germany)
GDR German Democratic Republic (East Germany)
GPO General Post Office
NAAFI Navy, Army and Air Force Institutes
PONTI Person of No Tactical Importance
RA Royal Artillery
RAEC Royal Army Educational Corps
RAMC Royal Army Medical Corps
RAOC Royal Army Ordnance Corps
RAPC Royal Army Pay Corps
RCT Royal Corps of Transport
REME Royal Electrical and Mechanical Engineers
RMP Royal Military Police
STASI *Ministerium für Staatssicherheit* – East German Ministry of State Security

Introduction

From 7 May 1945 we put our rifles away and got to work. After Hamburg we went to Duisburg. We cleared mines, stray bombs (our bombs!) from the autobahns. Our main job was bridges, started at Düsseldorf, on to Wesel, Marienborn, working all the way back to Hamburg. When you called [your book] *The Long Patrol*, you got it right. But think – it was men like myself and my comrades who had made it. A lot did not.

> Ronald Loveday, Lance Corporal, London Bomb Disposal

Shiny, chromium plated, it stood out amongst the other dusty bric-a-brac and caught my eye. It was five inches by three and even without my reading glasses I could see the familiar outline of a map of what was once called West Germany engraved on the front.

How this old cigarette case came to be in an antiques arcade in the cosy little market town of Louth in Lincolnshire will remain a mystery. The man on the stall couldn't tell me. Once I had my glasses on it intrigued me even more. The North Sea was engraved in German as '*Nordsee*'. At the bottom right-hand corner of the map was the legend 'The British Zone In Germany'. And there were all the towns and cities I remembered from childhood.

Back in the 1950s, when Judith Chalmers would get into her stride every Sunday lunchtime on BBC radio's *Family Favourites*, without fail those seemingly strange locations would figure largely: Osnabrück, Hanover, Detmold, Münster, Oldenburg, Sennelager.

It was hard to imagine how far away these places were. Back then, of course, before the British discovered holidays abroad, Germany still seemed as distant to us as Mars or Venus. Today we can leave the

Midlands at breakfast time and be in Frankfurt for tea – a journey which, in my childhood, would have seemed like a major expedition.

Yet in those mysterious places, from where soldiers wrote postcards from British Forces Post Office (BFPO) addresses requesting the latest chart hit by Elvis Presley, Little Richard or Lonnie Donegan, lived thousands of British servicemen. Many were regulars, thousands more were reluctant recruits enduring their two years' national service. Even as I grew older, 'our boys' in Germany continued to figure large in our lives. Well into the '70s and '80s it seemed as if there was a very large corner of that conquered foreign field which would be forever England – and Scotland, Ireland and Wales.

Today, the British are not afraid of Europe. They buy houses in France and apartments in Spain and Portugal. But Germany? That's a different place. For the British experience of life in Germany there are no Peter Mayle memoirs nor any wistful Stella Artois adverts. Although there's a lot of pleasure to be had in Deutschland, it seems to come across to us as too 'businesslike' for a holiday venue. Our experience of Germany is a military one, although prior to writing this book, having a German grandfather, I have frequently toured the country in an attempt to discover my own roots and study the German character.

The Germans have always been an industrious, law-abiding people. There used to be a cynical notion among some Allied politicians following the fall of the Third Reich that, with the establishment of the Federal Republic in 1949, the Germans had taken to their new-found democracy 'because they had been ordered to do so'. Yet there has always been a degree of obedience and correctness in German society which still impresses the more laid-back British visitor.

We have been conditioned over the decades since the Second World War to accept a stereotyped view of our European neighbours, the classic example of which is John Cleese's 'Don't mention the war' episode in the hilarious *Fawlty Towers* series. Often it was hard to resist.

I narrowly escaped national service in the late '50s by going to sea in the merchant navy. But that seven-year experience of living for long periods of time in the enclosed environment of a tramp steamer, with all its attendant traditions and comradeship, is not dissimilar to that which creates the bond between soldiers. The difference was that as simple civilian sailors, we were not armed or constantly expecting a Third World War. The only Russians we saw were passing vessels similar to ours, just enigmatic floating islands of the Soviet regime, with their hammer-and-sickle funnel markings and red flags. Their politics didn't particularly matter; like us, they were simple sailors.

Not coming from a military background, I did wonder just how interesting this project might be, yet after taking a look at the statistics that revealed that over those four decades hundreds of thousands of men, women and children had undergone this German experience, it became more intriguing. Although the RAF were also stationed in Germany during those years, the general perception of the period has always centred on the Army's presence. BAOR was an abbreviation known to all, so without wishing to make light of our flyers' German experience, it seemed simpler from my point of view to keep this story in khaki. To prepare a proposal for the book I placed a series of letters in provincial newspapers asking readers if they had been in the forces and stationed in Germany at any time between 1945 and 1990. The resulting mailbag plunged me into hours of fascinating reading, telephone conversations and face-to-face interviews, and within a very short time I realised that here was a hitherto neglected chapter of British social history, detached from the mother country.

Soldiers remember numbers, regiments, exercises and their mates. They also remember the countries they served in and how they felt about their locations overseas. Men like Bob Spragg, who emailed me his complete Army career, recalled that 'My total service was 22 years and 117 days'. The months, days and hours seemed even more important to the national service conscripts.

The German military experience had produced a new breed of Brit abroad. No matter what your opinion of the EU, as I discovered on my visits to today's Army bases, many of these fatigue-clad ex-pats seemed, by their attitude, to represent the new European just as much as Jacques Delors or Helmut Kohl. From the preparatory reading I had done I fully expected to meet young soldiers seething with xenophobia, living an insular life in their secure UK enclaves, complete with HP Sauce, PG Tips and jars of Marmite. To some degree the latter part of that expectation was correct, but on the whole my preconceptions were obliterated after my first hour at the

British Army's Wentworth Barracks in Herford, Northern Germany.

The end of the Cold War has altered the atmosphere. There are already many books in print which deal with the history of the Cold War, NATO and the various political upheavals Europe has undergone since 1945. These mainly academic studies are indispensable for anyone tackling a book such as this one. Yet the ordinary serviceman's individual experience of those four tense decades has, until now, remained isolated, confined to a hearty re-telling in the pub or at one of the many regimental association reunions which occur frequently around the UK.

Trying to marshal all the yarns collected over two years into a comprehensive, chronological manuscript has been a challenge. My first problem came when I realised that the bulk of responses coming in were from men and women who had served in the immediate post-war years, between 1945 and 1960. At one point I almost considered that the book might have to end in 1965, so thin on the ground were contacts from the later decades. Yet eventually more younger ex-servicemen got to hear of the project, and some of the elements of the original concept were saved.

However, the reader will note that those early years do dominate the book and for obvious reasons. One is that in the immediate post-war years the Allied presence in Europe was at its height. Another reason is national service. The experiences of those who were often reluctant conscripts rather than career soldiers seemed to have been burned into their memory much more severely. They were still in their teens. National service was a formative part of their lives and serving in Germany at a time when most of their countrymen only ventured as far as the British coast for a holiday was an exotic experience that they would never forget. In those early years the stark aftermath of the war left an impression that remains grimly intact above all other memories. Some of the memoirs, such as those of Alec Kingsmill, Adrian Cooper, John Saville and Iain Leggatt are gems of recollection that otherwise may well have never seen the light of day.

A large proportion of the men I have spoken to are now well into their 80s. I have had the distinct impression throughout that these memories, although dormant, have been aching to come out ever since the day these men were demobbed. I feel privileged to be the conduit through which so much simple, yet important, history has been allowed to pass. Therefore, I hope I have done them justice.

~ Introduction ~

When we examine the way the art of war has altered since that last great conflict, the growth of technology and the sweeping changes which have overtaken society, it is clear that the world of the soldier of the 1945 to '60 period differs enormously to the one I witnessed in 2002 in Sennelager. There, in the virtual-battle training environment, managed by the Land Warfare Collective Training Group (Germany) (LWCTG[G]), recruits spend many weeks before huge banks of computer screens, plotting and fighting sweeping land battles with cyberspace tanks and armoured vehicles. Alternate days are spent in a cavernous hangar containing tank simulators, their interiors accurate reproductions of the £2 million-pound machines they will eventually drive through German woods and over fields, and, ultimately, across the real battlefields of any future conflicts.

Much has been made in the media of our Army's poor equipment, of how during the first Gulf War British squaddies swapped their rations with the Americans for decent boots and other essentials. But listening to old soldiers over recent months has convinced me that such gripes and grumbles have, throughout history, formed a major part of the soldier's story and contributed greatly to a characteristic sense of humour. Even as far back as the fourteenth century it made common sense for an archer to build and own his own longbow – or any other essential kit. There may be lasting glory in a noble death but there's a lot more fun to be had by staying alive. Since the nineteenth century, however, governments have organised their ordnance, supplies and arsenals in a more unified manner. The fact that substandard items are still frequently foisted upon troops is more to do with big business – there's big money in arms manufacture. Since 1900, the arms industry has developed along the same lines as other manufacturing industries. Products need to be tested in the field, and not all of them pass muster. Guaranteed obsolescence in products ensures on-going development and new business. It took 100 years for the matchlock rifle to be replaced by the wheellock, another two centuries before the wheellock gave way to the flintlock, which 100 years later was superseded by the percussion-cap rifle. Yet the standard issue to US forces, the Model 1903 Springfield rifle, only lasted 33 years and the automatic M-1 Garand, standardised in 1936, only 21 years.[1]

In competitive arms manufacture, just as in the automobile industry, speed, efficiency and fashion – the constant desire for new models – rules the balance sheet.

When we consider the size of armies and their requirement for arms after the nineteenth century, their stock market potential becomes clear. At the height of his power Alexander the Great only commanded 40,000 men. Oliver Cromwell's New Model Army was only half that size. Yet in 1870 a million Prussians invaded France, and in the 1914–18 war, a staggering 66 million men fought on all sides.[2]

This is a big market. Armies need not only guns but uniforms. For instance, in the Second World War, even being a cowboy was a profitable occupation. It is estimated that to provide 2 million men and women with military footwear, it took 3,750,000 cows to provide the uppers and 4,462,500 steers to make the soles.[3] Like the Hollywood movie industry, for the stockbroker, arms manufacture remains a good investment in any depression.

Guns aside, as the following chapters hopefully demonstrate, the NAAFI (Navy, Army and Air Force Institutes) has had as much to do with our military prowess as weapons have. That's one thing Napoleon got right – the soldier's stomach is very important in peace and war.

This book, although concerned with soldiers, is not about war. It deals with long periods of that odd void we loosely called 'peace' – or the absence of war – that was filled in Germany by a military who were kept in a constant state of alertness. National servicemen simply counted their days, longing to be back in civvy street. However, despite much of their initial reluctance to be in uniform, one phrase seemed to repeat itself at the end of every national serviceman's conversation or letter: 'I wouldn't have missed it for the world.'

As for the regular soldiers and their families, in the main they too were just enjoying their day-to-day life in the hope that the politicians would keep their safety catches firmly locked and stick to diplomacy. Of course, they never do.

One thing struck me in particular whilst visiting our bases in Germany: everyone seemed relaxed and happy to be there. Although everyone was British, I felt foreign. I asked one warrant officer from Bielefeld (he wished to remain anonymous), who will soon be leaving the Army after almost 30 years of service, about what he would do back home.

'Back home? I can't see myself going back. It seems foreign to me. I go over, you know, [for] special occasions, weddings, that kind of thing. But it's all alien to me. I've got used to Germany. I have a

German wife. I live in a German house. I mix with my neighbours. No, it isn't the England I remember. I suppose I'll live out my days here in Germany.'

His attitude might have been unbelievable to those British soldiers in Germany back in 1945, yet the roots of this German love affair were planted even then.

M. V. Bayes, now living in Leamington Spa, served in the Royal Corps of Signals and was stationed in Hanover and Berlin from 1945 to '47.
  'When the war ended we were not allowed to speak to the Germans. We had a policy of non-fraternisation. Later this was relaxed. I spoke to few Germans, and the ones I did speak with seemed to regret losing the war, but didn't regret starting it. Some of the men in our unit had German girlfriends, and one man said he would never go back to his wife . . .'

The modern, favourable attitude to the Germans was more prevalent than I'd expected. When one considers the bitterness of Anglo-German history over the past century, it says much for the way Europe has picked itself up and dusted off the grief of two massive wars. In many ways, regular soldiers who have experienced long service in Germany have grown with that country, and not with Britain. They follow the flag, and do their government's bidding, yet when the time comes to hang up their uniform, many will be quite happy to stay in their beloved Deutschland. As the saying in Berlin goes regarding the Allies: 'they came as conquerors and left as friends' – but many have stayed.
  The period of history which brought about that transformation is a remarkable chapter. The Treaty of Versailles, imposed on Germany at the end of the First World War, would pale into insignificance in comparison with the events which were to be experienced by Germans after the defeat of the Third Reich.

A NATION DIVIDED
In 1945, Germany, once a powerful nation, was divided by the victorious Allies into four zones of occupation. The United States, the Soviet Union, France and Great Britain all had their own areas of administration. But this was in no way some vindictive sharing of the spoils of war by conquering powers. The reality was that

Germany had been so physically, materially and morally devastated by her defeat that in social terms, the country had become a wasteland. In no way could the victors simply retire and leave behind a moral vacuum that might easily have been filled by the all-powerful Soviet Union.

For 13 nightmarish years, National Socialism's violent stranglehold had throttled any remaining vestiges of political freedom. Democracy, and those who espoused it, had crumbled under the jackboot. The first priority of the Allies was to sort out the hard-line Nazis from those in the social administration who had simply done their jobs, run regions and cities or kept the roads, railways and utilities running. Yet the extent of damage, and the high civilian casualty rate (just under 4 million compared to Britain's 60,000) offered nothing but a vista of complete chaos, which could only be tackled by military efficiency. At first, strict rules of non-fraternisation were put in place. In a country which had seemingly thrown itself wholeheartedly behind the Führer's megalomania, no one was to be trusted.

Eventually, those 'good' Germans who had struggled to survive away from the constant scrutiny of the Gestapo, came blinking back into the light, and as their genuine credentials were finally revealed, they began to play a part in administering the four zones. Political parties were formed. Following the war's end, within a few months, despite the fact that all average Germans had on their mind was mere physical survival, elections were held. Although Germans would carry the Nazi period with them as a heavy burden of memory through subsequent generations, one can only respect the accomplishment of the nation in the period after the war, when a new economy, soon to be admired by the world, was built from scratch and cities were reconstructed – all simultaneous with the huge problem of assimilating millions of refugees, exiles from the eastern areas now lost to Germany following her defeat.

By the end of the 1940s, a new shadow had cast itself over Germany: the Cold War. The Soviet Union and the United States, now known as the 'superpowers', brandished their opposing ideologies at each other across the Iron Curtain. The Allied hope at the war's end that Germany would have remained a single, unified state had been dashed. As the 1950s dawned, the need for political and economic progress eventually required the three Allied-administered zones of Germany to be joined together, to make, in

~ Introduction ~

1949, the country we would know as the Federal Republic of Germany (FDR), more commonly referred to as West Germany. In the east, the Russians had no intention of moving, and thus the eastern zone became yet another Germany, the German Democratic Republic (GDR).

And so the scene was set for a continuing face-off for the next four decades. This cruel split down the centre of a nation must have seemed to many Germans some kind of divine retribution, an added slap in the face on top of defeat. Families could no longer see one another. If you lived in Dortmund and had relatives in Dresden, the days of getting together were over. The border was as tightly closed and policed as any border in history, and in Berlin, where political stubbornness reigned supreme on both sides of the wire, the city became a focus of vicious political propaganda for both Eastern and Western politicians. The Germans may well have wished to get on with their lives, yet were now caught in the vice of the hostility, suspicion and mutual hatred of the two superpowers.

Within 15 years of the war's end, rearmament had taken place in both the new Germanys. In the GDR, the old familiar uniforms of the *Wehrmacht* from the Second World War still proliferated, but were now adorned with the insignia of a totally different ideology: Soviet Communism. All along the border, from the Baltic down to Czechoslovakia, the new *National Volksarmee* (NVA), pressed their massed, western-facing heavily armed ranks against the wire, fingers on the trigger, waiting for someone to make the wrong move. In the west, the FDR's new armed forces, now called the *Bundeswehr*, joined with NATO and watched 'the enemy', now part of Communism's own international club, the Warsaw Pact, with bated breath. In 1961, the unthinkable happened when the Soviets erected the Berlin Wall. Little did they know it then, but this extreme posturing in concrete and barbed wire would be the catalyst for a distant, glorious occasion – reunification.

And so dawned the age of lie and counter-lie, mistrust, bitterness, suspicion and fear. Could the Allies ever have packed up and gone home in such an atmosphere? Hardly. Germany was the testing ground for two massive blocs of political thought. Occasionally the tension would snap, usually as a result of frayed nerves or trigger-happy border guards. We can be thankful that there were few reports like this press cutting from 1985:

~ The Long Patrol ~

RUSSIANS 'SHOT AT BRITISH OFFICERS'

A former British Intelligence officer yesterday revealed the shadowy 'James Bond' world in which US Army Major Arthur Nicholson died on Sunday. Although Major Nicholson was the first officer shot dead in Eastern Europe, a string of incidents since the Soviet and Allied liaison missions were set up after the Second World War have involved high-speed car chases in sensitive areas, detention by the Russians, interrogation and 'roughing up'. The 34-year-old former Intelligence Corps officer, who is now working in local government, is married with three children. He spent two and a half years as a member of the 21-strong British liaison mission before leaving the Army in 1983.

During his time in the section the captain made more than 50 visits into Eastern Europe. While he was there two British officers were involved in shootings, one in 1980 involving a lieutenant-colonel, the other in March 1981, when an RAF Squadron Leader was the target. Neither was hit.

He said 'There were a lot of incidents, car chases and detentions. About ten or twelve officers are detained and questioned each year for ignoring "restricted" signs, which we refuse to recognise. Although we were under strict orders not to go near certain restricted areas, we were told to ignore some signs in less-sensitive places. We also ran convoys – dodging in and out at high speed noting identification plates and other details. The Russians would try to block and ram us, and then chase us, sometimes for miles. I was once chased by two armoured cars over rough country and was once captured, pushed around and questioned. The same thing happens with the Russians over this side, although they are not as tightly controlled. Even after this incident I don't see these tours being stopped – they are too useful to both sides.'

The three-man British patrols leave each day in marked four-wheel drive Range Rovers or modified Opel cars on two-day or three-day visits to the East. Each patrol has a driver, an NCO and an officer, unarmed and with no radios, but equipped with sophisticated photographic equipment.

Although they avoid wearing camouflaged clothing, they camp overnight in forests in the East and use the British base in Potsdam, a former girls' school, only for face-to-face meetings with the Russians. The officer added:

'Although in normal circumstances there is tit-for-tat retaliation after incidents, I think this latest business will blow over quickly. The Russians will be as upset as anyone, and the soldier involved will probably get disciplined and packed off somewhere else.'[4]

Major Nicholson's tragic death seems such a waste when one considers that within five years of this report the so-called 'evil empire' was to dissolve with the fall of the Berlin Wall. An American report of the major's death goes into more grisly detail.[5] As the bullet hit the major, he cried out to his sergeant, Jesse Schultz, 'Jesse – I'm hit!'. Schultz later reported that the East German soldiers prevented him from giving the wounded officer first aid. Nicholson's body was flown back to Washington for a full military funeral, and he now lies in the Arlington National Cemetery, a sad reminder of a mad phase in European history.

Terry Barber, of Bolton, was a Guardsman in the Grenadier Guards. He served in Montgomery Barracks, Berlin, from 1953–5.

'Our barracks was right next to the wire which separated us from the Russians. (This was, of course, before the Wall was built.) One morning, our boiler man, a German civilian who worked in the Officers' Mess, told us that when he'd gone home the previous evening he found that the Russians had moved the barbed wire during the night and his house was now in the Russian sector. This was a regular occurrence. I recall one day in May 1954, the Russians just walked through our barracks. We were told to ignore them, and not to provoke anything.

'The thing which stood out for me was the total devastation of the city, and the reliance the people had on the Allies.'

It is tempting to hypothesise that the exercise of such restraint is part of the British character. It's hard to imagine the results of a similar incursion into premises occupied by the US Army.

One refreshing attitude has persisted with all the people involved in this book. That is their sense of making history. Of course, these contributors only represent a small fraction of the many thousands of more disinterested soldiers who passed through Germany. To them it was a foreign posting like any other, the memory of which would just pass into the pages of their lives and ultimately have little meaning. Yet every now and then that sense of history would come to the surface, as it did with Iain Leggatt of the Royal Army Service Corps (RASC), who prefaced his own German memoir with a quotation from Queen Elizabeth I: 'They pass best over the world who trip over it quickly; for it is but a bog – if we stop, we sink.'

Throughout this period, West Germany, this green and pleasant, hard-working land, with its chequered history, fine culture, wonderful beer and musical heritage, would at certain times become the home of thousands of ordinary Britons and their families who had chosen a military career. This book, hopefully, will offer a simple insight into how their lives were lived.

BAOR: A BRIEF HISTORY

The British Army of the Rhine was a peacetime force. It had a long lifespan, from the end of the Second World War to 1994. It was established and put in place to counter any possible aggression from the huge Soviet war machine which was poised, always ready for action, at the border. The end of the Second World War saw a massive reduction in the manpower of the British Army, so that at one time the Rhine Army only consisted of two British divisions – the 2nd Infantry Division and the 7th Armoured Division. By 1950 they were bolstered by the arrival of the 11th Armoured Division and two years later, the 6th Armoured Division. Combined, these became known eventually as 1st (British) Corps. This came under the command of NATO and that organisation's Northern Army Group, known as NORTHAG. Throughout BAOR's time in Germany, restructuring and re-equipping with new weaponry both went hand in hand with a steady reduction of the force's size. Bielefeld was to become the HQ of 1st (British) Corps, with re-supply being carried out from the British Rear Combat Zone from its HQ based in Düsseldorf. At Emblem in Belgium, the British Communications Zone had its headquarters, and through this passed the new reinforcements from Britain, who were to be dispersed to their various bases around Germany.

Berlin was a separate element where the 3,000-strong Berlin Infantry Brigade came under the auspices of the city's Allied Control Council, and therefore not subordinate to NORTHAG. Over the years' BAOR's strength fluctuated from 60,000 to 25,000 troops. From Rheindahlen, where the RAF also had its HQ, along with the

2nd Allied Tactical Airforce and NORTHAG, BAOR's troops were commanded by a four-star general. The 1st (British) Corps included the 2nd Infantry Division, who could be called upon should the need arise from their base in Catterick. The highly mobile 24 Airmobile Brigade could move rapidly with helicopters, at short notice, with all its equipment. Its three infantry battalions, equipped with Milan weapons systems, specialised in anti-tank defence. The Territorial Army made up two other brigades.[6] Spread throughout 20 areas in Germany's North Rhine Westphalia and Lower Saxony were three other armoured divisions, each able to call upon air support from Lynx and Gazelle helicopters from the Army Air Corps Regiment.

The requirement throughout BAOR's existence was for constant readiness. Thus regular exercises took place, which included units of the Territorial Army. In the NATO areas brigade-scale exercises regularly took place, and for battle-group-level experience the troops would move to Canada, where the wider open spaces of the Canadian plains stood in for the European landscape and allowed for live-ammunition exercises. At various times elements of BAOR served under UN command for peacekeeping missions, and often spent three to six months on tours of Northern Ireland. If war had broken out, NATO would have commanded BAOR.

The British Army of the Rhine was finally disbanded on 28 October 1994. The Prince of Wales was in attendance at a parade by the Devonshire and Dorset regiment and the Queen's Dragoon Guards took their final salute as they gave him three hearty cheers and raised their caps. His words on that day are worth recalling:

> The momentous events in Russia, Central Europe and Germany have brought changes for all of us in Western Europe, almost all for the better. Here today we draw together one of the consequences of these events with the disbandment of the British Army of the Rhine.

As I draw near to completing this book, what once seemed like the unimaginable has happened. Britain has been plunged into a war in Iraq. Many of the young men I met on our bases in Germany in 2002 will by now have had their training tested to the limit. In 50 years' time, like the men and women in this book, they too will have vivid memories of a life spent in a foreign land in tumultuous times.

I can only hope that whatever future scribe is given the opportunity to document their twenty-first-century experience, he or she enjoys the same generosity of spirit and openness from his subjects as this writer has.

Ladies and gentlemen, I salute you.

Now it's time for you to tell it like it was.

1

Stunde Null

One day a little German boy came and asked us if he could
swim in our pool. It was then that I noticed he had no hands.
He said he had picked something up and it blew his hands
off. But he certainly could swim.
Corporal Geoff Gilbert, Sherwood Foresters

Stunde Null: 'Zero Hour'. This was the term Germans came to use for
the immediate aftermath of their defeat. It fitted the situation well.
Infrastructure: destroyed; housing: over 25 per cent obliterated, the
rest severely damaged;[1] no working currency; thousands of bodies
with no one to bury them; transport decimated; no working
government.

They no longer had a national flag, as the Swastika was now
banned. After a heady decade of expansion, as the Nazis had
plundered countries and planted their evil standard around Europe,
Germany was no longer even the country it had been before Hitler.
In the east the unthinkable had happened. The Russians had
grabbed half of their country, and retribution for Barbarossa was
vicious, deep and all-embracing. The advance of the Red Army had
pushed thousands of homeless refugees into the west – men, women
and children with nowhere to live, nothing to eat and, seemingly, no
future. The only hub of organisation in this pitiful morass of
humanity was the presence throughout what was to become known
as the British Zone, an area which stretched from Bonn to the Baltic,
of almost 2 million British troops. This is where our story begins.

Will we ever get over the war? That was a question I put to an
elderly gentleman in a pub in Chesterfield. Harry Jackson had

landed, as thousands of others did, in Hamburg just after the conflict had ended. He was a private in the Royal Engineers, wondering what victory might feel like once he got to Germany.

'In some ways I was looking forward to it. I remember going over the sea on a fine June day. The sun was out and it crossed my mind as I lit up a cigarette that not many months previous we may have stood a good chance of being torpedoed. But I'd joined up too late and by the time my training was over the Germans had surrendered. I can't say I was relishing action; on the other hand, I was slightly miffed that I'd been kitted out as a soldier and now I'd probably end up as a glorified repair man, putting to rights the damage Hitler had made us cause. Looking back, it's funny how war turns the tables on things; Hitler started it, and we were all in Germany helping to put it back together again. I don't recall thousands of Germans coming over to repair what they'd done to us in the Blitz.

'It wasn't until I saw Hamburg that I realised how lucky I'd been. Whatever lay ahead, thankfully it wasn't war – it was to be a very difficult peace. No, we'll never forget the war – and that one in particular. Long after my generation, like the old blokes from 1914–18, have died off, the Third Reich will be remembered.'

The destruction of Dresden from 13 to 15 February 1945 by the RAF and USAAF was a three-day blitz no city could survive. It was a concentrated onslaught that left the Germans stunned and reeling. Hamburg's devastation had come in many waves, but the effect was the same. Huge civilian casualties, the almost total disabling of services and the infrastructure. It is difficult to think that anyone could survive such attacks at all, yet the people of Germany, even though they knew the end was in sight, still fought on. I spoke to an old man in Koblenz who was still at school in the last weeks of the war. He'd been a member of the Hitler Youth.

'Even by the end of 1943 I'd had quite enough of being told about "the glory of the Reich" and "fighting to the bitter end". Families on either side of us in our street had been wiped out by bombing and we too were homeless at the end of the war. But, of course, we had to somehow put on the brave face and look like good Nazis. As far as I was concerned, all I wanted was to survive. I knew the British and the Americans were coming – and as long as they got to us before the Russians, that was all that mattered. As for Hitler, yes . . . He was quite something before the war. But we'd had quite enough of him in our house by the end of 1944. What did I think to the British and the Yanks? Well, of course no one likes to be defeated. But at least we could start putting our lives back together again once you'd arrived. And thank God you weren't the Russians!'

The immediate post-war period dominates this book because it scorched memories, which have remained pristine and lucid to this day, into men's minds. They are recollections of a different kind to those well-catalogued experiences of armed men in dangerous conflict. The majority of the recruits and volunteers in Germany after April 1945 would never have to fire a shot in anger. Yet by being in devastated Europe – and Germany in particular – they could witness and feel the fresh legacy of those years of stupid hatred and destruction. It stood before them in the mute, bombed landscape and was etched in grimy silence on the face of a defeated population. Few could have imagined that 50 years later the British Army and RAF would still be there in the Fatherland (a dubious word even in today's German politics), still driving their tanks across the tundra of Sennelager, still marching around the parade grounds of Gütersloh, Herford and Mönchengladbach.[2] And of course there was national service. Thousands of young men found themselves in Germany as reluctant soldiers or airmen when they would far rather have been at home cutting a rug at the local *palais* to the latest Bill Haley record. Their memories have softer edges. With eighteen months or two years maximum to serve, they knew that by the time they'd worked themselves into a lather over being conscripted, they'd soon be on the boat or train home. Yet to many, those enforced months of militarism were still, to paraphrase the chronicler of national service, Trevor Royle, 'the best years of their lives'.[3]

Of course, there was always a war to be fought somewhere. At the same time everyone in Europe emerged from the rubble, blinking in the dusty light of peace, out in the Far East the war continued. It may well have been VE Day in Britain on 8 May 1945, but there was little to celebrate for Allied troops on the other side of the globe, out in the Pacific. It would be another four months before British troops would re-occupy Hong Kong, and the Japanese war machine would only be cowed in early August with the unimaginable horror of Hiroshima and Nagasaki. Korea would soon demand more sacrifice, and in just over a decade, Britain would be on a war footing yet again during the utter embarrassment of the Suez debacle.

If politicians had thought the world had changed radically after the Great War of 1914–18, then following the Second World War they had an even bigger surprise coming.

One of Hitler's great inspirations in his plans for a 1,000-year Reich had always been the British Empire. He had frequently looked at the size of Britain on the atlas and marvelled at the large swathes of pink elsewhere on the map, showing the expanse of the British Empire. How could such a tiny island in the northern hemisphere be in control of such huge colonies thousands of miles distant? One reason was that it had well-trained, highly efficient armed forces, and like the Romans, they were well-used to being far from home and dealing with 'Johnnie Foreigner'.

Yet Hitler, despite building one of the most efficient war machines in European history, was, in his blind racist rage, unwittingly assisting the demise of Imperialism around the world. Nothing saps an economy – and diverts political attention – more than war. What had begun in 1583 when Sir Humphrey Gilbert first planted the British flag on Newfoundland was about to end in India with the lowering of the Union Jack in 1947; this was to be closely followed by Burma and Palestine. Britain was left with fading bits of Africa, and among others, Jamaica, Honduras, and exotic, remote outposts such as Tonga, Fiji and Barbados, once staging posts on the road to riches and world dominance, now the paste jewels in a broken bracelet which once gripped the globe.

Now that six years of war were behind them, the British people began to look carefully at what lay ahead on the home front. The memories of the inter-war years, which had culminated in mass unemployment, the means test and the hunger marches of the 1930s, were still vivid enough to make the electorate think very carefully about what kind of world they wanted for their children after the war. Winston Churchill was undoubtedly the hero of the day, but he was about to be defeated – an incredible prospect for many – due to the fact that the electorate recognised the man who had steered the nation to victory, but not the Conservative party he led. It was time for change.[4]

This had also been a 'people's war', and as its anti-fascist thrust became more obvious after 1941, the route to eventual victory could only be opened up by abandoning the strictures of the class system. People really had 'pulled together'. Bombs were just as capable of falling on dukes and duchesses as they were on dockers. In addition to Neville Chamberlain, among Hitler's prominent appeasers there had been elements of high society, such as Sir Oswald Mosley and the socialite daughters of the 2nd Baron Redesdale, Unity Mitford, a regular associate of leading Nazis, and her sister, Diana, who became Mosley's second wife in 1936. It seems in retrospect no surprise that William 'Haw-Haw' Joyce should have had the epithet 'Lord' attached to his name. Now, as the British worker looked around his grimy, ruined world, he realised that whatever demands the war had made on him, the removal of the rubble was an even bigger task and the rebuilding of Britain could only be achieved by major social change. Another factor which influenced public thinking at this time had been the enormous sacrifice and bravery of the Red Army. The Nazi-Soviet Pact of 1939 had brought anti-Soviet feelings to a head, but the stubborn fury they later demonstrated in the face of the Nazi invasion became a source of inspiration and ultimately helped to tilt political thinking towards socialism.[5]

Churchill was no doubt disappointed with the result, but the shock of 26 July 1945 was met with a public joy which almost equalled the euphoria of VE Day. Clement Attlee's Labour Party swept to victory with 47.8 per cent of the total vote compared to the Conservatives' 39.8 per cent. Of the 640 seats in the House of Commons, Labour now held 393. They had the power to change society and they were about to exercise it.

Many men in khaki, new conscripts, began to wonder what this seismic shift in society might mean in military terms. If anything, it meant that a large army would be maintained. The world was still unstable and, having being caught with our proverbial pants down in 1939, no one, Labour or Tory, was about to let that happen again. Thus conscription was allowed to roll on, until in 1947 the National Service Act established compulsory peacetime military service for all males over 18. At first this was set at 12 months; it was then increased to 18 months in December 1948 and, in September 1950, the demands of the war in Korea pushed it up to 2 years. Of course, debate over the perceived benefits of this Act have rumbled on for decades. It spawned that favourite old taproom lawyers' adage: 'Two years in the Army would do 'em good.' But by 1957 it was decided to cut back on conscription and after 1960 no more men were called up.

Since then, a new kind of Army has been developed. Life in the ranks in Germany today would be virtually unrecognisable to the recruits of the 1940s and '50s. Being a soldier now is a vocation, a choice of profession. Gone are the rough uniforms, the bellowing drill sergeants and repetitive routines centred on kit inspection, cleaning and parades.

This twenty-first-century Army represents every change in British society over the past four decades. It is a highly technical, smoothly run operation. Yet things, as in any corporate body, can still go wrong. Thankfully, the camaraderie, routines and traditions of the British serviceman remain intact.

I recall one dull winter morning in Germany when I went to visit the public relations officer at Gütersloh. For many years Gütersloh was an RAF base, but today it is occupied by the Army. The site has its own railway line along which ordnance used to be delivered for the Air Force. This rail spur is still in use. I arrived too early for my appointment at the base and decided to bide my time in a lay-by along the road. I noticed that at the point where the railway line crossed the highway and entered the woods that surround the base, two very cold squaddies were standing, one at each side of the track, on sentry duty. It seemed a miserable job; they were flanked by dark pine trees and there was no shelter or sentry post – and it looked like it might rain.

They were patting their shoulders and stamping their feet and seemed to be waiting for a train. Forty-five minutes later, I drove back in their direction to the Army PR office, situated in a large ex-civilian house quite close to the track. The PR officer welcomed me and I commented on what a lousy duty the two nearby soldiers had.

'Ah,' she said, 'if you want to understand the British Army, there's a perfect example. They were sent out there early this morning to wait for a train coming in. What nobody's told them yet is that they've got the wrong day. The train they're waiting for isn't due until 3 o'clock tomorrow afternoon . . .'

If Germany feels closer and more accessible in travelling terms than it did 50 years ago, my experiences of talking to career soldiers stationed there today have revealed that to many of them, Britain seems more distant. We shall deal with this conundrum in a later chapter, but the time has come to return to the beginning and let the lads tell us the way things were.

Albert Winstanley now lives in Bolton. He was a member of the Royal

Army Medical Corps and was stationed in Hamburg from 1945 to '46.

'I volunteered for service in September 1939. After various postings I took part in Operation Torch – the landings in North Africa in November 1942. We opened up the first large General Hospital in Algiers a few days after the landings and were kept extremely busy with admissions. We remained in Algiers until 1945, when we moved to Marseilles in the south of France. We landed there the day the war finished.

'From there I travelled with the rest of the troops in cattle trucks through France, Belgium and into Holland, where we thankfully transferred onto road transport, to eventually cross the Rhine into Germany. The rumour flashed around that we were destined for "one of the most-bombed cities in Europe", and so it was that we arrived in Hamburg with the war just virtually days over.

'I shall never forget that experience of entering Hamburg in our transport, for almost as far as the eye could see, it was just devastation. What had obviously once been lovely buildings were now just ruins, shattered walls, great tumbles of stone, and a population seemingly staggering about like tired zombies.

'I recall the stench, too, as hundreds of bodies remained, still awaiting burial. This was, of course, all the result of our vengeance with our 1,000 bomber raids, which had followed on from the bombing of our towns and cities.

'We quickly set up the hospital at a place called Rubencamp, some six miles or so outside Hamburg, and naturally, we were kept extremely busy. I recall some victims of the concentration camps also being admitted. We were told in no uncertain terms that there had to be no fraternisation with the German people. This was extremely difficult, as many of the Germans seemed anxious to talk to us. Thankfully, the non-fraternisation rule was lifted.

'I was amazed that within days the excellent train service to the busy line from Hamburg to Ohlsdorf was running. Even so, there were several carriages reserved for British troops, with large notices in German forbidding Germans entry to these carriages.

'I have one vivid memory of that non-fraternisation period. There was a kiddie's fairground with roundabouts and kids' merry-go-rounds. And there were our soldiers, all sitting astride the miniature horses, whilst the sad little German boys and girls looked on in envy. I recall that this rather upset me at the time.

'Very soon, entertainment was organised and a cinema was

opened. I remember joining the queue one day, and seeing about 20 German men waiting around to stoop and snatch up from the gutter the discarded cigarette ends from the smokers in the queue. (I never smoked, but this was still upsetting.) Regarding entertainment, I remember clearly going to the theatre which had re-opened. That night it was a full house. One of the artistes appearing was Lale Andersen. Just as our own Vera Lynn was our "forces sweetheart", this lady had been the German's counterpart, especially with that famous song, "Lili Marlene".[6] She spoke English, and before singing, gave us a little history of that famous song. She was a little apprehensive as to how this British audience would react to her – probably worried that she might be booed off. She then sang a verse in German and one in English. When she finished there was loud cheering and huge applause, so she left the stage a very happy artiste. It was at that same theatre that I saw a performance of *Peer Gynt*, with Ralph Richardson in the leading role. Though I knew the music very well, this was the first time I had seen the stage rendering.

'Another little memory I have is of standing on the platform at the station in Hamburg, waiting for the train to Rubencamp, when a long train drew in, filled to capacity with homeward-bound German soldiers. A cheer went up from the German civilians on the platform, and there was a peculiar bit of soldier's camaraderie when several of our own men gave their German counterparts the "thumbs-up" sign. It was somewhat strange to witness this spirit between British khaki and German field grey, and to think that just shortly before we had all been shooting at each other.

'I had met my future wife whilst in North Africa. She was a sister in the hospital, and therefore a nursing officer, and fortunately she moved to Hamburg with us. However, we still had to keep our association secret, because officer–lower ranks relationships were severely frowned upon.

'Owing to the secrecy of Operation Torch in 1942, we had had no embarkation leave, which was a sore point with us. However, in July 1945 I finally got my first leave in three years. I sailed from Cuxhaven to Hull. En route I recall passing through Peenemunde and seeing all those V-2 rockets in position on railway wagons, all at one time destined for England. Thankfully they were never to be used.

'It was the onset of autumn when I returned to Hamburg after my leave. Soon the German people would begin to suffer from the cold. Most of the trees which had fringed the roads and streets had been chopped down for fuel. In many places there were desperate gangs of people digging out the remaining stumps, and everywhere people pulling little carts collecting any scrap of wood they could salvage.

'Owing to joining up very early in September 1939, I was fortunate to be demobbed early and I managed to arrive home on Christmas Eve 1945, just in time for Christmas with my family. Unhappily it was partly a sad reunion. My older brother had been killed in action in Italy. The following May, my wife-to-be was demobbed and we got married in September 1946.

'Though we who served through it all are now in our 80s, and our numbers are vanishing quickly, the memories of it all, both good and bad, will never die. '

Corporal E.A. 'Jed' Cressy started as railway cleaner and was promoted to locomotive driver in the Royal Engineers. He served from 1942 to '50, in the 954 Railway Operating Company.

'I joined up in November 1942 as a volunteer. Being in a reserved occupation, on the railways, I signed on for seven years.

'I entered the service at Blacon Camp, Chester, where we had six weeks' infantry training. (We were then known as the General Service Corps.) I spent my first Army Christmas there. Very depressing. I had to be assessed for whatever unit they had in mind, so, having been in civvy street a 'passed' [qualified] cleaner on the LMS Railway [London, Midland and South Railway], I was put in the Royal Engineers with a view to becoming a locomotive driver.

'But there was more training. This time it was at Weaversdown Camp for another six long weeks in demolition, bridge building, mine laying, all sorts of things. I thought that was it until we moved next door to yet another camp – Longmoor – where we finally got to grips with steam locomotives. They had a rare assortment of steam locos from all over the various railway systems. There was even one British Austerity 2-8-0 locomotive and an American diesel electric which had all mod-cons including a cab heater and even a cooking stove. Longmoor also had a wonderful model railway which was used for the training of signalmen. It was a bit like being a big lad with a train set but we were actually learning the job for real, whilst all the time wondering if we'd ever get to use all this knowledge in Germany. There were large areas on the site where field engineers practised the art of track-laying. By the end of our time there, I believe we got to the point where we could lay up to ten miles of track in a day. The Longmoor Military Railway which ran from Liss to Bordon surely deserves a place in military history.

'The next spot they sent me was Woolmer, the next station down the line, which was really a small holiday camp. From there I joined my company, the 954 Railway Operating Company at Weston-upon-Trent. This was a stretch of track from there to Ashby, part operational and part training track. There were quarries and an exchange sidings with the LMS and we had six to eight steam locomotives, including two American ones. Just down the track was King's Newton, where the British and Americans were bridge-building.

'There was great rivalry, but our sappers beat the Yanks every time, hands down. We moved to Newcastle-upon-Tyne and had more training in the loco sheds there. We were stationed in an old school in Bentinck Road. The people of Newcastle are some of the kindest and most generous I've ever met. Always giving us tickets to some "do" or other. Great folks. More military training, a battle course. We were sent out under canvas to Staindrop, west of Darlington, at the end of October and in November I was on my way to Scotland where we had a stretch of railway which glorified under the name of Stickenduff. This went down to the No. 1 military port on the Gare Loch, where five deep sea berths and some huge liners were accommodated. (Again the port had been built by sappers!) As Christmas went into New Year – 1944 – we were amazed at the volume of Naval traffic coming in and out of Gare Loch, in addition to American Liberty ships, each carrying 20 or 30 aircraft, all swaddled in canvas, on their decks.'

Germany
'Eventually, as the war came to an end, all this training took us to where we were bound, Germany. When we arrived after crossing the border I remember us pulling up outside the gates of a concentration camp – Belsen. We were only a few miles from our destination, Bremen. Lots of the ex-inmates were coming down the drive from the camp – which we couldn't see – but could smell. They were a pitiful sight, many of them still in their pyjama-striped uniforms. My abiding memory is of seeing what looked like an old lady dressed in black, who, upon reaching the road, began spinning

like a top until she collapsed in a heap in the road. That image stays with me still. We gave them what haversack rations we had but couldn't do much.

'The riding around on locos back home was nothing compared to what we'd be doing here. The first post was at Lohne, near Bad Oeyenhausen, which was Monty's HQ. We were "supervising", i.e. riding on locos all over the British zone, to such places as Bielefeld, Minden, Osnabrück, and Hanover. I later moved to Brunswick. Here we rode all the supply trains to Berlin.

'During my time in Berlin I spent two spells – including the Christmas of 1945 in Magdeburg – in the Russian zone. I was with a small detachment which specialised in attending to breakdowns where wagons or locomotives had overheated axles. I came back to Berlin on two more occasions. It was a desolate, awful time for the Germans. What had been beautiful streets were now lined with heaps of rubble. The only traffic seemed, for a time, to be military – jeeps, armoured cars. I wouldn't have liked to have been a German then. Yet despite all this, on both sides, there was a sense of relief that it was all finally over. All everyone could do now was rebuild things.

'My company broke up in early 1946 and went to the 960 ROC, which was still in Brunswick. After a few weeks I was posted to Detmold, to the 153 ROC. There we actually operated a stretch of German railway, which ran from Herford to Altenbeken. It was good to be in charge of locomotives again. Eventually the 153 became the 348 Railway Operating Squadron and remained so for the rest of my time in Germany. By this time my personal life had changed, too – I had got married.'

Married Life in Detmold

'By February 1948, the occupying forces had got things organised to such a degree that I was able to have my wife come out to Germany and live with me, which was wonderful. There was a good social life in the BAOR for married families – well, for everyone, really. There was always something going on. It wasn't all square-bashing. We'd had enough of that in war time. Now we could look forward to dances, outings, shows, films and lots of sport; often there were tournaments involving other bases.

'Still, although things were great in Detmold during 1948–9, my wife was now pregnant and had decided that she didn't really want our son to be born in what was still, to us, a "foreign" country. And my time was almost up, too. In the summer of 1949 we returned to the UK and I finished off my final few months.

'The war seemed like a distant, bad memory. Yet through it all, and especially in Germany, I had met so many great blokes. I am now in my 80s but I still treasure the many great memories of the friends I made and the places I visited and served in. I spent five Christmases in Europe: Dieppe in 1944; Magdeburg in 1945; and Detmold in '46, '47, and '48. I don't regret one of them.'

Jed's experience demonstrates how important the Allied presence was in those early years in restoring Germany's damaged infrastructure. It will be noticed from comments in later letters and interviews that many young soldiers arriving in Germany a decade or so after the war's end were surprised as they passed through Holland or Belgium at the standard of living enjoyed by the population. The first decade of peace was a time of hard work and constant rebuilding for the Germans, yet very soon, as the 1960s dawned, those observations about superior European living standards began to be applied to the Germans, too. Back in Britain, although much of the rubble and destruction in our city centres had been removed, the general aftermath of the war was evident for far longer than it was in our erstwhile enemy's homeland. Therefore, however much is made of that laudable German work ethic – and make no mistake, they really did put their backs into rebuilding – the whole process had benefited in no small way from the broad range of skills and craftsmanship of the occupying forces. It was perhaps that 'catch-all' net of conscription which had placed so many of Britain's building trade labour force not where they were most needed, at home, but in Germany.

Prior to 1939, there were a million men in the UK building industry. By 1945 this figure was down to 340,000. A great percentage of this reduced number were concentrated in the south-east of England, where the 'V' rockets and doodlebugs had done their worst damage.[7]

That great post-war politician, Aneurin Bevan, had a lot on his plate as Minister for Health. Simultaneous to building the new National Health Service from scratch, he faced the problem of housing those thousands of Britons who, like the Germans, had lost their homes. He vehemently badgered his cabinet colleagues, such as

Ernest Bevin, to make moves to demobilise those men in the Army who possessed the building skills the country so badly needed. It was an uphill task. One exchange in the House of Commons demonstrates his frustration.

Bevan asked the prime minister, Attlee: 'Where are all the people I need for my programme?'

Attlee came back with the witty yet perplexing riposte: 'Looking for houses, Nye!'[8]

The Germans, however, could look as hard as they could for houses but they would find few. At least Britain still had a functioning government – and a highly proactive one at that – to put plans into action. Politically and socially, as our boys were to find out when they arrived, the one-time Reich was back in the Stone Age.

John Appleby, of the Royal Northumberland Fusiliers, did national service in Germany. He was posted to 2nd Battalion Grenadier Guards at Sennelager.

'We crossed from Harwich to the Hook of Holland. I remember vividly a meal we had on arriving because it included white bread, something we hadn't seen for years. After the NCO course with the Guards, I was posted to the York and Lancaster Regiment stationed at Buxtehude, a few miles from Hamburg. The destruction of the city was unbelievable. Mile after mile of complete ruins. A vast number of people were living in sheds or greenhouses on various allotment sites around the city. As I was in the MT section of the battalion I travelled many miles around the Northern Occupation Zone. The city people were less friendly than those out in the country.

'When we were out on our manoeuvres the children's faces would light up as we gave them chocolate and sweets from our NAAFI rations. There were few smiles from the farmers, though, as we drove through their fields which had just been sown. Manoeuvres would start at the end of March through to October, beginning with the British Army, and end in October with the Americans and the French, the Dutch, Belgians and Norwegians. Quite an international affair. Often high-ranking personnel from home would be there to watch us. I remember one being Manny Shinwell MP.

'These training areas were mainly around Soltau, where the German Panzer Corps used to do their training. The barracks we were billeted in at Buxtehude were named *Spee Barracks* – they used to house the crew of the battleship *Graf Spee* when it was in port.

'I remember the Berlin Airlift, when the Russians stopped the movement of supplies to Berlin by road. I also remember well that some of our lads in our battalion were used as extras in a film they were making, *The Wooden Horse*. The film told the story of POWs escaping from Stalag Luft III by tunnelling under a vaulting horse. It was quite popular at the time. It turned out that one night we went to the cinema and actually found ourselves sitting alongside the stars of that film, Leo Genn, David Tomlinson and Anthony Steele.

'We didn't do too badly in Germany for entertainment. We got all the latest stage shows and films, and had a good radio service from BFN (British Forces Network), transmitted from Hamburg.

'I should also mention that at one time we were close to the Belsen concentration camp. The atmosphere around the area was uncanny. There seemed to be no signs of birds or other wildlife.

'One of my other duties was to take married family personnel on shopping trips with a Bedford QL truck, which had been converted into a 24-seater bus. Driving duties weren't bad and were often interesting. I also drove the second-in-command of the battalion around in a jeep. It was very interesting because it gave me the opportunity to see a lot of strategy in planning attacks.

'Although I only did 18 months of national service, and I certainly wasn't looking forward to the prospect, it was an experience which, in many ways, I'm really glad I did not miss.'

Jimmy King was a warrant officer in the Royal Engineers Railway/Transport Section. He joined the TA in 1938 and the regulars in 1939. He served for 30 years and was demobbed in 1969.

'Yes, that stretch of railway track – I knew every foot of it. If you like I can list all the stations between Altenbeken and Detmold . . . maybe not. We had a tough job on training our drivers and firemen on the German railways. Mind you, the Germans had an impressive selection of locomotives and rolling stock. At first relationships with the German rail crews – and there was a shortage of them – were very tetchy. We were housed in ex-German Wehrmacht barracks and we were frankly amazed at the quality the German serviceman had been used to compared to our own barracks. Still, it hadn't stopped us winning, I thought.

'I had 57 kilometres of track to work on and we covered all kinds of railway work. Not long after that bit of railway experience they shoved me so far north in Europe, that another foot and I'd have been in the sea – I was stationed for a while at the Hook of Holland. Eventually, stationed once again back in Germany, the barriers finally broke down a little. Although we had all paid heed (at first, that is), to Monty's firm instruction that we should not, under any circumstances, fraternise with the Germans, we were fit young lads and as far as we could see the war was over. We were as discreet as we needed to be and were soon seeing German girls. It was a mutual thing; we couldn't hold a grudge against each other forever. The world was turning.

'I met this rather attractive lady called Ottilie who lived at 149 Lageresch Strasse in Detmold. I suppose it was love at first sight. We started going out – pictures, the odd drink, stuff like that. Anyway, eventually, in 1947, we got married. It lasted 30 years but ended in divorce in 1977. Odd, really. Once my Army service was behind me, my marriage seemed to hit the buffers.

'Would I have had my life any other way? No. I loved my time in Germany and made some very good friends over those years. I saw the world change for the better – and certainly saw Germany overtake us. It was a great time to be young.'

Corporal Geoff Gilbert served from 1944 to '47. He was a physical training instructor in the Sherwood Foresters Regiment.

'I was called up for the Army in 1944 and had to report to the Burton Road Barracks at Lincoln, opposite the racecourse. Then it was battle training in Northumberland, which turned out to be much tougher than we'd expected – in fact our instructor told us he'd actually put us through commando training.

'January and February 1945 I remember well because there was about two foot of snow. We were given one week's embarkation leave before being sent overseas. My parents wondered if it would be Europe or the Far East for me – fighting the Japs. It appeared that all our Sherwood Foresters seemed to be in the Malaya/Burma area. But I managed to put their mind at rest, because I knew that if we embarked from Southampton, it would be the Far East, but if we left from Dover, then it must be Europe. We were allowed to send one censored postcard home; I wrote, "It's lovely to see the White Cliffs in the distance . . ." and it got through all right. So at least they knew I was on my way to Germany.

'We got to Calais and the town was in pitiful ruins. In a small town called Corby near Amiens, we were told that we were going on to the Rhine as reinforcements to help Monty get across the river. We broke our journey at Appeldoorn for a few days and joined the 4th Battalion of the Northampton Regiment. The Northamptons had been fighting in the Meuse in Belgium. We were transferred to this regiment.

'I was surprised to see cows next to the cookhouse tent. Apparently these animals supplied us with the milk for our tea, and every time the regiment moved on the cows went with us. We went on to Wesel and Goch, which to me looked like that photograph of Hiroshima: totally devastated, not a building standing. Our hardest job was picking up and disposing of all the dead animals and fishing human bodies out of the river. When we actually got to the Rhine, to our relief Monty had already got across and had the Germans on the run. Our orders were to guard the two pontoon bridges laid across by the Engineers. A real work of art – they became known as the London & Westminster. We were billeted in an abandoned hotel for a week.

'Our next accommodation was at Rheinberg, in the convent there. The nuns were at one end of the building and we were at the other. We never saw them at all. In the convent garden was a swimming pool, which we all really enjoyed.

'One day a little German boy came and asked us if he could swim in our pool. I noticed that he had no hands. He told us that he had picked something up, it had exploded and blown off his hands. I was so sorry for this little boy, who was about five years old. Mind you, he could swim really well.

'It was during our time at the Rheinberg Convent that we all heard that at last the war was over. The day after the good news my friend and I were told to go and patrol along a few miles of PLUTO (Pipe Line Under The Ocean). This had been laid under the channel and across Europe to supply our armies with fuel. After walking across a field we came to a gate bearing a warning, "Beware of Mines", and I think God was with us that day. As we got back on the road, two shots from a rifle rang out and the bullets screamed past our legs. I screamed at my mate "Down!" and we both dropped into a ditch. After a while we got up cautiously, but there were no more shots. We never did discover who fired at us, but whoever it was, if he'd hit us, it would have been a tragedy seeing as this was the first day after the war had ended.'

By Train to Berlin

'Our next move was to Brunswick to take NAAFI rations by train to our troops in Berlin. What a trip this turned out to be – it used to take all day. Our task was to guard against anyone getting onto the train and getting their hands on the food. We always seemed to be stopped in the Russian Sector for an hour. I recall a Russian soldier (a Mongolian, I believe) came up to the train and fancied my new wristwatch. He motioned to me that he wanted to swap his pocket-watch for mine. Well, his watch looked like one of those cheap five-shilling versions you could get from Woolworths years ago. I said to him, "Nothing doing, mate." He wasn't too pleased and went away. There was another Mongolian who had no less than five watches on his wrist, and claimed that they were all "*Kaput*" – broken. He simply didn't realise that you were supposed to wind them up to get them going!

'It was good to get away from the battalion for a few days and have a look at Berlin – or what was left of it. Women were shovelling rubble into lorries. It was hard work. A bomb had fallen on the zoo and only two animals had survived. One was a poor old lonely lion. It was a depressing place, but the Germans were working as fast as they could to try and return to some kind of order. There was something proud and special about the city, even though it had been pounded to rubble and ruins.'

J.G. Rooth, driver 23265376, was in the RASC 111 Company 8th Armoured Brigade. He was stationed in Verden and served between 1955 and '57.

'I was doing my national service and spent most of it in Germany. At first I was sent to Aldershot, then Yeovil and Borden for my basic training. After that we were shipped off to Verden in Germany in order to learn to drive on the right-hand side of the road. Our vehicles were Austin K4 three-ton lorries.

'One narrow escape I can remember was when, under instruction, we were going through a town and I had to ask the corporal which way I was supposed to turn – left or right. First he said left, then he said right, by which time I was in the middle of the road heading full tilt in the direction of a ladies' hairdresser's shop window. I just had time to pull up sharp about two inches from the window, and boy, did those ladies jump! Leaving Verden with our company, 111 Company of the 8th Armoured Brigade (Desert Rats) we went to a horrible place called Fallingbostel. It was out in the back of nowhere. We had an easy time there because there was no town as such, the only places for us to congregate being the TOC H and the NAAFI. Early in 1957 we moved to barracks at Celle to be near the 17th/21st Lancers and the Devon Regiment.

'I remember whilst we were at Celle we were enjoying a weekend break with two lorryfulls of men at a lakeside resort. At 1 a.m. we were all called back to barracks to get ready for Suez. A lot of us had been drinking quite a lot and I sometimes wonder how we got back to barracks at all.

'We got as far as the docks at Hamburg. Our lorries were painted with a large 'H' on their roofs to indicate to our aircraft that we were friendly.

'Once back in Germany (by the way, re. Suez – we never got a ribbon for going into action but I hear this is being looked into), I spent the last six months mainly wearing civilian clothes. The way this happened is one of those fluke strokes of luck you sometimes had in the Army. An officer was asking for volunteers, but he asked if we were interested in music. I thought perhaps we were volunteering to join the band, so me and four of my mates put our hands up. The music connection soon became clear – they wanted us to shift a piano from the Sergeants' Mess to the NAAFI!

'Well, we moved it but as we were getting it onto a lorry it slipped off and onto my foot. After this I was excused boots so I was sent to the Officers' Mess, where I landed a nice cushy number as a barman – a really good job.

'Lots of other things come to mind about that time in Germany. Delivering coal to married quarters, and getting cups of tea off the officers' and sergeants' wives, and arriving back late at the base. One weekend I was riding a motorcycle through a German forest and I fell off. The local people were very pleasant, and took me into their home where they washed my cuts and made me a cup of tea. I recall trying to get a date with their daughter. It was only national service, but looking back it was a good time. Pity it's finished now – the lads of today could do with it.'

That last comment is a common theme when talking to ex-servicemen.

But there is an undeniable truth behind conscription which often renders such emotion invalid: the British have never been fond of having a wholly conscripted army. Apart from the major points in our history where conscription was imposed on men over 18 – 1916 and 1939 – the National Service Act of 1947 was simply a contingency that the bold new Labour administration had to face due to the continuing instability in Europe. In addition to this, the old Empire was in a state of disintegration, and men were required to oversee this massive change in our colonial history.

As an island race, Britain's defensive power had always been on the high seas. There are references going back to Alfred the Great, who had a fleet of ships built specifically to fight against the Vikings. But the sense of obligation to form a defensive force which might be recognised as a 'navy' did not come into play until long after the Norman Conquest. This force was supplied to the Crown by the Channel ports – Sandwich, Hythe, Romney, Dover and Hastings. They were obliged by a number of kings to supply 57 ships, all expenses paid, with crews, for 15 days per year.[9] These were merchant ships, adapted for fighting. Other kings, such as Edward III and Henry V, also gave great importance to strength at sea. But it was Henry VII who laid the foundations of a 'proper' navy as we know it today, with a permanent corps of officers and men, such as boatswains, gunners and carpenters, all of whom eventually saw this as a career of sorts.[10] Henry Tudor's navy was impressive, but only consisted of 20 ships. As for 'conscripting' men into this force, especially into the lower decks, the press gang ruled right into the nineteenth century. It was not until the middle of that century that navy sailors were offered a proper career and given a uniform to wear.

The history of a standing army, a 'King's Army', has its roots in Anglo-Saxon times, when it was called the *Fyrd*. The obligation to military service was laid on the shoulders of landholders by kings when they granted their subjects estates. Referred to by historians as the 'Commons Burdens', there were three obligations: to serve in the King's Army when required, to repair fortifications, and to maintain and repair bridges. What professional soldiery there was then consisted of mercenaries, land-owning knights and loose-knit militias, often hastily thrown together to meet some threat. With a little imagination one can see in this trio of demands the distant genesis of what centuries later became the Royal Engineers. By Tudor times troops received wages yet armies were still only raised on a temporary basis at times of war. The first proper 'standing army' did not appear until the reign of Charles II when, in 1661, he established 'His Majesty's Guards and Garrisons'. The Declaration of Rights of 1689, issued in the face of James II's expansion of the Army, established that without Parliamentary approval any such force was illegal.

By 1751, incorporating the Royal Regiment of Artillery, which had been formed in 1716, what we can now recognise as a real army finally received a Royal Warrant. But it was still a relatively small affair. It eventually became an acceptable vocation for members of the lower gentry, as officers, and for the very poor working class, and as the Empire grew, it was at least a way of seeing the world – which to most common soldiers meant India. The creation of the now familiar 'county' regiments did not come about until as late as 1881. It seems surprising, therefore, that throughout all of Britain's many famous campaigns and battles between the seventeenth and nineteenth centuries, unlike the many enemies we fought, Britain's Army never laboured under conscription. The truth is, the British never trusted their kings and queens when it came to founding armies. Henry VIII may have had his personal protection force, the Yeomen of the Guard, but the commoners knew that the expansion of such forces was always going to be a possible threat to their internal freedom.

Thus the idea of being 'called up' was always regarded in the past as an alien concept, and as such, a threat to British liberty. In 1639–40 one of the root causes of the Civil Wars was Parliament's refusal to give Charles I the money he needed to raise a force to repel an invasion by the Scots. The founding of the New Model Army in 1645, a force in which men received wages and officers were appointed on their military ability rather than their social connections, confirmed general suspicions of dormant despotism. Long after it was disbanded the memory of this highly efficient unit, driven along by pious religious belief, served to stop any notions of assembling such a potentially dangerous force again dead in their tracks. This did of course cause the more avaricious rulers, politicians and military leaders some frustration. Britain had always maintained her position of power by checking states or countries who were on the rise and likely to become too big for their ambitious boots. The method was simple; in response to a perceived threat, we would raise our army, and form a coalition of states or countries against the object of our suspicion. Echoes of this procedure still exist in the Iraq adventure.

By the later nineteenth century our lack of conscription undermined this method when the Franco-Prussian War (1870–1) broke out. Britain was simply unable to raise an effective force for intervention, leaving the field open for Prussian expansion. Similar difficulties came to a head during the Boer War (1899–1902). During this conflict Richard Haldane (1856–1928), as Secretary of State for War, reformed the Army. He established a much-needed general staff, as well as the Territorial Army, and the British Expeditionary Force (BEF), which was to have a positive effect in the First World War and a less successful one in the Second World War.

Yet between 1914 and 1916 it was still the many thousands of volunteers who enabled Britain to fight the 'war to end all wars' – the Great War. It was only in January 1916 that, with the death toll rapidly rising, the politicians and generals got their way – conscription was introduced.

Six decades after the Second World War the notion of conscription is once again generally unpopular. It may have a hearty resonance with the many men who served their national service, and it remains the popular hobby horse of those politicians who believe that the whole of modern society's ills – and they are manifold – might in some way be swept aside by 24 compulsory months of square-bashing and weapons training. But a visit to any base in Germany today, and a conversation with an officer, will dispel any notions that conscription could make an early comeback. The following memoirs, from Private Booth and Lance Corporal Kingsmill, both illustrate in some small way just how much British society – and our Army – has changed since their arrival in Germany over four decades ago.

J.E. Booth was a private with 4th Infantry Workshops REME. He was stationed in Glamorgan Barracks, Duisburg between 1950 and '51.

'When I was posted to Germany I wasn't sure what to expect in Europe after five years of war with heavy bombing and the land assault after D-Day.

'We travelled to the Hook of Holland via Harwich on the overnight ferry. When we arrived we were put on an International Wagon-Lit train to travel into Germany.

'The train compared very well with the trains back home, with very comfortable carriages, and the food in the dining car was far better than we had been used to in our barracks in England. After passing through a reception centre in Hanover, I was posted to Glamorgan Barracks, Duisburg, where I stayed until demobilisation.

'The barracks were ex-SS and of a very high standard. For instance, we even had central heating, double glazing and there were only two or four of us to a room. When we were in barracks we served as a repair and maintenance unit for the brigade. It wasn't very exciting work. Outside the camp it was much more interesting. We were paid in British Armed Forces Currency Vouchers (commonly referred to as "baffs"). These were only accepted in the NAAFI or in the YMCAs. But Nescafé was a very desirable commodity for the German civilians and a few 4 oz tins sent over from home could provide us with enough German marks to have a good time and enjoy a bit more liberty. A group of us with similar interests visited Düsseldorf, Cologne and Bonn by train and tram. Cologne was a surprise. Up until then we hadn't come across too much bomb damage, yet in Cologne the cathedral stood virtually undamaged in the midst of acres of rubble. TOC H had acquired a large private house which they had turned into a bed and breakfast for servicemen. So, we spent our weekend leaves there in order to see more of the area.

'I remember taking a river cruise on the Rhine and visiting Bonn and the Dragonfels near Königswinter. I have intended to return to this area with my wife several times over the past years, but 50 years on, sadly, I still haven't managed it. So I am grateful that I was given that opportunity whilst in the Army.

'We took part in two exercises whilst I was there. This involved taking the mobile workshops into the area where the exercise was taking place and carrying out repairs. On one occasion myself and two others with a breakdown truck became detached (lost, that is!) from our unit for three days. When we eventually got back we had a three-ton truck with two motorcycles on board, plus four more "bodies". We had simply left our unit in the morning and not realised that they had moved on without us.'

Alec Kingsmill was a lance corporal with the REME. He was stationed at Hamburg, Finkenwerder and Minden and served between 1948 and '49.

'The trip from Harwich to the Hook of Holland in the old *Empire Wansbeck* was uncomfortable – 176 souls in 4-storey bunks in a space which was usually only occupied by 36. But we did get two Mars Bars off the ration. We disembarked about 0830 and we were given a "jolly good meal" of white bread. It made me realise just how dark the stuff we'd been eating at home was. The train for Germany was good, German rolling stock with big picture windows. I was impressed with Holland, its clean streets and healthy-looking people. Perhaps they'd managed their post-war recovery better than we had. We had another good meal when we temporarily got off at the German border, and it was a long haul to Hamburg but we had the accompanying NAAFI coach dispensing tea and cakes. We hadn't yet learned of the commercial value of cigarettes and few, at least in our group, took advantage of the "new" price of ten pence for twenty. Money came in a new form – baffs, which were notes down to 3d.

'British government fiscal policy forbade the export of British currency.

'We went through Osnabrück, which gave us our first view of the results of Allied bombing. The people looked really fed-up – a sad contrast with the perfection of Holland behind us. The darkness set in and we saw very little, until we arrived in Hamburg. On the way, various groups got off, including some German POWs, who were travelling under a light guard. They looked pretty crestfallen.

'We were billeted in ex-German naval barracks. Between two to five to a room, with the luxury of en-suite washbasins with hot and cold water. Things were really looking up. The barracks were associated with the one-time adjoining U-boat facility at Deutsche-Werft. I was to work in 22 Heavy Workshop, REME, BAOR, which occupied the ex-Blohm and Voss seaplane works. My job was to learn "field radio", i.e. tactical radio as used by the Army in the field, including those used by tanks. The next six months were a mixture of the strange, the interesting and the frustrating. Our workshop employed 2,000 German workers – many of whom were extremely skilled, especially in optics and instruments. All fatigues were done by Germans. They cleared the tables after us, swept our rooms, they even cut our hair and did all the washing up. For the lowly rank of private at the time I found that the food I ate was excellent. Our accommodation at what we now called Pilbright Barracks was very pleasant, and we had an added bonus, because Hamburg at the time was a Mecca of entertainment. Fortunately we were virgin soldiers enough not to really realise what a wholly male environment we lived in.

'There were seven cinemas for British troops, besides the State

Opera, the Garrison Theatre and the studios and the concert hall of the British Forces Network. It was in Hamburg that I went to my first symphony concert. On Remembrance Sunday in 1948 I was among the congregation of the BBC's *Sunday Half Hour*, which was broadcast from the Garrison Church in Hamburg. Above all stood the NAAFI facility – Victory House – reputed to be the best NAAFI in the world. Saturday-afternoon tea, accompanied by a string ensemble, was really rather fine. During that time the concept of "victory" was becoming almost politically incorrect. The NAAFI club was eventually re-named "Hamburg House". Getting to Hamburg was a bit tedious for us, having first to catch the launch across the Elbe, then perhaps a lucky hitchhike in a lorry, but more likely a half-mile walk to the S-bahn, the local suburban train service at Klein Flottbeck. By then the non-fraternisation policy had officially ended, but we still travelled free in compartments labelled *"Nur fur besatzungsarmee"* (Only for occupying forces). At first, travelling around the Hamburg region, I assumed that all the war damage was concentrated in the industrial and dockside area.

'It was what subsequent histories would say "reflected our accurate bombing". But slowly, what I saw begin to reveal this was not the case. In October I wrote home to my parents:

> My God, the damage. I have never seen such a lot of wilderness in all my life. As far as you could see from the railway it is just rubble and wrecked buildings . . . all the stations are just twisted girders and a platform. It is amazing that anyone gets out of the train at these stations, but I suppose someone lives beneath all that rubble.

'Then there was the black market in cigarettes. It was illegal, popular and extensive, generally administered through the camp barbers, who were the only Germans we were in contact with. The official rate of the German mark at that time was 13.5 to the pound. However, cigarettes could be bought at 10d for 20 in the NAAFI and sold for 5 marks. That was the equivalent of 120 marks to the pound. With this unofficial exchange-rate through cigarettes some of the high-tech products Germany was renowned for, which, unlike food, were slowly re-appearing in German shops, became very accessible to us. Our ration was 100 cigarettes per week, plus 3 bars of chocolate, and 3 packs of chewing gum, all for 6/9d. (34p).'

Like the other contributions from this period, Alec Kingsmill's observations on food, travel and the legacy of living accommodation for soldiers left behind for the Third Reich's conquerors amply reveal the massive task which lay ahead for the British government in bringing society up to speed and, eventually, allowing the Army to reflect such social improvements.

As a bright, confident young tank officer told me in Sennelager:

'I chose this job – no one pushed me into it. Today's British Army represents every social advance made at home since World War Two. The bull's gone – and nobody shouts at anyone anymore. Nevertheless, *we still get the job done.'*

2

'Please Throw Sandwiches'

I wondered how one Christian country could do this to
another Christian country. When the train entered Münster
I had been a nominal Methodist. When the train finally
cleared the ruins I had become an agnostic and have
remained one ever since.

Lance Corporal Gordon Cox, RAMC

Considering the warlike state of mind Hitler had forced upon his
beloved *Volk* during his 13 mad years of power, it is worth
remembering that throughout history the German philosophical
mind has had as much to offer on the subject of peace as the Nazis
did on conflict. Thomas Mann famously said that war was only a
cowardly escape from the problems of peace. Desiderius Erasmus
(1466–1536), although a Dutchman, took most of his inspiration
from the German religious tradition, claiming he had 'a Catholic
soul, but a Lutheran stomach'. One of his phrases still serves to
point out the harsh truth behind any recruiting poster: '*War is
sweet for those who do not have to take part.*'

The ordinary foot soldier, sailor or airman, seeing his friends and
comrades wounded or killed, soon realises that smart uniforms,
parades and exotic travel are all much more enjoyable when you're
not being fired at. However, you'll rarely hear the soldier voice such
an opinion, and he's always ready to do the job. That was what
Germany was all about for the British – being in a state of readiness.
The idea of firing in anger may seem a world away as you sit with
your mates over a few beers in the cosy confines of a German bar on
a cold night. However, as the Gulf, the Falklands and Belfast have
proved, if you're looking for a safe nine-to-five job with a pension

52

and few risks, don't join the Army. As one sergeant at Sennelager remarked, 'Danger? It comes with the territory – part of the job. You wouldn't become a milkman if you hated early rising and cold glass bottles . . .'

Whatever reservations soldiers may have about their lot, these usually come out in a resigned sense of humour. Consider this song from the Great War:

> Why did we join the Army, boys?
> Why did we join the Army?
> Why did we come to France to fight?
> We must have been bloody well barmy.[1]

Such a ditty bears comparison with one recalled by Lance Corporal John Saville of the RASC four decades later – it goes with the tune of *Shotgun Boogie* by Tennessee Ernie Ford:

> Round about sun-up every day,
> I grab my Brasso and I'm on my way,
> I march down the road,
> A bullin' and a willin'
> Down to the square
> To do some shit-hot drillin'.

One of the more pleasant aspects of the period in Germany covered by this book is that as the shadows of the Second World War recede, death and injury, with the exception of those Germans who attempted to escape from the east, take a back seat, to be replaced by different shadows, those of impending nuclear doom. Thankfully, despite the grim expectations following Nagasaki and Hiroshima, the much-predicted Third World War never happened, although, to paraphrase Harold Wilson, the time spent writing a book is a long time in politics.

The keenness to talk about and write down their memories among soldiers who served in Germany between 1945 and 1960 has by far surpassed any desire by later generations to recall their service. Perhaps the explanation for this lies in the less-dramatic circumstances, even allowing for the continuing Cold War stand-off, that our troops found themselves in by the 1970s. By that time Germany's economy had steamed ahead of Britain's. Social conditions both at home and in the Army had improved dramatically.

Based on the collected evidence, conflict and its immediate aftermath have provided those earlier servicemen with indelible recollections and remembered images which for obvious reasons would remain far more memorable. Army life in a well-heeled peacetime is one of routine, even though in Germany vigilance was the watchword. Army life in the immediate aftershock of war offers a different scenario.

Allen Parker, now living in Grimsby, was a corporal with the 113 Company of the RASC. He was based in Sennelager and Mülheim from 1952 to '54.

'I am one of a family of nine, plus mother and father, with six boys surviving. Dad was in the '14 to '18 war in France and Russia, about which he would not talk. Five of us were in the services; four in the Army, one in the Navy. Three caught the '39 to '45 war and survived. I arrived in Germany on 25 February 1953.

'When we reached the German border at Dalheim the engine changed and armed border guards checked the train. The border guards and military staff looked far more military than us 18-year-old "sprogs". As a schoolboy in the war, most evenings I had watched bomber command leave Waltham aerodrome on their ops to the very places I was now passing through. In 1953 the damage seen from the train was still extensive but the town centres were not too bad. As you can imagine, my first impression of Deutschland on that dark winter's day was pretty grim: 113 Company was based in Wrexham Barracks with 11 Company. Our function was to supply the Infantry Division with food and fuel. The barracks was a superb set of buildings, double glazed, tiled corridors, washrooms, centrally heated. The canteen had curtains, tablecloths and we had waitress service. This, after our UK billets, was five star. We had a good NAAFI, WVS, a football pitch, tennis courts and a swimming pool.

'I started in the CQMS stores and then became GOL – "Gasoline, Oil and Lubricants", and by the end of my national service had reached full Corporal. Because we were a supply unit we were always on "schemes". I think I did about 13 in 19 months. One scheme in March 1954 was called: "Applejack" and it was so cold that even the wagons with anti-freeze were freezing up – hence the name was changed to "Rednose".

'Exercise Triple Cross was a Royal Engineers scheme, and they had to get us across the River Weser three different ways. This they managed, but sometimes it was a bit hairy. Every September there was the big exercise. In 1952 it was called Grand Repulse, 1954 it was Battle Royal, which I just missed because my demob was due. I was pleased to miss it but it was sad waving the lads off, knowing I would not see them again.

'On one scheme I was responsible for a whole train load of fuel. It was a nightmare; stacked everywhere by German GSO and issued to all and sundry. At the end we were 157 Jerry cans light. The contents were covered by a generous 2 per cent leakage write-off. Still, I thought, "I'm in trouble now." But my captain happened to mention on the phone to a fellow officer at the supply depot our dilemma, and to my relief was told that the other officer had plenty of surplus and we could help ourselves. I was round there in a three-tonner before you could blink.

'Our wagons were Austin K5s; 11 Company had long-nosed Bedfords. When you were out on location and one of our K5s was approaching in the middle of the night, you could hear it from miles away with that high-pitched whine.

'The food on schemes was very good, mainly compo meals cooked on hydro burners. The latrines were, as usual, always the hole in the ground with sacking screens, poles to sit on, and a shovel. It was always super to get back to camp, take a shower and enjoy a proper bed after living in the backs of wagons or bivouacs. On one scheme we didn't scrim up quick enough (that's putting camouflage nets on the wagons) so all the next day on our travels they made us do it many times.

'The winter of 1953–4 was one of the coldest on the Ruhr for many years and the river was used just like a street; you could drive a jeep across it. We used to kick a piece of ice all the way from the town centre back to camp along the river.

'I had two leaves of 21 days back to the UK and I sailed on the *Wansbeck*, *Vienna* and the *Parkestone*. A work colleague was a deck officer on the *Wansbeck* and he said they were known as the "ghost ships" because they always slipped in and out of port by night. On one leave I left Mülheim and there was a huge hole in the town centre. When I returned after three weeks there was a large building there. I think it was a store. The builders used to work all night under floodlights.

'The shops in Germany had more choice of food than in the UK. Back home we still had rationing.

'I recall one time when we were on an exercise involving atomic warfare and we all got lost in Wuppertal. We were in blocks of six wagons. There were wagons coming out of every street, with everyone looking bewildered. It was complete chaos.

'I could ride a motorbike and we had big side-valve BSAs. If you got stuck in a tram line on a wet day it was very dodgy. I was given a new Matchless to run on Wednesday afternoons for a few weeks to get it ready for the September Army scheme. I really enjoyed that and saw a lot of our area. I had a super time apart from Guards, Vehicle Picket Duty, Clerks and lost Jerry cans! I often used to think of the lads of 1944–5 and of how it must have been for them over the same area where I now was, just a short eight years later.

'I remember Karl, a German on our camp. He said he'd woken up one morning and the city of Essen had been flattened. All those who could – i.e. the rich – moved to Cologne, and the next night that too was flattened.

'I left Germany in mid-September 1954 and arrived back at Bordon Camp to be demobbed on 30 September. On the last weekend in the Army at Bordon I was on a scheme somewhere guarding a river.

'I am now 69 and retired 9 years ago after 28 years working at the Humber Oil Terminal. What a difference – from Jerry cans to supertankers.'

For those of us who lived in Britain during that period, our memory is of a grey, dull time. Its high points were perhaps the Festival of Britain and the Coronation in 1953, but with rationing still in full flow, acres of bomb rubble and legions of still war-weary men and women taking on any work they could find, even the reappearance of Stork margarine in 1954, after years of that standard yellow utility grease in its brown-printed wrapper, seemed a major focus for celebration. With this monochrome world to escape from, it seems little wonder that to many young soldiers, Germany was a big adventure.

Gerald Gurney, now living in Colchester, was a corporal with the RAOC, at Bad Oeyenhausen between 1950 and '52.

'I was surely the only private soldier to arrive in Bad Oeyenhausen, then the headquarters of BAOR, in a staff car. It was 1950. Our group of national servicemen had disembarked from a boat at the Hook of Holland after surviving conditions reminiscent of that great slavery epic, *Roots*. We were then interviewed by a major in my own regiment, the Royal Army Ordnance Corps. He selected me for his office. This was altogether more promising than a posting to Korea – the fate of those soldiers at our training camp in Aldershot whose surnames began with any letter from M to Z.

'The office was set up in a private house requisitioned from the Germans in 1945 and had a staff of five – the major, a sergeant, a corporal and a private as well as a German postal orderly affectionately known, on account of his shaven head, as *"Kartoffelkopf"* (Potatohead). We handled the manpower administration of all Ordnance Corps, Dental Corps and Intelligence Corps personnel in the British Zone, including establishments, postings and promotions.

'I replaced Ian Ball, later to become a distinguished journalist, and, apart from typing letters and orders, maintained a huge plastic wall-chart of Ordnance Corps statistics covering all the units. It was, to say the least, undemanding, and only occasionally was there any relief from the daily routine. But sometimes the sergeant, having fallen out with someone – quite probably of a higher rank – would look him up in the records and transfer him to some dreary, out-of-the-way unit. We often indulged in the common office practice of throwing waste paper into a distant basket and using mock German, as in *"Holdenzie* on a moment" on the telephone. On one occasion we had a call, ostensibly from the commander-in-chief's office, which informed us that "a courier is now on his way to pick up a secret file". This was, of course, an Intelligence Section test of our security – we didn't fall for it. In our small group it was natural that the usual differences of rank were rather blurred, and the major took a keen personal interest in our welfare. On one occasion he went out of his way to break the conventions. One afternoon, when he was away from the office, a telephone call from the War Office granted me instant compassionate leave on account of my father's serious illness. I was at the station within an hour, and, just before the train came in, the major arrived to offer comforting words. Arrangements were also made for the train from Harwich to make an unscheduled stop at Colchester, where my family lived.

'After a time, I was promoted to lance corporal, but promotion to corporal, which soon followed, required that I should attend a course in stock control, etc., although I never saw the inside of an Ordnance store. The major had little interest in the Medical, Dental and Intelligence Corps, so I took on more and more of their administration. Some months later, I took particular delight in drafting and typing my early release – by a few weeks – in order to take up my place at Oxford University in the autumn of 1952.

'An order came from above that we had to take part in an exercise. We were to be "Blueland", retreating westwards across Holland along the autobahn, hotly pursued by the mythical "Redland". As we had to be self-supporting, we were required to cater for ourselves, and I was appointed cook for about 30 officers and men. The major asked me what I needed to make an open fire – a large number of bricks and a heap of wood – and it was no coincidence that our first stop was close to a building site. He gave the necessary orders, saying *"C'est la guerre"*. Just as the stew (what else?) was simmering nicely, the order came for us to move on, whilst at the same time we were being "bombed" from above with bags of flour. (What happens if someone is hit on the head with a bag of flour dropped from a great height?) This could have been a scene at Captain Mainwaring's Walmington-on-Sea. More hilarity was to follow; we were supposed to practise our administration skills – receiving and responding to pseudo-messages sent by radio. For the first time in my life, I had no sleep at all and passed the time receiving such messages as "Colonel Snodgrass killed in action" and replying "Promote Major Goodenough".

'Fear of the Redland forces was nothing compared with the possibility of losing one's rifle, which had to be carried at all times. Despite these war games and camping out in the bitter cold, my doubles partner and I won the BAOR table-tennis championship on the day after our return.

'It was not quite a life of luxury but we lived in a private house – nothing like a barracks – where I had contrived to get a room to myself. As became headquarters staff, we suffered hardly any Army routine – no parades (not even for pay) and no inspections – but we did have occasional guard duty, which could be avoided by payment to some hard-up mate. The nearest we got to a parade was to form an orderly queue before the seated medical officer, drop our trousers and pants, and suffer the indignity of an FFI involving the deft use of a pencil. FFI in Army jargon stands (ungrammatically) for "Free From Infection". Returning to the subject of guard duty, it seemed that duty officers rarely attended to their duties, so it was a profound shock when late one night, one made an appearance. We were all sheltering from the rain and cold when some should have been out on stag patrol. The officer was very drunk, but we could hardly use this in our defence when hauled up before the commanding officer in the morning. We were merely given an informal reprimand, suggesting that he was well aware of the situation.

'Baths were taken in the wooden tubs which remained from the pre-war days of Bad Oeyenhausen when it was a spa, and they were even filled for us by an attendant. Astonishingly, we had free use of taxis, Volkswagen Beetles with German drivers. When I first went out to Germany, we were required to wear uniform in public but later on we were allowed to wear civvies. Cookhouse food was appalling. I often went to the canteen, took a look at what was on offer and finished up in the NAAFI. Was there, perhaps, a conspiracy so that NAAFI profits were boosted?'

To gauge the atmosphere in Europe in the immediate post-war period, the following statistics on the Second World War reveal the full misery this great 'war of liberation' had caused.

The Second World War – the Costs[2]

	Probable Military Casualties	Probable Civilian Casualties	Probable Costs in £ millions
USSR	13,600,000	7,700,000	£23,253
Germany	3,480,000	3,890,000	£53,084
Japan	1,700,000	360,000	£10,317
Great Britain	452,000	60,000	£12,446
Italy	330,000	85,000	£5,267
USA	295,000	none	£62,560
France	250,000	360,000	£27,818
Poland	120,000	5,300,000	unknown
Totals	20,227,000	17,755,000	£194,745

Well over half a century later, these statistics, even allowing for two atomic bombs, remain shocking. The physical results of all this death and destruction would continue to have their effect upon the young men and women who, although they had no part in their creation, were now old enough to be called up for service in Germany. What they witnessed and remembered so vividly makes Germany's recovery even more remarkable. By the 1960s political commentators were referring to Germany's recovery as the *Wirtschaftwunder* – the 'economic miracle'. However, without being disingenuous to the hard-working Germans, it could be argued that this miracle may not have appeared so rapidly without the imposition of a state of order amidst chaos, courtesy of a lot of uniformed youngsters from across the Channel.

Here's how one of them saw it all:

Lance Corporal Gordon Cox was with the RAMC at Bielefeld. He was a part of the 'The Linseed Lancers' between 1946 and '49.

'Sometime in the summer of 1947 a cloud of blanco descended from a train at Waterloo, wafted across to the station exit and disappeared into a dozen or so TCVs to be carried to Liverpool Street, bound for Harwich and the waiting *Empire Parkestone*. Inside this cloud were 120 medics, glad to have escaped from the severe regime of the Royal Army Medical Corps Depot, where the daily bullshit included blancoing *all* your webbing and, for Pete's sake, your tin hat! Most of us had been out at UK military hospitals working shifts and hours, so returning to the bawl and shout of a barracks had, to put it mildly, been a culture shock.

'We disembarked from the *Parkestone* at the Hook of Holland where a small garrison of railway sappers, cooks and Pay Corps occupied a small enclave to organise the unloading of troopships carrying reinforcements and men returning from leave. We boarded a troop train bound for Bielefeld Reinforcement Unit and as the train chugged across Holland we were surprised that there didn't seem to be signs of the country having been involved in a war. The war had been over for two years so perhaps the Dutch had cleaned up. Passing Rotterdam it was hard to believe it had been blitzed by the Luftwaffe, but it had. At Appeldoorn on the German-Dutch frontier we were issued with sandwiches in cellophane packets bearing the legend "Keep Death Off The Lines".

'As the train crossed the frontier, groups of German boys stood on the embankment with little placards which said "Please Throw Sandwiches". The train was now rolling along quite slowly on tracks which had probably not had much maintenance in recent years. We eventually reached the outskirts of Münster. My comrades and I had to stand up for 20 minutes or so at the windows, gazing at a scene of devastation unbroken for five or six miles, courtesy of the RAF and USAAF. I wondered how a Christian country could do this to another Christian country. When the train entered Münster I had been a nominal Methodist. By the time it finally cleared the ruins I had become an agnostic and have remained one ever since.

'In the late evening we arrived at the barracks in Bielefeld. It was a fine modern building – Hitler loved his Wehrmacht – quite different to the wooden pigsties most of us had been kipping in for the past year. We remained in Bielefeld for about a fortnight, killing time with square-bashing, PT and a run-and-a-jump over an assault course, while our future postings were determined.

'It had been a pleasant surprise to go into the NAAFI and collect weekly cigarette rations of 105 snouts for 15 pence. Ten pence in the beer bar could buy you six pints.

'We went into Bielefeld town several times. The currency was cigarettes. Four of the soon-to-be-discontinued Reichsmarks could be had for one cigarette. The average German earned 60 Reichsmarks per week. Seven Germans were paid the equivalent of one of our weekly fag rations – 15 pence. Privates suddenly became very rich.

'The DNAFM draft was eventually scattered to the eight British military hospitals and to the many Camp Reception Stations (sort of mini cottage hospitals) attached to battalions and other large formations. I was posted to the medical branch HQ, BAOR, at Bad Oeyenhausen. "Baddo", as it was called, was a very pleasant spa, about twice the size of Southwell in Nottinghamshire, with twice the population. Unfortunately the 10,000 "Deutschers" had been evicted from their nice little town to make way for 1,000 officers and 2,000 other ranks who acted as clerks, batmen, drivers, runners, and every kind of dogsbody to the officers.'

Sausage, Chips and Music
'The centre of Baddo was a large park, the perimeter being well over a mile long. It contained the opera house, which became the Garrison Theatre, scene of regular visits from top UK entertainers. It was also the venue for regular sit-down parades. Up on the stage would be the Medical Officer (MO) and the Padre, who would not

mince words about the perils of consorting with the platoon of doxies who hovered around the garrison. For medics, it was coals to Newcastle, but we still had to parade with the rest of the troops, who were mainly teenagers.

'The other buildings in the park were the *Badhaus* (bath house) where we had our weekly tub, and the large *Kurhaus* (hotel and pump house), which had been converted into a NAAFI. This was well patronised. On pay day, and for a couple of days after, we would go into the Kurhaus in the evening and have a plate of sausage and chips (7p). Whilst enjoying this feast we were serenaded by an eight-piece string orchestra of high quality which would have brought shouts of "Bravo!" from Mantovani or even Nelson Riddle had they been with us.'

Brasshats Everywhere

'Surrounding the park were hotels and large houses. The largest hotel was the Konigshof, which accommodated "G" people – the general staff. The GOC, chief of staff and major-general administration were based there. Other hotels and houses were taken over by Ordnance, Signals, Engineers and other units, usually led by a brigadier. The place was alive with brasshats. There were cookhouses, where we peasants ate, sergeants' messes, officers' messes, and that rare establishment, a brigadiers' mess. Full colonels and above made up the membership.

'The medical branch occupied a large convent. Major-General Sir Edward Philips, (at one time Monty's head sawbones), was in charge. There were two brigadiers, three full colonels, a lieutenant-colonel, and several majors and captains. Apart from a couple of quartermasters, they were all consultants, doctors and dentists. There were about 20 or so other ranks all serving the brass, led by a no-nonsense regimental sergeant-major. He was extremely tough with us young conscripts, but looking back he was like a strict father and we all benefited from his regime. On one occasion half a dozen of us were arrested after tottering and singing our way back to the billet from the beer bar. He pulled strings with the garrison police to get the fizzer cancelled. In return he paraded us and gave us the ear-bashing of a lifetime. "Disgrace to the Corps! Not fit to wear the badge . . ."

'The rollicking lasted a full five minutes. We were shaking like leaves when he dismissed us, but it was better than the inevitable seven-day jankers [punishment duties] had he not intervened.

'Our neighbours just up the road were the War Crimes Commission. Apparently they spent a lot of time going into Poland and Czechoslovakia, gathering evidence. They had no connection to the Rhine Army but Baddo was a handy place to make their base camp.'

The Wehrmacht's Revenge

'My first job at the Medical Branch was in the CSR (the Central Syphilis Registry!) – I kid you not. Three of us, behind locked doors, recorded names of soldiers who had reported sick with VD. They had completed questionnaires which included questions such as:

> *What was her name?*
> Answer: Don't know.
> *Was she fair haired, dark haired or a redhead?*
> Answer: Can't remember.
> *How old was she?*
> Answer: I didn't ask her.

'This information was subsequently passed to the Redcaps who would attempt to apprehend the girls with the help of the German *Polizei*. The *fräuleins* had taken over the job of wounding the British Army from the Wehrmacht. One squaddie in seven had been hit, despite the constant propaganda about the dangers of using the services of the streetwalkers.

'Eight months after arriving in BAOR I was approached by an attractive girl as I stood waiting for a bus. "Coming my way, soldier?" she said.

'"No thanks," I replied. The bus came two minutes later. It was the number 29 from Portland Street, Manchester Piccadilly to my home in Ashton-under-Lyne. I was home on my first leave. It seemed ironic, after so much lecturing and warnings in BAOR, that the first time I was to be accosted had to be home in Blighty.'

Hugh Martin now lives in Jersey. He was a sergeant in the Army Education Service at Finkenwerder between 1950 and '52.

'I seemed to spend all of my pay, about £5.50 per week, eating out. At Finkenwerder, it was assumed I played the piano. Apparently it was thought that all education sergeants did so. We were expected to entertain. In fact, I used to get suspicious looks – "Are you *sure* you don't play?" Never volunteer. I think a lot of soldiers were puzzled by the Royal Army Education Corps (RAEC). So, at one point we toyed with the idea (which we didn't pursue, fortunately), that we'd inform anyone mystified by us that we belonged to the Royal Atomic Energy Commission and were all scientists. It was our own version of Baldrick's "cunning plan", but it may well have contravened the Official Secrets Act. My own puzzle was a simple one – I still wonder why Army washbasins never had any plugs.

'As education sergeants, a group of us once toyed with the idea. In the Sergeants' Club at Hamburg House, we had a delightful old waiter. He was 83 years old. He'd been jailed during the war for listening to the BBC. He insisted on serving us his own choice of wine, "The beautiful German Mosel – not that French rubbish!"

'We heard all kinds of stories from the Germans. One Hamburger told us that they always knew when an air raid was due long before the sirens went off. Apparently, the local dogs would start howling.

'As I recall, there wasn't too much animosity between us. I recall walking down the street in Hamburg once. There were three of us. Some passing Germans swore at us. We couldn't translate it, but we knew they were swearing. And my wife, Anne, was pushed off the road once in Brunswick. But in general, we were accepted, and after all, we weren't the Russians.'

Dennis Pell was a signalman with the Royal Signals in 1948. He served at Fassberg in the 11th Air Formation Signals Regiment.

'When I knew I was to be posted to Germany I was quite pleased in a way. I left school at Christmas in 1942 and started work at the age of 14 at our local airfield at Little Staughton in Bedfordshire. The Americans were there by then and I worked with the Air Ministry electricians. I enjoyed the job and the life very much.

'When I finally got into the Army I knew it was going to be interesting for me to see what effect all those bombers we'd helped to send off had had on Germany. I suppose whatever the bombers had done, in some way I'd contributed to it. It was 1948 when I got to Germany and I got on well with the Germans. To me they were simply people, just like us.

'Although I was in the Army, my job with Royal Signals meant that I was attached to the RAF, which I found fortunate, because I loved planes and still do. At RAF Station Fassberg, our parent station, many of the buildings were built among the fir trees, which provided excellent camouflage. I worked alongside three German linemen, two of whom had been in the German military air force. One had been a navigator who told me that he'd made at least two flights over the UK during the war. We both got on well together, although I didn't always swallow what he told me. Another of these guys had been stationed on Jersey during the German occupation at St Helier airfield. He'd never agree to me taking a photograph of him, but he wasn't opposed to a couple of us taking some chocolate down to his house at Christmas!

'I did have one or two romances in Germany. Troops always seem to respond to a nation's ladies as opposed to its men. I met one girl who I really fell for when I was despatched to the officers' base housing at Fassberg, where the RAF adjutant was based. In addition to my romance the adjutant became very friendly towards me and I to him, and he would always pass the time of day when seeing me at the base.

'I did manage to get put on a couple of charges whilst in Germany. The first came as a result of my working alongside a chap called Geordie Mayne. We were both detailed to lay a quad cable from Fassberg to a small railway station at Poitzon. It was only a few kilometres and we had this darn great steam locomotive pulling a long flatbed wagon on which we had our cable layer. The Army term for this cable-laying device was a "drum barrow" and this was mounted on two wheels with brand-new pneumatic tyres. The engine would pull us slowly along the track and Geordie and I would lay the cable as we went along. At the end of the day back at Fassberg we knew we should have taken the drum barrow back to our stores but Geordie persuaded me that we could leave it for the night on the flatbed wagon so it would be ready for us to carry on the next day. Come the next morning, we turned up for work only to discover that the cable layer had been nicked!

'Needless to say, we'd all been thoroughly briefed about taking particular care of vehicles. There was an acute shortage of tyres and inner tubes in the German economy.'

In such an atmosphere of deprivation the Germans had to find space for another emotion: shame. A few of the soldiers who have contributed to this book briefly mentioned Bergen-Belsen. Most avoided going into detail; one summed it up with the phrase 'I won't go into that.' The story of the liberation of the camps has been told in all its gory detail many times. Belsen, for those who saw it in the immediate post-war months, remains a dark memory.

Adrian Cooper, now of Lostwithiel, Cornwall, was a private in the REME, BAOR, between 1947 and '49.

'It was while we were staying in the hostel in Celle that someone suggested a visit to Belsen concentration camp, so I instructed our coach driver – a German – and we went the next day. You turn off the road at a hamlet called Bergen into a side road that leads to open moorland. The camp was spread over a large area, some of it under trees. The main entrance consisted of a few buildings including a dark, sinister-looking Gothic eye-catcher on rising ground with an imposing flight of stone stairs. This had been the SS and camp guards' quarters. Some of the perimeter wire fence had been flattened by tanks when the camp was liberated and we drove through to the central area. There were three long, deep trenches and big square mounds nearby, each with a wooden notice which read "3,000 buried here" or "5,000 buried here", or "800" – they were numbers too great to comprehend. In another part there were the concrete bases of the gas chambers and a huge tank sunk into the ground. It contained thousands of pairs of shoes – men's, women's and children's. A sickening sight. And the silence was very real, a shocked atmosphere.

'All the accommodation huts had been burned down. There was nothing more to see except the ironical sight of a group of elderly Jews enjoying the sun on the steps of the SS building. Our driver had stayed in the coach and declined to get out. He told me later that he had spent four months there as punishment for deserting from the Russian front. The sights and sounds, beatings, killings, filth, cruelty, starvation and disease, and the tasks he had to perform haunted him. He was ashamed.'

Prisoners, displaced persons and refugees were all some of the many problems the Army of occupation had to deal with. A number of soldiers have mentioned the Yugoslavian DPs, in their ill-fitting navy-blue uniforms, many of whom would sit around the fire in their huts at night and sing poignant songs from their homeland, filled with a heart-wrenching longing. And there was that most persecuted nation, who, next to the Jews, had also suffered the brute force of the Nazi's boundless hatred – the Poles. Like many other refugees, they too had to be accommodated in camps.

K.O. Airey of Middlesbrough was in the Royal Artillery at Bielefeld between 1947 and '48.

'The week after arriving we were sent with a working party to cut down trees in the forests near Hanover. They called us "The Woodpeckers". This was just one of our duties. The other was to keep a camp full of Polish refugees in a nearby compound in order. They were displaced persons, homeless, and kept having uprisings. So we were kept very busy indeed.

'We worked in the forests until January 1948 when the German Timber Corporation took over. Until then there had been virtually no employment in Germany. After that we did our "Army of occupation" duties. It was called "showing the German population who won the war". In our SS-built billet we had an ex-SS man scrubbing the floor. We paid him two cigarettes for cleaning up. The German workers in the camp were usually badly treated. At this time there was still a blackout and most Germans lived in cellars. I remember one of our tree-felling crew – his name was Samson, from Nottingham – was killed by a falling tree. Also, one of our majors shot himself. Both were given military funerals and are buried in Hanover cemetery.'

With all the devastation, and the new atmosphere of dull, challenging reality presented to the conquerors after the years filled with the high-adrenaline thrust of combat, the British troops stood at the threshold of a massive task. Not only did they have to keep order; it would be the military who would be the catalyst for the re-organisation of the very country they had fought against. Eventually, through the gloom, hope would appear, but it seemed a long time coming.

Geoff Gilbert of Swadlincote was a PT instructor corporal with the Sherwood Foresters. He was based at Rheinberg in 1947.

'Outside of Stuttgart we passed two hills, and my friend said that they were all the rubble and bomb damage from the city. The hills were now grassed over and paths had been made, so that the local people could now walk to the top of the remains of what had been their homes and enjoy picnics. I was told that General Rommel's son was the Mayor of Stuttgart, and highly thought of.

'In 1951, with my friends who lived in Göttingen, we all walked about three miles to a clearing in a wood. There, against a backdrop of rocks, we saw the opera *Carmen* performed. The company of actors and actresses were all very professional. I was told that this was a regular event during the summer. I found it very unusual, being outdoors, but a most enjoyable experience.'

For the Germans there was no way to go but up. Four decades later, in 1984, the good people of Stuttgart would still be picnicking on their grassy rubble hills, whilst down in the city, British bricklayers, having said '*Auf Weidersehen*, pet' to their wives at home, would be demonstrating their skills in the re-shaping of Stuttgart's skyline.

At least in Germany they could find some work which paid a decent wage. According to the city's authorities, their craftsmanship, like that of the British Army, was very good indeed.

3

Living with Herman

At the camp where I was eventually based, there were several German civilian employees. What contact I had with them always seemed amicable. Outside the camp, in bars, shops or restaurants, I found it quite easy to get along with the local people. I did try and learn the language, and can't remember ever falling out with a German.

Stan Roberts, Staff Sergeant, REME

As it has always been between Britain and France, there will forever remain an undercurrent of xenophobia between us and the Germans.

No doubt there was an atmosphere of mutual hostility between the Germans and the occupying Allies in the immediate post-war years. Yet the memories of the soldiers who served in BAOR during that time often display an openness and an observational curiosity which seems a long way from any hatred or mistrust. Living with the Germans, who had been such an implacable foe, became a strange reality upon which some soldiers meditated.

Alec Kingsmill, of Nottingham, was in the REME between 1948 and '49.

'There was, I suppose, also a sense of worldliness. Extensive travelling was not the norm in those days and to those who were prepared to be interested, Germany was definitely overseas and definitely different. Somewhere in the pysche must have been some reflection of superiority in being part of an Army of occupation and the perks that went with it, following the defeat of a rather disliked enemy.'

Unlike the American Army, the British Army in Germany has never had the notion of fraternisation forced upon it. As the memory of the Nazi period began to fade, the Americans, with the best of intentions, carried on their policy of 'host nation relations' to such a degree that at one time they produced daily statistics on how well their soldiers were mixing with the locals. Our own reticence to adopt such a procedure probably resulted from the fact that although we share a common language with America and eagerly soak up their bright shiny culture, domestically we have much more in common with the Germans than we'll ever have with the Yanks. No doubt the cosmopolitan nature of American society, as represented by its army abroad, with so many genealogical European roots, including the descendants of German, Polish, Italian and other emigrant families, helped to form a different quest for international understanding between them and their hosts – especially when it came to the appearance of Jewish soldiers and African Americans in the midst of Hitler and Himmler's failed project of an 'Aryan Nation'. Among Britain's more static, broadly Anglo-Saxon forces, however, there were exceptions which had the Germans slightly puzzled.

Phil 'Tommo' Thompson of Kirkby-in-Ashfield, Nottinghamshire was a member of 54th Squadron RCT BAOR. He was stationed at Minden from 1962 to '65.

'I can remember going on exercise somewhere in Westphalia in the winter. Being the only black man in the outfit, I caused a few surprises. Some German women, having never seen a black man before, came up to me and rubbed my forearms to see if it was dirt which made them look like that. They then went on to pull my hair – there was nothing nasty about all this – they were honestly just curious. They would comment on my hair, saying, "*Starke . . . starke*" meaning "strong". My English friends were shocked and asked me if I was going to stand there and take all this. My response was, "They're just curious – they've never seen a black fellow before." You can imagine the laughter and the jibes afterwards. I continued to enjoy a very happy stay in Germany, having quite a lot of success with the ladies, and many good German friends were made, too.'

Many British soldiers, their families and children, formed warm and lasting relationships with their German hosts, even in those early post-war years.

Allen Parker of Grimsby was a corporal with the RASC. He served at Mülheim between 1952 and '54.

'Ernst, a German clerk, became a good friend and he still is to this day. One of my Army comrades in Germany, John, and I went back to stay with Ernst and his wife Inge in 1979 for Karnival weekend. We went back for a look at Wrexham Barracks and had a walk back down to the Ruhr. Everywhere was covered in snow. It was a fantastic weekend. We have since had many holidays with Ernst and Inge both over here and all over Germany and Austria.'

Thankfully, we've moved on from the situation in the mid-1960s when, after a few drinks, both officers and the rank and file could still rub a German's nose in history's dirt by reminding him 'who won the war'. It was not uncommon even as late as the 1960s for those less-sensitive members of the older officer class to express their role as victors in a less than magnanimous fashion. Without doubt the Germans, like the French, poke fun at us, but throughout history, such xenophobic ribbing has been part of every nation's culture.

Although Corporal Allen Parker expressed his surprise at the German work rate after seeing a Mülheim department store built during the duration of his three-week leave, this was not, apparently, too unusual. Yet another ex-soldier stationed in Germany not long after the war told me that he had passed by a devastated town square in Hamburg on his way home for his three weeks' leave.

'There was some scaffolding and a few trucks. When I came back that way three weeks later, there was a four-storey building there. I was amazed, and asked the tram driver how they'd built it so quickly – he told me that the men had worked 24 hours a day, 7 days a week. Within another fortnight, the building was occupied.'

What friendships did develop between squaddies and their German hosts often grew from a more opportunistic root – money. With NAAFI-issue cigarettes and chocolate being an exchangeable currency, one needed to get to know which Germans were keen to trade and supply you with those valuable Deutschmarks.

~ The Long Patrol ~

Ted Levy of Yeovil did national service. He was a mechanic with the
REME and served at Mülheim and Sennelager in 1950.

'As a vehicle mechanic I worked with two German fitters who did
a lot of the heavier work and were especially good with
Volkswagens, which most of the officers seemed to have. We also
employed German drivers, one of whom had driven a Panzer tank.
The workshop consisted of two REME, and a Cockney corporal,
who seemed out of place somehow in the Gordon Highlander's
Regiment! The two Germans were Heinz and Hans. They were both
hard workers, both good fun and had been fighter pilots during the
war. Their star turn was to be able to lower a VW engine onto
Heinz's shoulders to save us using jacks and hoists. Heinz had a
huge BMW bike. They both acknowledged the supremacy of the
Spitfire over their own fighter planes, although neither of them had
flown the Focke-Wulf 190.

'I used to sell Hans and Heinz my cheap NAAFI allowances for
Deutschmarks. This was common practice, at least in our HQ. With
the Marks I could buy goods in the town, mainly for presents for
relatives; souvenirs etc., which weren't available in the NAAFI shop.
The Deutschmarks also came in handy for other activities in town. I
used to make the most of my off-duty time of being in a foreign land
and travelled around to see the sights, or went on walks along the
river to pursue my hobby – watching wildlife.

'I remember when a deserter absconded with a 15 cwt truck and
I had to go and recover the vehicle when he abandoned it. I was also
part of an escort for a Scottish chap who had run off with a stolen
pistol. There was excitement and street-fights at night – sometimes
involving bottles. We were billeted in private houses which all had
nice gardens where we could relax and chat when off-duty. There
were constant reminders about mixing with German women and
sexual diseases, and a few men learnt the hard way. I had pen pals
and a girlfriend at home, so never took friendships too far. One or
two of the squaddies had married German girls and had private
houses in the town.

'After being moved to Lippspring, near Sennelager, I discovered
another amenity which I made full use of – learning to ride.

'About five ponies were available. There were two of us
squaddies, NCOs and an officer. We were trained by a German ex-
cavalry officer. The cost was one shilling per one-hour lesson.

'I also honed my piano-playing in Army "quiet rooms". I had

inherited my dad's untaught ear for music and became one of the sing-song "key bashers" in a restaurant in the town, which became our NAAFI club. None of the German mechanics or drivers had moved east with us from Mülheim so I no longer had an easy way of getting hold of Deutschmarks.

'I enjoyed my time in the Army and made the most of it. The tank range was just up the road, a huge heath and pine forest, where I went whenever I could to enjoy the wildlife. I count myself lucky.'

For the British serviceman and his family, getting along with the Germans is far easier today than it was 40 years ago, and even more so since reunification. Since the entry of Britain into the EEC and the more recent removal of borders between modern European countries, Germany feels no different in many ways than another British country. Its roads, towns and countryside have become almost as familiar to generations of military personnel as the ring roads around their home towns in the UK. One soldier in Sennelager told me that he felt far more foreign and disliked in Belfast than any other posting he'd had. Whilst this example is hardly surprising, considering the continuing political tensions in Northern Ireland, at least in Germany, despite the threat of terrorism, the likelihood of someone taking a pot shot at a British soldier seems minimal.

Since the wider availability of married quarters after 1970, an increasing number of soldiers have been able to enjoy a fuller domestic life in Germany. As the social barriers between the two cultures have begun to fade, there have been other positive developments. Ever since the Second World War single soldiers have been discovering that the German way of life has many attractions – as do its women. By the time the Berlin Wall had fallen, it is estimated that of approximately 65,000 British soldiers stationed around the world, over 2,500 had married German girls.[1] In addition to this, in Westphalia, an area which includes many of the well-established British bases, over 40,000 British servicemen have adopted Germany as their homeland. As we've discussed elsewhere, the reasons for this are many, but one fact is that unlike their British counterparts, German wives are far less happy to leave their home country to settle elsewhere. For a German girl marrying an Englishman, the move to the UK would seem to be permanent, whereas a British Army wife knows that once her husband's tour of duty is up, at least she'll be heading home again.

Judging by my own conversations with servicemen stationed in Germany, that 1990 figure of 40,000 has probably increased substantially by now.

In Germany, the British Army's transformation from conquerors to friends has been a long journey of mutual discovery. In the immediate aftermath of the war, non-fraternisation was the military rule. Young conscripts, faced with the tragic sight of hungry, innocent children, many of whom had not only lost parents but also their homes, found the idea of not mixing with or talking to these defeated people very difficult. Fortunately, the restrictions didn't last too long.

Stan Roberts of Spital in the Wirral was a staff sergeant in the REME. He was stationed in Hamburg, Trelde and Wenzendorf in 1946.
'The fraternisation ban as far as children were concerned was lifted quite quickly and Letter No. 3 on non-fraternisation was issued by the commander-in-chief on 14 July 1945. This allowed us to "engage in conversation with adult Germans in the streets and in public places", but "not for the present enter the homes and houses of the Germans nor permit them to enter any of the premises you are using except for duty or work".

'At some time this last restriction was removed, shortly before Christmas, I think, so that we were able to organise a party for the children at which we hired a *Kasperltheatre* – a marionette show. At New Year we had our first dance in the dancehall of the *Gasthof*. This was a converted barn, but it did have a very good floor for dancing. As I had learned German at school, very soon I became the MC and was made responsible for running the weekly dances. Normally I was able to hire a band made up of DPs (Displaced Persons – often Poles who had worked in the Reich as slave labourers). The rumour went out that the DPs had been locked in a room with a stack of Victor Sylvester records and told not to come out until they could play like that!

'No doubt the story was exaggerated in the telling, but they were an excellent strict-tempo band. I was never a very good dancer, I had attended classes in Bury in 1943, but we were able to organise classes run by one of our craftsmen, who was also an excellent pianist. So that I could enjoy the dancing, as MC I was able to make the band play only those dances I could do, except when I wanted a breather at the bar, when I let them play the more exotic dances such as the tango or the rumba. This formula turned out to be a great success and our dances were always well attended by soldiers from other units.

'We of course were able to go to their dances, but sometimes theirs were not as good as ours. They let the bands do their own thing, which often meant more tangos etc., than the average soldier could cope with, together with lengthy elimination dances, which became rather boring for those eliminated. I never had them, but relied on spot prizes. Before the ban, "fraternisation" was not a word in many people's vocabulary, but it became common usage, leading to a German girlfriend being known as a "Frat" or "a bit of Frat".

'As a sidelight on the German economy I remember when I visited a German dentist I paid him in Marks, but tipped him a packet of cigarettes. He nearly danced with delight as these were worth far more to him. I visited him for a small filling and to have a plate made to replace two front teeth I had lost due to an abscess. The *Zahnarzt* (literally translated – "tooth doctor") operated in a wooden hut similar to a large garden shed in the woods not far away, as he had been bombed out of his surgery in Hamburg. There was no electricity, so he had a treadle drilling machine. His stock of teeth was limited and he was quite upset that he could not exactly match my own, but in fact the slight irregularity disguised the fact that they were not natural. On home leaves my mother was always saying I should get a plate but on my next leave she never noticed until I pointed them out just before returning to my unit!'

Apart from the Germans who worked alongside the Army in those early days, there were many thousands of displaced persons and refugees, many of whom found menial jobs on the periphery of the Army of occupation. There were many Poles, Yugoslavs, Czechs and others who, as either ex-prisoners or slave workers, faced a difficult choice in their lives. Some feared the return to their country of origin, where the politics had changed. Others had lost both their homes and their families during the war. Many Russian POWs who were returned to the USSR received not a hero's welcome, but faced the harshness of Stalin's victorious Red Army; that they had seen out the remaining months of the war, not in sacrifice on the front line, but as unwilling slaves of the Nazis, counted for nothing.

Beyond the comparatively comfortable situation of the young British soldiers and their families, with their regular income, their NAAFI and ordered lifestyles, stood a shadowy, tragic mass of people whose pasts had vanished into history and whose futures were far from secure.

Understandably, in that first decade after the war there was still a degree of reservation amongst those young Germans who had survived their own military service towards the occupying forces. Even in the 1950s, by which time fraternisation had become more common, some soldiers came face to face with this opposition, which sometimes boiled over into open revolt.

Gerald Gurney of Colchester was a corporal with RAOC at Bad Oeyenhausen in 1950.

'Contact with the local population was minimal, partly because a large area of the BAOR HQ – with the finest buildings and hotels – was surrounded by a high fence. But there was a thriving market in cigarettes, a monthly ration of which could be bought very cheaply in the NAAFI and sold on, entirely, of course, in the interest of Anglo-German relations! As a non-smoker, I was well situated to take advantage of this, and I remember receiving tins of coffee from home in the post – with no intention of drinking it. The Germans were quite remarkably acquiescent, but on one occasion they gathered on the town's football pitch for a demonstration against the continued occupation and we were all issued with rifles – but with no ammunition or instructions. In Hamburg, when similar trouble arose, units of a (nameless) regiment with a reputation for drunkenness, rape and pillage, were moved in.

'Visiting Cologne one weekend, in uniform, I encountered three young Germans, who linked arms across the pavement in my path, only to separate at the last moment. I also felt distinctly uncomfortable, for no palpable reason, when I went to an opera performance – but it was insensitive of me to be there.'

It seems unlikely that the 'nameless regiment' referred to by Corporal Gurney was anything to do with the Royal Artillery, who figure in the next contribution.

Peter Daniels of Truro was a gunner with the Royal Artillery. He was based at Kiel and Münster between 1947 and '48.

~ Living With Herman ~

'I was in BAOR during the long hot summers of 1947 and 1948. I was 18, in the Royal Artillery, and the world was my lobster!

'There was an incident in Kiel in late 1947. The Control Commission Germany (CCG) had laid down that all factories in the area which had previously been making torpedoes were to be shut down. However, most of them had already changed over to civilian production and when the CCG insisted on closure the whole area revolted and we were sent in to crush it. It didn't take long. We stood in line and from behind the Sergeant said, "Daniels – when I tell you to shoot the man waving the banner *do not* kill the little old lady next door to him! We're going to push them down the road until they disperse – we may have to fire a volley over their heads. That's *over their heads*, Daniels, not *through* their heads!"

'My marksmanship was legendary and remained a laughing stock for some years. (But then, I was in the RA!)

'The revolt in Kiel finished quite peacefully with no casualties on either side, I'm happy to say; although there were a few further jibes at my marksmanship. We were all very young. I was a regular with six whole months' service but the rest of my squad were national servicemen. We didn't speak the language and at that time weren't allowed to fraternise. Our only contact with civilians was an old gentleman who came around each day to collect our washing. "*Guten Morgen*," he would say, "*Mein frau waschen in der morgen, wen sie will, mir dem bringen zurück . . .*" [This was "cod" German, as used by soldiers on the base, but an approximate translation would be: "Good morning, my wife will do the washing in the morning and return it later on."] It was a kind of little song we'd made up for him. It still seems a little strange to think that we had no military laundry to do our washing. Our other local contact was in the NAAFI, where we were all in love with the same blonde girl.'

Of course, love and romance pay little heed to politics or square-bashing. Many British soldiers and German civilians put their humanity first and in a time-honoured fashion, let their hearts rule their heads. For a number of years after our first family holiday on the Rhine we had a correspondence running with an elderly couple in South Shields, both of whom have since sadly passed away. George and Gerda Walker typified in many ways the relationships which were struck in that period after fraternisation became legal. We met them whilst staying in the *Gasthof* [guesthouse] of the ebullient Frau

Olbricht in the small town of Bacharach. Frau Olbricht was a big, jolly woman whose husband was a member of the local fire brigade. Over breakfast we would listen to the conversations in very basic English between herself and the Walkers. George would speak slowly and clearly in a strong Tyneside accent, then be joined by Gerda who spoke in German, steady and deliberately, yet still with a discernible Tyneside accent. It transpired that George had met Gerda in the late 1940s whilst serving with the Royal Artillery. She had been a civilian nurse and worked in a hospital near Osnabrück. George, as a regular, had seen action in Germany during the war and had developed a deep loathing and mistrust of the Germans after witnessing the results of a massacre carried out by the SS. Eventually, we got to know one another.

'As far as I was concerned, they were all bloody Nazis and you couldn't trust 'em. But when I met Gerda it was as if something else had taken me over. I just went ahead and asked her if she'd like to go to the pictures. Oddly enough, we went to see a war film – it was *Five Graves To Cairo*, about British spies trying to destroy Rommel's secret supply dumps in North Africa. Gerda spoke very little English at the time and I only had a few phrases in German, but she did comment that at least the director, Billy Wilder – who was no stranger to Germany – had chosen a proper German, Erich von Stroheim, to play Rommel, and not some "Britisher with a funny accent".

'I later found out that Gerda's parents hadn't voted for Hitler but, like thousands of others who didn't either, they lived in constant fear of stepping out of line. I also realised, once I'd been to a few of Gerda's relatives' houses, how much more the Germans had suffered than we had back home. I know we were blitzed, but every branch of her family had suffered awful tragedy, and most of the young men, cousins and brothers, had died with the Wehrmacht; some had vanished into Russia as POWs and were never heard from again.

'After a while I met more and more Germans and realised that the only way I'd begin to appreciate being stationed there was to knock that chip off my shoulder. We [Gerda and I] became inseparable and after marrying in 1949 she made the brave sacrifice of coming to live in South Shields.'

By the 1950s Britain was still a long way from recovery after the war. Gerda remembered feeling very homesick.

~ Living With Herman ~

'Somehow we thought it might be "safer" living away from Germany, what with all the damage. But England seemed very grey and dull after Germany. The people accepted me, although there were a few unpleasant comments in the shops sometimes. I slowly picked up the language and started making friends, but I missed my mother so much. We always had to go back and have done every year, long after my parents had passed away. I never for a minute during the war imagined that one day I would be married to a British soldier and live in England. I never regretted it, though.'

For a single serving soldier, (known today as 'Singlies') the concept of family domesticity is left behind once you join the ranks. Barracks life in the new century may be more relaxed than it was 50 years ago, but the modern squaddie based in Germany enjoys his own culture, the same as any group of young single men away from home would. This may revolve around sports, drinking, or simply seeing more of the host country, but their social base and circle of contact differs from that of the Army's married couples. Yet there is a limit to how much fine German beer you can drink and the number of clubs you can visit on a weekend. Now that we're all part of Europe and any trace of Anglo-German enmity has long since vanished, mixing in with the people of Mönchengladbach or Minden is a far more relaxed affair. But it wasn't always like this.

Corporal Geoff Gilbert served from 1944 to '47. He was a physical training instructor with the Sherwood Foresters Regiment.
'My favourite place in Germany was soon established when we were moved to Göttingen. This is a university town, on a similar cultural level as Cambridge or Oxford. It was in Göttingen that I met a German family. It was Christmas 1945. With the war over we had begun to fraternise with German people. It all began one evening when we were visited at the house we were billeted in (the Army had confiscated one side of the street and moved us in) by a young boy aged 12. The lad had a little four-wheeled trolley and said to us, "Does anyone want any washing doing? My mother will wash your clothes and iron them and I will bring them back to you in two days." He spoke good English, which he had learned at school.
'At this time we had to do our own washing. Of course, my roommates said, "Don't do it – you'll never see your clothes again." But I gave the lad a pile of my gear and off he went with his little

trolley. Two days later, sure enough, he arrived with all my clothes neatly washed, ironed and folded. All his mother wanted for this service was a few cigarettes which she could exchange for food and clothes, etc. So, naturally, I gave the lad his cigarettes. The next time he came I got a surprise, because he told me that his mother wanted to know if I would like to come to tea at their house on Sunday. I was quite touched by this and told him to tell his mum that I would love to come. And so began a wonderful friendship, which still carries on today.

'When I look at the photograph of the 12-year-old Helmut and think of the older, bespectacled Helmut and his lovely family, with whom I have spent so many happy times in Germany (and he's been to stay with us in Derbyshire), it makes me realise what a piece of my life would have been missing if I had listened to my roommates when that little lad came around with his washing trolley.'

There are many examples of friendships such as this forged in darker times. Today, many Army families enjoy a much broader relationship with their hosts than ever before, but to really feel at home in any foreign country an understanding of the culture and social framework is essential.

A popular sport in Germany among both civilians and British soldiers is shooting, but this is only permissible with a German hunting licence – a *Jagdschein*. Soldiers must inspect the British Army's order 5200 to pick their way through the application process. Once you've loaded your gun and stepped into the woods, never think that you can take a trusty hound with you to pick up your prey. Dogs are not permitted to hunt or chase game in woods and country areas, and gamekeepers are within their rights to shoot on sight any uncontrolled dog. Germany's administrative regions, the *Länder*, have local rules and by-laws any mythical 'Disgusted of Tunbridge Wells' would pray for. This is a country where you can't wash your car in the street or on a garage forecourt – or even in front of the barracks on a British base, unless it is in a designated 'washing area'. If you use a public car park, then it is you, the motorist, who will keep it clean – local councils do not clean car parks.

If you're a family living in Sennelager, there is a raft of local legislation, all designed for that different, more ordered German lifestyle, to contend with. Here's a sample:

Identity documents must be carried by everyone over 8 years of age at all times.

Noise: The following are 'quiet' times:

Workdays: 1300–1500 hours and 2200–0700 hours;

Sundays and Public Holidays: All Day.

During these quiet times the following activities are not permitted:

lawn-mowing or hedge cutting;

hammering, sawing or chopping wood;

mechanical drilling;

playing music loudly;

beating of carpets;

creating noise which annoys neighbours, such as parties, etc.

Washing: In flats, it is prohibited by German Law to hang out washing which shows above the flat balcony level.

Sundays and Public Holidays: In Germany, Sundays and Public Holidays are treated as days of rest and you are not permitted to hang laundry on outside lines, clean windows, clean outside areas, mow lawns, clean or do maintenance on your car.

Pavements: Householders are responsible for sweeping and cleaning rubbish and weeds from pavements adjoining their property. The Stadt (Town/City) will only clean up to the kerbstones; beyond this it is the householder's responsibility, including clearing autumn leaves.

Snow: Householders are responsible for clearing snow from all footpaths adjoining their property by 0700 hours in the morning, or within a short time after the snowfall ceases during daylight hours.

Barbecues are not permitted on the balconies of flats.

Children: Liability for Children's Actions: In Germany, parents are held generally to be responsible for the misconduct of their children. To protect against possible legal damages, insurance must be taken out against such a liability. The cost is nominal and policies which provide such cover are regarded as essential by the vast majority of German parents.

The laws go on and on. Children's play areas cannot be used after dark, no pets are allowed in such areas, and ball games are only permitted in designated areas. Children cannot ride their bikes on the road until they have a thorough knowledge of the German Highway Code. The German Police even set up checkpoints to look at bikes to test their roadworthiness. Fines are issued to parents who allow a faulty cycle to be used and riding on the pavement is strictly forbidden, as are skateboards and roller-skates unless in specially designated areas. Climbing trees is not allowed, begging is banned and drunkenness is swiftly dealt with. You could receive a hefty fine for using a UK-manufactured baby alarm – they have a different frequency to German ones and can interfere with TV and emergency channels. You cannot burn garden rubbish, nor can you park a car on grass or convert part of your green area for car-parking.

Although the British Military Police have always dealt with misdemeanours promptly and efficiently, the German civil police have remained vigilant throughout our Army's tenure there.

Norman Baldwin, of Gloucester, was a corporal in the Royal Signals at Delmenhorst between 1954 and '56.

'One evening, four or five of us were wandering around the local town, not out of bounds but not within an area normally frequented by troops. Suddenly we were surrounded by a couple of German police cars, bundled into the back and taken to the local police station, where we were detained overnight. Next day we were handed over to the Military Police. As the senior soldier, I was the spokesman and tried to explain what had happened, which was rather vague. We were returned to our barracks without charge. Next day I was called before the RSM, a man of some charisma. I told him all that had happened and that as far as I was concerned, we had not committed any crime. The RSM telephoned the MPs and told them that if Corporal Baldwin said they had done nothing wrong, then "that's the way it is". The case was dropped. I learned some time later that a private car had been stolen and that British troops in the area had been blamed.'

Most young men in those early post-war days soon realised that their status as members of what was still an army of occupation afforded them certain privileges and opportunities to explore Germany and attempt to get to grips with her culture. Some recognised, during their short tour, that – especially if one was a national serviceman – this was a one-off chance to get around

Europe. Those who did received a bonus of memories that have gone into family legend.

Iain Leggatt of Carnoustie, Scotland was a private with the RASC in Rheindahlen, Mönchengladbach between 1957 and '58.

'On arrival at the Hook of Holland, we were shouted at by Royal Engineers senior ranks, marshalled, shouted at again, and then shepherded onto British Military Trains to take us to our various destinations mainly, I guessed, in West Germany.

'My biggest surprise came when the civilian staff on the train, on which we had enjoyed a five-star breakfast and possibly a six-star lunch, addressed each one of us privates as "Sir", and sounded as though they meant it. They were all Germans – the first I had encountered since the prisoners of war at Greenwood Road a decade before. My travelling companion, Private Taffy Arthur, employed his recently acquired German to find out from one of them that they not only worked on the train as waiters, chefs and stewards, but they *lived* on board the train which was their only home. Their original homes had been in *"der Ost"* (the East) and they had been among the lucky ones who had escaped and found somewhere permanent to live and work in the West.

'Rheindahlen was known to the Germans as *Kleine England* (little England), because HQ BAOR and its supporting units numbered around 6,000 servicemen and women, and the co-located HQ Allied Tactical Air Force plus its units, another 3,000. And then there were all the British and German Civil Servants and NAAFI staff, wives, children, and voluntary organisations such as Red Shield, Civilian Volunteer Women Workers (CVWW) and Women's Voluntary Service (WVS)!

'My heaps of spare time, coupled with the copious amounts of pay and Local Overseas Allowance, enabled me to travel to Düsseldorf, Bonn, Cologne, Aachen, Duisburg, Krefeld, Dortmund and Münster. My travels were all by civilian train, the carriages of which resembled cattle trucks, and all I had to do to obtain free travel was to wear my uniform and flash my Army Identity Card, AF B 2603/4. As Prime Minister Harold Macmillan was to tell us all a couple of years later: I'd never had it so good. My Army Identity Card was enough for me to travel into and around Holland as well, so I visited Eindhoven, Venlo and Nijmegen.

'Some Sunday mornings, the entire off-going SMC (Staff Message

Control) nightshift would go across the Dutch border to Roermond, 15 miles away (misusing a War Department Volkswagen Beetle, petrol and German semi-military GSO driver in the process) for an *enormous* Dutch breakfast of ham, eggs, fried potatoes, crusty bread, butter, jam and tea – all for the equivalent of a couple of bob.

'In those days, 1957–8, one pound sterling got you twelve Deutschmarks. Twenty years on, in 1977, one pound bought only five Deutschmarks. By the 1990s the rate had dropped to about two and a half Deutschmarks for a quid. I was the first to appreciate that I was a very rich young man indeed.

'I visited Düsseldorf for that *phantastisch* German festival, *Rosenmontag*, in the company of ex-RASC Regimental boys Tommy Lawton, Taff Davies and Duke Barron. The *"fest"* involved much carousing, with happy drunks swaying down the streets wearing funny hats and noses and shouting *"Karnival! Karnival!"* but before we had left on our trip we had been led to believe a lot by other soldiers. Yet not once did we discover any signs of hugely attractive young females flinging their apartment keys into the middle of the floor of bars and nightclubs, followed at a given signal by a mad, lust-filled scramble. Maybe we were just never in the right place at the right time.

'One evening, I went to Mönchengladbach for "a few drinks" with Duke Barron. This was the first occasion on which either of us had ever drunk schnapps, which we did in a bar near the railway station, and we had a couple of slugs because we liked the shape of the bottle. Warmed by the liquor and feeling adventurous, we decided to try some other tastes and were introduced to *Dunkel*, which is a dark beer with a slightly sweet taste. We both liked this and decided to ask for it in the next bar we went into. When we asked for it the bartender laughed. *"Was? Dunkel!? Das ist für wimmin und childs!"*

'So we went back to Dortmunder Export Pils. Four Germans were playing a very noisy game of cribbage in this bar, with much slapping of cards down on the table, and Duke and I realised that one of them bore a startling resemblance to the pictures we had seen of Adolf Hitler.

'Inevitably, we drank and chatted too well, missed the last bus by a mile . . . well, a kilometre. We walked back in what we hoped was the direction of our camp and, after an hour or two, came across a stationary *Polizei* Volkswagen. We asked the occupants if they knew in which direction HQ BAOR was. *"Bitte? Wo ist die Hauptquartier?"*

'They politely wound their windows up and showed deep respect for the Army of occupation by completely and pointedly ignoring us. Farther on – and a good deal farther on – just as it was getting light, we saw something to the right of us up ahead, in a field near the road. Duke said, "I think it's a tank." As we got closer, we decided it was something smaller. I said I thought it was an ack-ack [anti-aircraft] gun. It was a horse.'

Following a failed pretence that they were French students, Iain and Duke, with the assistance of two passing Redcaps, finally made it back to camp and escaped any indictment. Iain continues:

'On one of my lone visits to Düsseldorf (they were many – I really liked the city and even met up with my parents one July day when their Rhine cruise stopped for a two-hour break), I was walking out of the railway station when I passed the office marked "RTO" – Railway Transport Officer. I saw a man sitting behind a desk so, full of "we-British-sticking-together-in-a-foreign-landness", I spoke to him. He seemed glad of the chat but his history was what made the occurrence remarkable. He had been a British infantryman in the First World War, and had stayed on when his battalion became part of the Army of occupation, and had remained in Germany after his discharge, obtaining employment on the railways. He had been there ever since – right through the Second World War, during which he had been merely required to report to the local *Polizei* station once a week. He had never married. I said that surely he must have had some problems.

'"Oh yes," he said, "when the RAF came over, I had the devil's own job trying to dodge their bloody bombs!"'

Understanding the Germans and eventually mixing with them wasn't an overnight process. In the immediate post-war years the whiff of mutual propaganda about the enemy still hung in the air.

John Saville of Wallasey was a lance corporal with the RASC at Sennelager between 1952 and '54.

'In conversations with many Germans, it became evident that after discovering that British soldiers were ordinary people (not inhuman beasts, as the Nazi propaganda had portrayed them) average Germans came to appreciate that they had a much better bargain in us than they would have had if "Ivan" had beaten us to the Danish border. Working for us were three German drivers, all of whom served on the Eastern front, and it was evident that they were still extremely frightened of the Russians. Walther Priess was the usual driver of our unit Volkswagen (00 XB 59) that served as Captain Sherwood's staff car. Walther walked with a very pronounced limp, which he had acquired on the Russian front. Hermann Dittmann drove the big Humber that took Major Scotter out on exercise. Herr Dittmann liked to maintain a military appearance; he had obtained a beret, military overalls and gaiters. Herr Kuhl was a giant ex-SS man who had grisly tales of the Russian winter to tell. He usually drove the Bedford 15 cwt or the very old Fordson (the white star from D-Day still visible beneath the green paint) that served as our mobile office on schemes. All of these men had much more military experience than we national service men, but they were in no way condescending and were cheerful and helpful in their dealings with us.

'As we were such a small unit, we did not justify having an AA cookhouse and our food and laundry were looked after by two German ladies, Anna and Mia (Maria), both of whom had unpronounceable Polish-sounding names and had escaped from East Prussia. We communicated with them in a mixture of simple English and even simpler German. *"Essen bitte"* (let's eat) summoned us to our meals, and from us *"Mehr Kartoffel"* (more potatoes) brought extra helpings of potato. With no on-camp NAAFI we found most of our off-duty distractions in *"Die Stadt"* (the town). As we didn't have to be back in barracks until 2359 hours, long evenings were spent in local hostelries and we found that, as often as not, we didn't have to pay for a single drink during the entire evening. Enough basic German was soon acquired to carry on quite good conversations and I found my fluency increased in proportion to the amount of beer I consumed.

'Britain seemed to be in great favour with many people and quite often former prisoners of war who had enjoyed their time in camps in England regaled us with their happy recollections of their wartime sojourn in the UK. Typical were the party who had been in a camp in Sheffield, and who, after their day's work was finished, would go down to the pub to while away the hours until "time" was called. In buying drinks for us, they felt that they were repaying all the hospitality they had received in the UK. *"Politik ist ein grosser schwindel"* (politics is a huge swindle) summed up our host's attitude to their former leaders. In frequent travels around Germany by train, approaches to railway officials for directions to the correct train always evoked a polite and helpful response.

'Out on exercises, we would have to find somewhere to sleep every night. The farmers of Schleswig Holstein were quite taciturn people but I don't think there was ever an occasion when we were refused permission to go onto their land and find somewhere to sleep. It was soon discovered that if we could put our bedding down in an outbuilding occupied by animals, a warm refuge from the bitter winter weather was assured. The heat generated by pigs was fine but one always woke in the morning with a headache. Cattle also provided life-saving warmth, without the troubling headache. Even better was to find refuge in a village bakery. The ovens were on all night so a warm sleep was assured, together with freshly baked bread and fine coffee in the morning before we went on our way. That the rural German population were pleased that the British Army was present is really beyond doubt. I don't think that we ever left a location without being invited into the farmhouse and treated to breakfast and the best-tasting coffee I've ever enjoyed.

'I regret that we were not able to express our thanks more fully – thinking back a mere *"Dankeshöne"* now seems very inadequate.

'In Itzehoe, people wanted to talk about Britain, and with my German vocabulary increased, I began to feel very much at home. On one occasion, we went to the cinema in the town and saw the famous British film *The Cruel Sea*. It had been dubbed into German and re-titled *Der Grosser Atlantik*. With the war only over just under eight years I wondered what the German people thought about the story.

'If we went out in the evening we would visit a local bar or dance hall. Lots of girls came into Itzehoe from outlying villages. We seemed to attract a better class of girl. I think that they wanted to practise speaking English in social time spent away from their homes. Towards the end of my stay in Itzehoe, my friend Brian Crampin and I made the acquaintance of two sisters, Lizzi and Ulla (Ursula) Lutz. They were very high-class girls, way above our social station, and spoke excellent English. Their parents owned a furniture and removals business and they lived in a big house in a nice part of town. We were often invited into their home, where we amused their family with humorous parodies of our attempts to speak German. We were invited there to watch a World Cup football match, which West Germany won, but I'm afraid that we rather insensitively expressed amusement at the seriousness which greeted the playing of the German national anthem following their football victory. Lizzi very seriously explained that *Deutschland Über Alles* meant that Germany was above all in their hearts, not supreme in the military sense. Another time saw us canoeing with the girls. They were members of the local *Kanuverein*, which had its boathouse on the banks of the fast-flowing river which ran through the town. Ulla and Brian went off in one of the two-seater canoes while Lizzi and I took another. Unfortunately, she had put her sunglasses down in the boat, and stood on them when getting in. *"Ach, mein brille!"* (Oh, my spectacles!) she said. Today, I would buy her a new pair, but sadly in those days we were lacking in the social graces.'

From Berlin to Bonn, the legacy of our coexistence with the Germans seems to be one of mutual respect and even close friendship. With a few exceptions, settling in Germany seems to have been no different for the British than it would be for a Yorkshireman moving to Cornwall. In fact, John Saville's coda to his national service seems to sum up the general attitude.

'One summer, Captain Sherwood and his family took a month's leave to go back to the UK. I was asked if I would spend my off-duty hours "house-sitting" for them. I would leave work at 1600 hours and walk down to the pleasant suburb where the house was. The family's German maid looked after things during the day and always had a meal ready for me when I turned up. Having never been waited on before, it was very nice to be treated in such a deferential manner. There cannot have been many lance corporals who experienced such luxury. During my national service, and on later visits, I always found the German people to be polite and obliging and, even today, on arriving in Germany, I have a feeling that I have, in some way, "come home".'

4

A Woman's Touch

When you get to a man in the case,
They're like as a row of pins
For the Colonel's Lady an' Judy O'Grady
Are sisters under their skins!
                    Rudyard Kipling (1865-1936), 'The Ladies'

There is a generally held view in the forces that if you marry a soldier, you also become married to the Army. Over the years since the Second World War many women have found the strain too much to take. Divorce between couples either separated by a foreign posting or even living in married quarters abroad was not uncommon. Romance, courtship, the attraction of the uniform – these factors can soon evaporate when a girl finds herself stationed on the military equivalent of a housing estate, surrounded by an alien culture and a different language.

The Army's top brass over the years could prove obstinate in the face of social change. As long ago as 1975 the unhappiness of Army wives was temporarily addressed by an independent study that resulted in The Spencer Report, but whatever recommendations this contained, they were unacceptable to the Army Board. Back then a wife was not even regarded as 'Mrs', but always referred to on documentation as, for example, 'Wife of Private Jones' – which almost gave the poor woman the status of part of his kit. Ten years later came The Gaffney Report. This was more of a breakthrough because the commission to write the report was given to Colonel Michael Gaffney – and his wife. With a woman on board, and a real Army wife to boot, the report's recommendations on how to improve married life for those in the services may well have enraged the older misogynists in the ranks, but society at home was changing rapidly and the new wave of recruits and officers expected a better deal. Today, things may not be perfect, but at least these days the problems of life in married quarters are no longer entirely overlooked, as they seem to have been in the early post-war years.

For some soldiers, though, being granted permission to have their wives in Germany, rather than enhancing morale, could have the opposite effect.

Brian Morris was a sergeant with the 50th Royal Artillery Regiment at Minden between 1962 and '63.

'On arriving in Minden I was informed that there were no married quarters available. My wife and two young daughters were living in a married quarter in Rhyl, North Wales. I had to make myself comfortable in a bunk in the accommodation block. In the May or June of 1962 I was allocated one of ten Bluebird caravans that had been sited outside the rear gate of Northumberland Barracks. The late Jim Bradley and his wife Anne were my neighbours. Christmas 1962 found Jim and I carrying jerrycans of water from the camp to our caravans as all the water systems had frozen up. Eventually, sometime in 1963, my family and I were allocated to an accommodation block which had been converted to serve as family accommodation. During this period an arsonist was running amok in the barracks, and consequently we were having to do guard duty as well as regimental guard duties. My battery commander informed me that I was to be promoted to sergeant. I was disturbed to discover that the fire bug had prepared materials to set fire to the family accommodation block.

'I decided to leave 50 Regiment as soon as possible. In October 1963 I left BAOR to join the Commando Gunners. I was reunited with my family in December. Alas there were no quarters available in Plymouth. All in all I was not happy in the regiment.'[1]

One of the bonuses for the lonely soldier of having unattached women in the Army, and serving in the various ancillary services such as the WRVS or NAAFI, was that, should you prefer not to try your luck with the German female population, a romance with a comrade was always a possibility.

Hugh Martin, now living in Jersey, was a sergeant with the Army Education Service at Finkenwerde between 1951 and '52.

'The last thing my mother said to me before I went off to the war was "Whatever you do, for heaven's sake don't bring back a Kraut!" I didn't. I met my wife-to-be at the Allied Services Sailing and Rowing Club, where I was rowing and she was sailing. I said to the chap I was with, "You see that girl over there? That's the girl I'm going to marry."

'She was with the WVS, running social clubs for the troops. Fifty years later she's sitting across the room re-reading *Dr. Zhivago*, checking on the current TV rendition thereof. Hamburg was a good place to do one's courting.'

As a 'good place to do one's courting' Germany worked equally as well for the women.

Betty R. Radley of Lutterworth, Leicestershire was a part of the Control Commission for Germany, Hanover, Goslar, Bunde and Münster between 1946 and '49.

'I lived and worked in the CCG from late 1946 – our soldier friends called us "Charlie Chaplin's Grenadiers". In May 1948, I married an Army lieutenant and moved to Goslar, where he was stationed at the Kaiserworth Hotel – one of several hotels in "T" Force Group, which looked after businesspeople passing through. Goslar is a delightful small town at the foot of the Harz Mountains, which provided scope for skiing, sleigh-riding and walking. Whilst there I worked in the detachment office of "T" Force.

'My husband was demobbed from there but after several months in civvy street he decided to re-join the Army. Almost immediately he was posted to Suez during that crisis and I remained in England. My elder son was born at this time. After [my husband's] posting to Cyprus, where we joined him, we returned to Germany, this time to Bunde. We were happy to be going there, remembering the good times we had in the past. The environment contrasted favourably with my earlier period in Germany when the streets had been strewn with bricks and mortar. I remember Hanover railway station being just a shell of steel girders. We lived in a beautiful house in Bunde, which had been requisitioned from the owner of a cigar factory. My younger son was born then, at the military hospital 30 miles away from Bunde at a place called Rinteln.

'I spent some time helping the CO's wife on welfare work at the camp. From there we went on to spend a year in Münster. My elder son attended the school for British servicemen's children and gained a good knowledge of the German language. It was at Münster that my husband was promoted to captain and subsequently became a major. After some time in Nairobi and then home postings, my husband retired from the Army in 1975. We made a nostalgic visit back to Germany to celebrate our Ruby Wedding anniversary, visiting all the places we had known. Sadly, my husband died in 2001.'

As the twenty-first century opens up, the British forces in Germany have a social infrastructure which contains many of the elements which would justify calling any British base there 'Little England'. Although the British Army of the Rhine is no more, and what troops we do have there have been greatly reduced in number, the basic set-up they still enjoy makes this home-from-home impressive.

Apart from having their own newspaper, TV and radio station, the following statistics speak for themselves:[2]

> *Family Accommodation*: 14,680 homes (8,456 owned by the Federal Government, 6,227 rented)
> *Service Children's Education Schools*: 32 (26 Primary, 2 Middle and 4 Secondary)
> *Pupils*: 8,531 (5,807 Primary, 621 Middle and 2,103 Secondary)
> *Teachers*: 700
> *Churches*: 25
> *Padres (Ministers of Religion)*: 39
> *NAAFI Stores*: 50
> *NAAFI Entertainment Clubs*: 34
> *Cinemas*: 12

As in most occupations, being an Army wife was what you made of it. The more dedicated military spouse with a penchant for socialising would always find something to do to fill in the time. For others the stress of moving from base to base could be very depressing, a fact which would not escape the more sensitive soldier.

T. Clark, BEM, of the Royal Artillery was stationed at Oldenburg between 1942 and '44.

'After being posted to Crowborough, I joined the 44th Heavy

Anti-Aircraft Regiment, who had just been brought out of mothballs. We then left for Oldenburg in Germany. My wife joined me after a couple of months with two children – and when we returned home to the UK to join my parent regiment, 3rd Royal Horse Artillery, we were blessed with six children. The time in Germany was stressful to my young wife. Our Married Service Quarters (MSQ) was five miles from camp in Falklandstrasse. We were then moved to new MSQ in Gloyesteenstrasse – about the same distance from the camp. I can't actually remember the number of exercises I attended, but I do know I took part in every one – they were long exercises. I well remember "June Primer" and "Spearhead One".

'We always seemed to be travelling around Belgium and Holland. This was extremely hard on the wives. Where we were it was around five miles to the NAAFI, though all the rations were brought round to them by a three-tonner from the camp. I am very proud of my wife as she bore me four more children before we returned home to the UK. Although she was married at 18 and a very shy, demure girl, she always seemed to be consulted when chickenpox and measles were around, when the more mature wives were flapping. We now have two more children, making eight – and she even managed, to my satisfaction, to have four boys and four girls. She was the one who took the brunt of being a soldier's wife and shed the tears during my absence on schemes. I left the Army in 1974, having served for 32 years.'

As opposed to being soldiers' wives, women who join the forces could also be regarded as distinguished in the military ranks by the fact that, in pre-politically correct terms, as 'the fair sex' it has always puzzled some men as to why a woman would seek to opt for a uniform, bull and barracks life. More humorous to note, however, are the British press reports that some women seek to retain their femininity despite anything the Army throws at them:

> The drab corridors of the Ministry of Defence were echoing to the groans of senior officers and civil servants today as Lance Corporal Roberta Winterton decided to junk her Army career by becoming the first serving soldier to pose topless for the Page Three photographer of *The Sun*. Her decision to pose topless is another embarrassment for the

MOD, following the appearance last year of a 24-year-old
female soldier who had appeared in publicity shots
highlighting the role of women in the Army. She went
AWOL with a married sergeant and has still not been found.[3]

Women are able to serve in 70 per cent of posts in the Army, 73 per
cent in the Navy, and 96 per cent in the RAF, yet the female
membership of Britain's armed forces only adds up to 8 per cent of
the total manpower.[4] However, the urge to serve one's country by
enlisting has never been an exclusively male domain. Much has
been made by at least two of my female interviewees – who wish to
remain anonymous – of the subject of lesbian tendencies in the
female ranks. One girl who enlisted in the early '80s told me that of
the eight girls she joined up with, she discovered once she'd settled
in Germany that four of them were gay, and that within a year of her
posting her best friend, who had enlisted with her at the same time,
was 'persuaded' by their sergeant into a more or less Sapphic
lifestyle. Feeling more and more isolated, this interviewee decided
against re-enlisting once her time was up.

It would be salacious to dwell on this subject. All that can be said
is that what bonds or relationships are formed in a military
atmosphere, and what goes on in the bedroom or outside, should be
regarded as little different to what occurs in society in general.
What matters in the end is the ability to do the job, and by all
accounts the women seem as capable as the men in whatever duties
are allotted to them by the Army. That is not, as you will see, the
official view. Judging by the attitude of many women who have left
the service, many of those same 'duties' often don't match up with
their aspirations. Although certain elements of the MOD's views on
female soldiers may seem valid, in an obstinately male environment,
sexism is still capable of making an all-too-regular appearance.

However, the way in which the forces – or at least the politicians
– have sought to move with social change at home was amply
demonstrated in the British press in 2001, when the thorny subject
of same-sex relationships raised its controversial head.[5]

The same-sex partners of gay men and women serving in the
British Armed Forces will soon be recognised as fully fledged
spouses, eligible for all the rights and benefits now afforded to
married couples.

The move, which would mean that gay partners could also receive pensions and other benefits, is highly controversial. One senior military officer called the move 'political correctness gone mad'. But the MOD concession has been robustly welcomed by gay and lesbian service members. Lieutenant-Commander Craig Jones, one of the most senior officers to 'come out', said he greatly welcomed the idea of having his male partner quartered with him in Royal Navy-supplied accommodations.

As in the United States, homosexuality in the British Armed Forces was forbidden until January last year. The ban, which routinely prompted some 200 forces dismissals a year, was lifted after the European Court of Human Rights ruled it unlawful. Prior to its removal, the ban on gay service personnel was justified on the grounds of military effectiveness. Conservative Armed Services Minister Nicholas Soames said the services should not be 'bludgeoned out of the *esprit de corps* which has won every war since 1812. Many senior officers fought the lifting of the ban. Last week one called moves to allow same-sex marriages 'madness'.

'It's a monstrosity. We are becoming an army of social workers not soldiers. There is all this focus on issues of gays and women and very little recognition of the fact that we have tens of thousands of soldiers doing a very professional job with increasingly limited funds.'

All this has provided some tongue-in-cheek fun for our erstwhile enemies, the Russians. The Cold War may well have ended, but even several months before the 'same sex' controversy broke, that old Moscow propaganda warhorse, *Pravda*, had a few chuckles by linking the following stories in order to have a crack at the British Army:

DONALD TRUMP TRIES BUT FAILS TO BED MISS UNIVERSE
A novel attempt by billionaire Donald Trump, American sponsor of the Miss Universe competition, to 'examine' the French candidate Elodie Gossuin, has made the headlines around the world. Trump wanted to have the candidate 'examined' after claims that she had been born a man.

~ The Long Patrol ~

BRITISH ARMY PROVIDES SEX-CHANGE TREATMENT
FOR SOLDIERS

The British Army has admitted that it offers sex-change treatment to male soldiers who wish to become women. The Ministry of Defence admitted that it pays for male members of the armed forces to have sex-change treatment and for female members to have breast enlargement operations. The operations are carried out in civilian hospitals, since the Ministry of Defence does not have doctors capable of performing the operation. If one is on a battlefield where British armed forces are deployed, and sees what looks like a woman carrying a gun, it would be wise to call Donald Trump, who would insist on an 'examination' to confirm the sex.[6]

This may well be a farcical fragment of Russian tabloid baloney, but it's a bit rich coming from the Eastern bloc, whose steroid-stuffed 'female' athletes during the Cold War had all the feminine allure of Geoff Capes in knickers. It is also sad to note that the new generation of laugh-a-minute thigh-slappers at *Pravda*, like many of their Western counterparts, in their search for a cheap chuckle, tend to forget the part their mothers and grandmothers played in wartime, creating the very liberated environment in which they can write such tripe today. For instance, the Red Army and the Soviet Air Force were noted for the bravery and ferocity of their female recruits. As ever, sacrifice can soon be disregarded for a low-priced laugh.

The term 'total war' arose in the twentieth century. In previous conflicts the military machine went into action, supported by the government and with the moral support – or, in some cases, indifference – of the public. By the First World War every economic, human and ideological resource was required to be mobilised if we were to win. Hence 'total' war. Germany's devotion to this all-embracing cause in the Second World War is a tragic example.

Women had always been of prime importance on the home front. However, during the eighteenth century they had often joined the Army disguised as men. As many as 5,000 women accompanied the British Army during the American War of

Independence.[7] The larger part of these were the wives of common soldiers, with the usual privileged few at the top such as Baroness von Riedesel and Mrs Thomas Cage, both wives of generals. In those days it was unthinkable for the Army to recruit married men, and those who did join were discouraged from marrying. In an age where medical inspections were non-existent, this nevertheless must have been a difficult existence. Biology demands differing hygienic behaviour from the sexes, so in addition to the rigours of campaigning and the constant threat of death, a woman dressed as a man occupying a testosterone-driven battlefield must have been a very determined character. One conversation I had with a Women's Royal Army Corps (WRAC) soldier in Germany illustrated these difficulties. She told me that there are certain scenarios – such as tank warfare – where being a 'Lumpie' (Army slang denoting women soldiers by the 'lumps' in their uniforms) can turn you into a 'Ponti' – a 'person of no tactical importance'.

'It's all down to what happens when you want to pee. When you're fully kitted out on an exercise it's fine if you're a bloke. Men can, to put it crudely, "whip it out" whilst standing up. It's quick and doesn't involve the long process of getting your gear off. For a woman, first of all you have to find somewhere to pee – unlike the blokes we can't just wee up against the tank tracks – we don't have the aim – and Army or no Army, there's still modesty to consider. So we have to find some cover – a bush or vegetation – then unzip everything and take everything down. In a real battle situation, I suppose we'd have to wet ourselves.'

Even as recently as 2002 the male attitude to women soldiers was further bolstered when Defence Secretary Geoff Hoon said that a 'practical test of female capacity in close combat could not be justified'. A Ministry of Defence report prompted the statement that 'Women will continue to be barred from close combat roles in the armed forces because it would be too risky to find out how their presence would affect operations.' The report further concluded that women had a 'gap in the capacity for aggression' and that their capacity to develop muscle strength and aerobic fitness were such that only about 1 per cent of women could equal the performance of the average man. When exposed to the same physical workload, women had to work up to 80 per cent harder than men to achieve the same results.

The challenge to women continues in the RAF, too:

> Britain's RAF has rejected all applications from women pilots
> who want to fly the new Eurofighter because their limbs are
> too short for the cockpit. Senior officers found that all the
> female applicants so far for the multi-role combat aircraft
> have 'builds' incompatible with the cockpit layout. In
> particular, there was concern that they could not safely use
> the ejector seat.[8]

Although it would be another year before they got the vote, women
were recruited into the army for the first time during the First World
War in 1917. Prior to this they had been involved in nursing duties,
until the Women's Army Auxiliary Corps (WAAC) was founded,
which later became Queen Mary's Army Auxiliary Corps (QMAAC)
with Queen Mary as their Patron. They served with some
distinction with the British Expeditionary Force (BEF), winning
three military medals for gallantry.

King George VI ordered the founding of the Auxiliary Territorial
Service (ATS) on 9 September 1938. It soon had in excess of over a
quarter of a million members, including the present queen, who, as
Princess Elizabeth, served in the Second World War and was
commissioned in March 1945. The ATS served around the world as
drivers, orderlies, cooks and in stores, and they are particularly
remembered for their work with Anti Aircraft Command. In total,
313 of them were wounded and 72 women lost their lives. There was
a man behind the founding of the WRAC as we know it today:
Emmanuel Shinwell MP submitted the idea of a regular corps of
women and on 1 February 1949 women became subject for the first
time to all sections of the Army Act when the Women's Royal Army
Corps was founded. They were soon serving in over 40 different
trades in 20 different branches of the Army. Today there is nothing
unusual about a woman doing a man's job in the Army. In my own
travels around Germany to various bases, my first point of contact
with any regiment was invariably a woman. As in the Navy and the
Air Force, the forces in general have become an exciting career
option for young women and their influence in the ranks has
inevitably broken down quite a few of the old barriers.

Maintaining a significant peacetime military presence in Germany offered the married regular soldier the opportunity of preserving some vestiges of home domestic life whilst on duty. Germany, foreign country though it is, was considered a 'home posting' and as such married families and their children could be accommodated on bases. For wives, in those grim early post-war years, it was not always the most pleasant of experiences. If your husband was sent away on a 'scheme' – as major exercises were then called – it could result in six weeks of separation. If you were about to give birth, this would be doubly traumatic.

Margaret Shelley, of Grimsby, served in the Royal Army Nursing Corps between 1957 and '58, where she met her husband, a soldier.

'After a small separation he was posted to Münster in Germany. I joined him after a short while. We moved into private accommodation, staying with a lovely German family. Army houses were like council houses, given out on a points system. (To this day I could never work out how it was done . . .)

'This was a new world to me. I was newly married in a strange country, with a strange language. At least I didn't have to cope with Deutschmarks, as the Army dealt in pounds, shillings and pence, although we used German money in the shops.

'You would meet up with other wives in the NAAFI and TOC H, and that was fine until your husband "went back to work". In those days there were no social workers or counsellors to help you through this. You were on your own, and then there'd be another blow: sent on a scheme, your husband would be away for six weeks. Luckily, my German family were great – I still keep in touch with them today. Eventually we started a family and were given Army accommodation, but it was miles away in Bückerburg, and my husband only came home at weekends. As I was pregnant, it was very lonely. However, there were other wives in the same boat so we had to build up our own community-within-a-community, and eventually got to make friends with wives from other regiments.

'I had my first boy in Iserlohn British Military Hospital, where we shared services with the Canadian forces. It was so far away from my husband that he couldn't visit me. In fact when I was discharged after ten days an officer from another regiment took me home. My husband arrived the next day – that was in April 1960. Just about a year later I was pregnant again, and we moved to Detmold. There it was lovely as my husband came home every day. Sadly, this was to be short-lived.

'A year later, now with two sons, we were on our way home to England. My parents in the meantime had moved from Mansfield in Nottinghamshire up to Grimsby, so we joined them there. My husband and I divorced in 1972, and I've lived in Grimsby since.'

Apart from Army wives, women soldiers and children, there was another category of British women in those early years in Germany.

Mrs H. Roberts, of Stockton-on-Tees, was a civil servant in Hanover between 1946 and '48.

'A large number of civilians, mostly ex-Civil Service, were enlisted to work in Germany, probably starting early in 1946. I started there at the end of that year and stayed until late 1948, but most people stayed much longer. We were called the Control Commission for Germany and we took over mostly clerical jobs from the Army. We were billeted in large private houses known as messes and in many ways had similar conditions to the occupying forces. Life for the Germans then was very hard, as food for them was short and their cities were badly damaged by the bombing, with many of them still living in the ruins. Life for us, in contrast, was very good, with plentiful and varied food, much better than we had ever been used to at home. The social life was good, too. We were young people and enjoyed parties and dances with our forces friends. We also had "local leave", which meant skiing in the Harz Mountains. There was also "Continental leave", which was taken in Brussels and Paris, both cities trying to recover from the ravages of war. During my stay, the Russians, from their advantageous area of command in Berlin, cut off the supply routes to the city. This prompted the Berlin Airlift, resulting in an aeroplane carrying food flying past every few minutes in the skies above Hanover.

'I remember that winter of 1946–7 for its extreme weather. I can't remember ever being so very cold. The electricity would be cut off for hours at a time, and the only way to keep warm was to go to bed with all your clothes piled on top of your blankets. Cigarettes were widely used as barter. Two would buy you a shampoo and set, five cigarettes a perm – although this was against the rules, of course.'

As the memory of the war began to fade, British society changed. Women, as ever, still lacked equal status, although some politicians were now making the right noises about equal pay.

There was a new assertiveness and confidence developing among

British women, so it was hardly surprising that many would take the military option as regular employment. Although joining the forces may not have been the most fashionable thing to do for most working-class girls in the 1970s, those of a more adventurous bent with a yen for travel discovered that the Army could offer a decent career. For some girls, this wasn't an afterthought or a late decision – they knew early in life what they wanted to do. To succeed as a woman in the Army requires determination and stamina, and some have more than others. The following recollection is one of the longer ones encountered whilst preparing this work, but it is included almost in its entirety because in many ways it encapsulates the challenging life of a female recruit better than most.

Carole Gladman of Colchester served in the Royal Military Police in Germany from 1978 to '83.

'I was born on 6 August 1960. I can always remember as a very young child telling everyone that one day I was going to join the Army to become a Military Policewoman, and that I wanted to do parachute jumping. No one in the little town of Bideford [Devon] took me seriously. Apart from the local Bobbies, you would never see a uniform or even anyone of foreign nationality and, as for London, as far as we were concerned that was a foreign country. When I was due to leave school, my English teacher became annoyed with me, as I didn't want to join any of the groups going on to college. I just kept telling him that I wanted to join the Army. I wasn't even 16 when I first wrote off and of course they told me I was too young. So from March 1976 to January 1978 I worked in a factory, AMP (Aircraft Marine Products), biding my time until I was old enough to join up. I worked a good 50-hour week with overtime and my take-home pay was £30 per week.

'The big day came on 23 January 1978. My mum had to sign the Army consent form as I wasn't yet 18. But I was in, and off for my six weeks' training at Guildford. I'd never been away from home, and when I found out that my Army pay was only £5 per week, it didn't compare well to the £30 I'd been earning in the factory. Still, I had somewhere warm to sleep and they fed me too. After a couple of weeks a lot of the girls left as they had become homesick. They couldn't cope with the training, keeping your kit nicely pressed and clean and trying to learn the knack of bulling your boots. There were lots and lots of parades and learning to march was especially funny when someone turned the wrong way. The most embarrassing part of physical training was having to wear what looked like your granny's large green bloomers. My training was interrupted by a bout of influenza, but after recovering I completed my training and made it to the passing-out parade.'

As with men who joined up, Carole was soon to be dismayed by the knowledge that the job you hoped to do in the Army didn't always coincide with the brass's plans. Carole was at first pleased that although she only gained five 'O' levels at school, she had at least been accepted. Yet her hopes of eventually donning a red cap were at first dashed when she found herself posted to Woolwich in March 1978, where she was to learn the less adventurous trade of laying tables and serving officers with their dinner as a silver service waitress. She was soon attached to 19th Field Regiment of the Royal Artillery at Larkhill. Working in the Officers' Mess was hardly the job she'd hoped for, but there were a few significant high points.

'Whilst at Larkhill I was fortunate enough to meet Prince Charles. I also met the Prime Minister at that time, Jim Callaghan. He sat down with me for a while and asked my opinion on certain issues. I was also pleased to go out for a day on the ranges with the 19th Field Regiment, where I loaded heavy shells into cannons that we fired at old tanks. What a noise they made! I started a parachuting course in August 1978 at Netheravon, not far from Bulford Camp – the place any soldier dreaded being posted to. Eventually I had a great time at Larkhill, but I was still determined to become a Military Policewoman. So I tried to reallocate my trade, but was told that I would have to learn to drive first. So I was sent off to Leconfield in East Yorkshire, to the Normandy Barracks. I passed my test first time. I had great fun as I also got to drive a Stalwart and a Snowcat.'

Carole had progressed from the less challenging position of waitress, but now her designated trade was 'driver'. She was intrigued as to what posting would result from this. She soon found out it was Germany, this time with 68th Squadron Royal Corps Transport. After learning to drive on the left-hand side of the road, now she'd be driving on the right.

'I thought "Wow!" – I'm going to be miles away in a foreign country with all those Germans we fought against in the war – and for a whole two years. I wondered how I would understand the language and the money, but the excitement of it all was just great and I was straight on the phone to my friends and family.'

And so on 9 September 1979, just 18 months after all that square-bashing in Guildford, Carole arrived at Rheindahlen, more commonly known to squaddies as 'Little England'. There she found everything she needed: cheap drinks in the Marlborough and Queensway Clubs, discos and live entertainment.

'We even had the chart group "Mud" come to play one night. There was a German restaurant where we used to go and have half a chicken with nice crusty rolls and a few beers, followed by plenty of cherry schnapps. As a driver, it meant being away from the squadron sometimes – when I had an officer who needed to travel to certain units throughout Germany, even as far as Hanover, and sometimes across the border. Other times our duties might include driving the civilians who were employed on the base to and from work. We did go out on exercises – such as exercise "Snowqueen", and we were quite often in the field.

'Driving on the autobahns was interesting, as the Germans would drive really fast – like maniacs. You needed to carry at least 20 Deutschmarks with you when driving, just in case you were caught speeding or illegally parked. The German Civil Police would fine you on the spot. You wouldn't want to get on the wrong side of the German Police. You knew that their handguns were definitely loaded with live ammunition, and I always felt that they would rather hit you first and talk later.

'I took a course in the German language, which I passed.

'At Flagstaff House I spent time working for the Commander-in-Chief, General Scotter. My job was to drive his wife, Lady Scotter, wherever she wanted to go. This was mainly to Mönchengladbach, where she would do some shopping. The general and his wife were very nice and they regarded their staff as their family. At Rheindahlen it was difficult sometimes when you had to salute officers, because there were so many ranks and nationalities: Americans, Dutch and the RAF. Being there was the best two years of my Army experience. But I still wanted to move on – and was still determined to become a Military Policewoman. When I told 68 Squadron my aims, they weren't too pleased. However, I got to sit a selection-board exam. Unfortunately, I failed on some of the tests. I sat them again and although I passed, my grades still weren't high enough. But the interviewing officer told me that she could see that I had improved and had been studying hard, and because of this she said she would "open the gate" for me because of my determination. I could start my training, but she said that I must not let her down. I couldn't believe it – I was finally being given a chance to prove myself, and I certainly did.'

From this point Carole discovered in no uncertain terms that Army life was still primarily a male domain. She was sent back to Britain, this time to the Military Police Training Camp at Chichester. She was 21, and to her dismay found that she was the only woman on the course.

In terms of training, it was back to square one – only this time much tougher and more rigorous than at Guildford. As the lone girl she was given the task of cleaning the whole block herself – corridors, toilets and the four-girl room she occupied on her own. The gentle life of Rheindahlen seemed like a distant memory.

'The worst was cleaning up after the corporals. And there was my own kit inspection, just me, alone. Every morning started the same at 6 a.m.: outside in squad ready for our long, long run. I would have to go to the front of the squad and stand on my own behind the RSM and the OC, who just happened to be a fitness-mad person who loved running. Behind me would be lots and lots of men, with me the only woman. I always started at the front but couldn't keep up and would always end up at the back of the squad, far behind. The lads would smack my bottom and call me names as they ran past me. In the distance I would see the squad come to a halt and mark time, whilst the RSM would be screaming at me to hurry up. No sooner had I caught up than off we went again, with me still out of breath. The worst runs were those during which we had to carry huge heavy logs through mud and water. After a few months of this, I gradually got better but I never finished at the front.

'Then one day a squad of girls got posted in to start their training. There I was one morning, stood with the men as I had always done, and to our left stood the new girls, ready for their first run. The OC told me to go and join them. I even astonished myself with my response: "No, sir. No disrespect, but I've been running with the men for all these months now sir . . ."

'He responded: "Are you trying to be funny?"

'"No, sir," I replied. He then sent the girls' squad off on their run, led by the female physical training instructor.

'He then told the men that this morning, they would run a full eight miles, and that they could all blame me for "trying to be clever". Great, I thought – just when I've started getting less grief from the lads, this is all I need.

'I started at the front that morning and that's just where I stayed. Afterwards, the RSM praised me, and some of the soldiers who had given me grief in the past came up to me and said, "Well done!" – and I got lots of hugs, because they were actually proud of me. They weren't annoyed about the long run and I'd earned their respect that morning.

'From then on I ran every day with the girls and yes, I was ahead of them every time. I think the woman instructor was glad she didn't have to run with me.'

Carole's progress was temporarily halted soon after when she broke her collarbone during a physical training exercise in the gymnasium. Put on light duties, she became bored. But once recovered and back into the tough old routine, she faced another problem – sexism – which was probably more widespread than some soldiers would care to admit.

'My food intake would be monitored at every meal, and the OC would stand in the canteen and order the chefs to take food off my plate. I was always hungry.

'I remember one of the corporal training instructors getting me on my own one day. He told me that there were only two ways that I would complete my training to become a Military Policewoman: "On your back, or up the commanding officer's behind." I told him "No way!" From then on he made my life hell.

'Yet I made it out of training with not one tear being shed.

'I was the only female on my passing-out parade photograph. My mum came up for that day, and she was proud of her girl.'

After the years of dreaming and determination, Carole had made the grade – at last she was in the Military Police. On 4 May 1982 she was back in Germany, this time with 110 Provost Company Royal Military Police, at Sennelager. Nearby at the parachute centre she was able to complete 123 jumps. She was able to practise live firing on the ranges with a 9 mm pistol. As for the work, some of it seemed routine, such as attending accidents or working with the German police in settling disputes between German civilians and the British. One job, however, seemed slightly unusual:

'I worked with the SIB [Special Investigations Branch] for a while. But the most I got to do for them was visit an Army house where the husband, a British soldier, had supposedly been cheating on his wife whilst she was in England. I had the lonely task of taking the sheets from his bed and placing them in a plastic bag for investigation – well, that's what I was told to do anyway.'

Carole's prowess in skydiving soon saw her spending a month at a time away from Germany, this time in Dhekelia, Cyprus. There she took part in the Cyprus Combined Services Parachute Centre Championships, which were held annually. She won the 'Leading Lady' section – for accuracy – both years. She was back there as recently as 2002, wearing her Spurs football shirt. Football was another of her passions, but her abiding affection for Germany forms the happiest part of her recollections.

'I used to go into Paderborn quite often as I thought it was a lovely place. I liked eating out in the German restaurants where you would always get very large plates of food, no matter what it was on the menu that you'd ordered. I loved the German lager. Sometimes they would put fruit in your beer – that was lovely, too. It was nice to enjoy the good food and drink from nice glasses. It was all very special. I had German friends, Marlize and her husband, Winfried, who I visited quite often. They would visit the camp and come into the Corporals' Mess to have drinks with us. They were very nice people. Marlize spoke good English but Winfried didn't, so it was good to practise my German on him. In Germany there always seemed to be fairs and festivals throughout the year. My experience of Germany was that everything was of better quality than in England – their food, houses, clothes, everything. Obviously there were poorer areas – for instance I would see the people working in the fields all day near the British Military Hospital in Rinteln. But I loved living in Germany. I never had any animosity at all with the people there. They simply accepted us and it is hard to even imagine how different it had been in the Second World War.'

Whilst stationed in Sennelager, Carole found romance. She married a corporal in the same unit. She was soon pregnant, and her first children – twins, Crystal and Cindy – were born in the British Medical Hospital in Rinteln. In 1984 her husband was posted to Lisburn in Northern Ireland. During the two years they spent there, her third child, Nathan, was born.

'I found it difficult becoming a wife of a soldier, especially as I had been in the Army nearly six years. I felt I was treated with less respect than when I was actually serving. My husband left the Army in 1987 and returned home to Essex, where he joined the civilian police force. Unfortunately, we got officially divorced in May 1991. Ironically, I ended up living in Colchester garrison town, still surrounded by the military and all the parachute regiments. I did join the 45th Signal Regiment, Territorial Army, for a while, when my children were younger, but I couldn't put the time in. Two of my daughters are now in the TA, one of whom has just returned from Germany on exercise, so I still see lots of Army uniform in my house.'

'It's different for girls' is indeed an understatement. One can see by Carole Gladman's experiences that it takes a special kind of woman to sustain a career in the Army. Thankfully, they keep appearing and joining up. Some see it more as a fine way to spend their youth, and providing there isn't a shooting war, spending time out on the range in Germany certainly beats secretarial work or fending off complaints in a call centre.

Corporal Janine Soyer of Mansfield, Notts was a WRAC driver. She was in service from 1971 to '75 and was stationed in Lübbecke in 1973.

'The idea was simple – I fancied seeing a bit of the world, so I thought I'd join the Army. It was a four-year signing. I fancied being an Army driver and that's what I became. We did six weeks' basic training at Guildford and then I went on to Aldershot to do my driver training. That was in June 1971 until August. Although I was only in Germany for six months in 1973, it was one of the best times of my life and quite exciting. We were sent to a place called Lübbecke, which is not to be confused with Lübeck, which is in the north. Lübbecke is between Osnabrück and Minden, more in the centre of the country.

'I was part of an Army experiment. There were just 14 of us girls and we were sent out to Lübbecke because there were no women there; the only bases at the time with women on them were Rheindahlen and Mönchengladbach. The only other girls at the time were involved with the Military Police and they were scattered around all over, a bit thin on the ground. So, as you can imagine, 14 young women arriving on an all-male Army base – and there were hundreds of men there – we were going to be very popular. I was actually down at Folkestone when the news came, driving ambulances on the range at Hythe. When I discovered I was part of this 14-girl experiment it all seemed a bit exciting – and it was. Me and my friend Lou were happily on duty at Folkestone one day and our Sergeant came along and said, "You two have been picked for Germany." We looked at each other and said, "Oh . . . right!"

'Our sergeant for the group was brought over from duty in Berlin, and we had a corporal from somewhere in Germany, too. We flew out there in the first week of January. There was heavy fog over Germany so we couldn't land anywhere near Lübbecke and ended up landing somewhere near Münster. We stayed overnight there and then had one hell of a long ride the next day to get to Lübbecke.

'I'll never forget arriving at the base. When we got off the coach the men were queuing to carry our bags: "Can we help you? Shall I carry your luggage?" That first week we had no end of lads asking us out for drinks and for meals – it was absolutely unbelievable. We were billeted separate, of course, around the back of the offices by the dental and medical centre. We had the top of a two-storey building. There was a kindergarten nearby for visiting Army children, because there were some service families living in the area, but they were a good 15 minutes' drive away, so we were still the only females on the base itself.

'We were split up into pairs for duty: two drivers, that was me and Lou; two cooks; two clerical workers; two signal girls; a woman officer; a sergeant; a full corporal; and a lance corporal. My duties involved driving the camp doctor. I'd drive him to the surgery at the barracks. We also had a neighbouring camp which was a half-hour drive away and he used to do a surgery there if their doctor wasn't on duty. I drove officers to their mess functions, to parties and dances, things like that. We soon got settled in and had a whale of a time. Before long I was going out on various dates and then I met up with an old flame from back in England. I know one of our girls got married out there – I went to see her years later. I know it was "duty", but frankly it was just like one big holiday. We'd only been out there a few weeks when in March we went on a five-day break to Berlin. Our sergeant was one of those characters who was always planning and doing things. Going to Berlin was fascinating, because the wall was up then of course and there was Checkpoint Charlie. We were able to stay in this special forces "hotel" called Edinburgh House and in there you could use English currency.

'Then there was so-called "adventure training". Our sergeant – she knew all the skives and how to waste time, but we didn't mind. We were due to go on this trip to the Hartz Mountains. Some training – I always got to go in any case because I was driving Land-Rovers, but it was a week's booze up. That was in the June and it was hardly over when the offer of going down Bavaria came up. We were off like a shot. In Bavaria we met up with other WRACs and the beer didn't stop flowing. Bavaria in July is beautiful and the beer the best in Europe. I know that if I'd stayed there, then I'd certainly have become over-friendly with the booze. It was just too easy. Every night it was kit inspection, get your dinner and off to the bar. The exchange-rate was brilliant at the time: about eight and a half marks to the pound. When you consider that we could buy a large bottle of beer for just 50 pfennigs, that meant 17 bottles for a quid. That's dangerous ground to be on, but it was very enjoyable, I must admit.

'You couldn't come home at weekends and the only vehicles we had were the Land-Rovers. So all there was to do was drink!

'We never really stopped to think much about the Cold War; I mean, yes, we were capable of rapid mobilisation and that's what everyone was trained up for all the time, but as for the Russians . . . yet come to think of it, they were often around, even where we were, because they had this nickname, the "Socksmiths". These were like Russian "ghosts" − there would often be two guys hanging around in a car and they'd follow you wherever you went. We were told by the Military Police that if we saw these Socksmiths, then we had to tell them and they'd "deal" with it. It was a bit spooky, but all part of the game.

'We were busy enjoying ourselves. We often went nightclubbing. There were two nightclubs in the town. One was very good − the DJ was a coloured lad who was in the Army. The other we avoided − it was full of drugs. Yes, even in those days there was a drugs problem. You could get anything if you visited that other place but we steered clear of it. There were fights, too. There was a cinema run by the camp, and sometimes at the weekend we'd maybe pair up in fours and go to the pictures in town. We used to go to Bielefeld for our sports on a Wednesday afternoon. We didn't really mix with the Germans too much. There were civilian Germans working on the base and we got along with them all right. We had some German drivers on the motor yard, too. They were run by Mike Shannon's dad − that's Mike Shannon who used to play for Southampton Football Club. Germans were employed in the kitchens, too. There were a lot of MSO's (Mixed Services Overseas). These were displaced eastern Europeans − Poles, people like that. They did odd jobs around the camp.

'I have always had a deep interest in the Second World War. My grandfather was a leader in the French Resistance. You'll have noticed my unusual surname, Soyer.

'He was Jean Soyer and he's mentioned in *Jersey Under The Jackboot,* a book about the German occupation of the Channel Islands. But when he was in Northern France he kept a radio set in an old couple's home. The Germans were searching for this radio and he escaped, on his bike, and cycled around the back of the Germans. They told him to halt; he didn't, and they shot him dead. At his funeral, there was a lad named Roger Le Bell who ran a bicycle shop. When the funeral procession arrived at the church, Roger went into the belfry to toll the bell for my grandfather. The Germans thought he was a sniper and shot him. As they shot him the bell rang just once. On a scroll presented to my grandmother by the Resistance the inscription reads: "The bell tolled once for Jean Soyer".'

'In 1976 I went over to Germany to visit my friend Jan who had married over there. But it didn't last. I wasn't all that keen to get married at that time. I'd joined up to have an adventure and a good time, and certainly got that. I remember going to Checkpoint Charlie in Berlin. We went past Spandau Prison where Hess was held prisoner. As we were driving along we could see all the watchtowers. We visited an American PX store – that was interesting. Near Checkpoint Charlie there was a little museum showing the various methods people had used to escape from East Germany. I was amazed to see how someone had wrapped themselves around the engine compartment in a bubble car – it was unbelievable. Barbed wire, minefields, loose Alsatians. A scary bit of countryside between them and us.

'When I came out of the army I joined the Territorials for a couple of years. Looking back on it all I just have very happy memories. In fact if my house caught fire, there's only one thing I'd go back for, and that's my Army photograph album. You can recreate most memories, but I couldn't recreate my Army days.'

For the women, both wives and soldiers, their lifestyle has altered dramatically since that bleak decade following the war. Service conditions, routines and social life have all moved ahead progressively with the times. The Army may always be primarily a male machine, yet today there's more than a few female cogs to keep it turning over. Yet the fact remains that women still have some way to go before their male colleagues in the ranks take them seriously.

~ A Woman's Touch ~

Cheryl Ciccone was a WRAC Clerk at Rheindahlen between 1987 and '97.

'I actually joined the Army in 1987 as a supply specialist. After one years' service I retraded to military clerk. After completing my trade training at Worthy Down, my posting request was for Germany.

'When I was 13 years old, the Army Recruitment Team visited our school and gave a chat. It sounded really great so I made the decision to join the Army if I could not be a nurse. As we moved from my home town just before I left school I was unable to go on to further education so my nursing dream went out the window and I joined the Army instead.

'My parents were extremely proud of me, as it actually took me a year to get in, as I have a heart condition and had to undergo a number of tests by the military hospitals before I was declared fit enough to join.

'The training itself was quite good fun, but tiring. The one thing you never seemed to have was time for yourself, as you were constantly on the go, learning new skills and learning to cope with new personalities. I do recall a number of girls taking the bed springs out of one of the cadets' beds (don't think they were too keen on her) and then putting the mattress back on, so when she actually did sit on it she fell straight through; the whole floor heard her scream, which sent everyone into fits of giggles as by this time everyone knew what had happened apart from her. The hardest thing was learning to stand still for so long – still haven't a clue how we managed to do so.

'I also recall the disco they put on for us; it makes me chuckle to think of it. They brought trainees in from the Royal Electrical and Mechanical Engineers (REME), who were based at Bordon doing their basic training. We were marched over to the gym, doors opened and there were these guys all standing on one side of the gym hall and us on the other. It was like a picture out of a pre-war magazine – didn't take us long to mingle, though!

'When I finished my trade training as a military clerk, we were all brought together to be told where we would be posted; we all actually got the postings we requested. Over the moon was my feeling at the time, and excitement at going to another country, yet I wish I had asked for Cyprus or Hong Kong.

'The accommodation was good. The actual camp was an old

111

German Army camp, with cobbled paths (not nice to run on, I can tell you). The female accommodation was set out so that there were two to a room; we had a kitchen and sitting-room, and of course wash facilities. It was quite modern. Not what I was used to, as the accommodation in my first posting was very old-fashioned.

'I was employed within the regimental headquarters and lucky enough to have a warrant officer who believed that we should get experience in all departments. So every six months we were moved around to learn different aspects of providing services throughout, which was a huge benefit and great way to learn. However, during the last year of my service in Germany I actually spent six months on guard, doing two days on and two days off, working twelve-hour shifts. Which would have been fine, but for a regimental sergeant-major, who decided that to build character we should work on what should have been one of our days off, which actually left you shattered and unable to have a social life.

'Compromise wasn't a word used in Germany; it was a case [of if] you [were] told to do something, you did it. Being quite a strong-headed person, I did challenge those things I thought were wrong, not a good idea.

'The social life in Germany was great. I and my friends used to get the last tram to Düsseldorf, which would arrive around 10 p.m., and the first tram back in the morning (6 a.m.). Many a time I have gone straight onto duty clerk (lucky it was a sleeping duty) after a night out in Düsseldorf.

'I got on reasonably well with the girls in the camp; there weren't many of us – about 25 in all. You would speak with everyone but you had your main group of say two or three friends. There were four of us who used to go clubbing and to the NAAFI; we used to call ourselves the four musketeers.

'Unfortunately, us youngsters tended not to mix with the Germans. They, in my opinion, were quite hostile to us military personnel, so we tended not to mix with them. Obviously they would be very friendly to us females if we did approach them, but we were mainly surrounded by English people, there being a military base in Düsseldorf.

'However, I did notice that the people who lived in Bavaria were much more friendly and approachable than other Germans. I really do think this was down to them not being surrounded by squaddies.

~ A Woman's Touch ~

'I recall being in the NAAFI one day, buying some goods, as I was being posted back to England. They were selling bits of the Berlin Wall, which I thought bizarre. As a 20 year old, at that time I couldn't understand why anyone would want to actually pay for a tiny bit of concrete or brick.

'I actually served just over ten years in the Army. I left in June 1997. I did feel like my left arm had been torn off for a quite a while after leaving, but I was so angry with the Army – its treatment of female staff was very sexist. An Army career for a female is extremely difficult, as promotion is easier if you are willing to sleep with those who have the authority to get you promoted or if you work extremely hard. For a man it is a lot easier, as in a way they are only competing with one another, whereas females are competing with one another and males, and those old-school believers who still hold onto the knowledge that woman should not be in the forces.

'I also had a child whilst serving and did another four years before leaving after my child's birth – an added cross against my name when it came to promotion.

'I can honestly say, as a person of mixed race, that whilst I served in the Army I came across indirect racial discrimination, direct sexual discrimination and indirect discrimination. As long as the forces stay in the old institutional way of thinking this will continue, and I do not envy any female joining the forces today. Whilst it is easier in some respects due to law change, which does affect the forces, it is still a man's world and a world where females should know and have their place as some would say. It's about time it did modernise and learn from the past.'

It may seem a sombre note on which to end this chapter, but being a soldier's wife, apart from the stress of being in an unfamiliar country, can always provide a further background tension. The following contribution – as the conflicts in the Falklands and Iraq have sadly demonstrated – reminds us of what armies are for, and the possible consequences of joining up. This story does not culminate in Germany, yet starkly reminds us that soldiers based there were often sent to other, less-friendly locations.

Mrs Shirley Houston of Brightlingsea, Essex was stationed in Berlin with her husband Jim, a private with the King's Own Scottish Borderers, between 1987 and '89.

'With my husband Jim, I lived in Berlin for two years from February 1987 to February 1989. We met in August 1985 as he was based in Colchester and I lived with my parents in Wivenhoe [Essex]. We got married in August 1986 and then went off to Berlin in the following February, 1987.

'We had a great time there. I missed my family a lot at first, but I had to get used to it. We lived in Spandau District — just five minutes away from the prison where Hess had been a prisoner. Jim did a lot of guard duties there, which he said were very scary as there were supposed to be ghosts in the prison and they used to hear voices.

'We then found out that we were expecting our first child. We were so happy. Daniel was born in January 1988 at the British Military Hospital. We were in hospital for a week and then we went home. By February 1989 we were based in Edinburgh, which is a lovely place. October came and Jim was sent to Northern Ireland for six months' duty there. My son and I went to my parents' to stay. Jim came home for his leave, which was for six days. We had a great time, and had Christmas a little earlier. Jim travelled back to Ireland on Monday, 11 December and on the 13th he was tragically killed — ambushed whilst on duty. It totally devastated our family. Daniel was only 23 months old, so was too young to remember. Thirteen years on I still miss him, but Daniel looks his double, which sometimes is a help. I have since met a lovely guy who has shown me you can love again, and we have a lovely daughter, Katie, who is now four years old.'

5

Der Britische Kinder

> I had never thought of my time in Germany as important; not
> until fairly recently, when I began to think how
> extraordinary it was that in the 1960s I had spent time in this
> country as part of something called The British Army of the
> Rhine . . . what an Imperialist notion . . .
>
> Hilary Plews, schoolgirl at Iserlohn in the 1960s

Bringing children into this kind of world could be regarded as a
depressing prospect, but thousands of British children have been
born and bred in Germany. For teachers working for the British
Forces Education Service, this must also have been a very different
environment to be in compared to working in an ordinary British
school. During the day the atmosphere, with its classrooms and
corridors, plus the fact that English was spoken, was probably very
familiar. The difference came off-duty. Being mainly civilians, they
had a choice: they could enjoy whatever facilities were available on
a base, or circulate with German friends. Many did both. Education
for Army children today in Germany follows all the basic tenets set
down for schools back home. The curriculum may have changed and
accommodation may have improved, but being in school in
Germany follows a familiar pattern. In the early days, however, a
posting to Germany could be a mixed blessing for parents and
children alike.

*Hilary Plews's father was a lieutenant-colonel in the RAMC and an
ENT (ear, nose and throat) specialist. The family were stationed in
Iserlohn from 1960 to '66.*

'My dad was posted to the British Military Hospital, Iserlohn, in

1960. I was six years old. He was a lieutenant-colonel in the Royal Army Medical Corps (RAMC), an ear, nose and throat specialist. My parents stayed there for nearly six years, coming back to Catterick Camp before the World Cup in 1966. I was sent to boarding school in 1964 in Staffordshire and was only part-time in Germany after that.

'We drove to Germany from Aldershot. My parents didn't speak any German and I remember finding being in public with them, when they were trying to order meals in a restaurant, buy sweets, petrol, etc., extremely embarrassing.

'The Army house we were given was an enormous flat in a small town called Hemer, a couple of miles away from Iserlohn. There were four of these huge two-storied flats, with attics and basements, in the street where we lived. British Army personnel lived in our flat and Canadian Army personnel lived in the remaining three flats on our side of the street. The German families lived on the other side in neat terraces. A German single mother, Frau Gründa and her two children, Siegfried and Hannelora, lived in the attic flat of the block next door to us. I think Frau Gründa cleaned for the Canadian families.

'The flat felt very strange; it was so huge and I'd never lived in a flat before. There were two balconies and an enormous garden – plus *radiators*, which I'd never seen. Army houses in England at that time were freezing affairs heated by open fires. I remember being amazed that the German children opposite only went to school for half a day whereas I went to the British Forces Education Service (BFES) school in Iserlohn all day. A small minibus with a soldier escort used to pick up me and the English child who lived downstairs every weekday and drive us to school along with a few other Army children who lived in smaller houses around the corner.

'The school (primary only) was also amazing. I had attended an old Dame school in Aldershot housed in a Nissen hut which had three classrooms divided by curtains with an outside toilet. This German school seemed huge. It was purpose built, single storey, had a proper playground, a big hall where we had cooked dinners every day and loads of staff – not just three! And men teachers, too, which was unheard of at Miss Seed's establishment in Aldershot.

'The first thing I did there was fall off the back of my chair and split my head open on the radiator behind me. The school had a proper curriculum, school trips to places like the Mohne Dam, famous for the Dambusters raid. There were after-school activities such as the Brownies, open days, school reports, etc.

'Everything was in English – all the teachers were English. The kitchen staff were German. No foreign languages were taught, not even German. You would not have known we were in Germany; all the kitchen staff spoke perfect English.

'We hardly had any contact with the German civilians, except in German shops, which my mother avoided as she did most of her shopping in the NAAFI. The NAAFI wasn't just a food shop, but more like a department store. We also went to the Maple Leaf Services, the Canadian version of the NAAFI. We had a German cleaner who seemed to come with the flat. Her name was Klara, but although she had lived in Germany a long time, she was originally Polish. She spoke good English. She lived in a tiny attic flat in the terraced houses opposite our flat. The "Molly Man" was a regular caller. He delivered my parents' Mollige beer supplies. He married Klara and built his mother, Klara and him a big new house in the forest which surrounded Hemer. Myself and the Canadian children in the other flats used to swap insults with the German children opposite (but not with Siegfried and Hannelora – they were somehow off-limits). The insults went something like this: we would shout "Krauts!" at them and they would shout "Danish Cheese!" at us (don't ask me what this referred to). Then there was Herr Schader, an enormous man who stoked all the boilers in the Army flats. His wife sometimes babysat me and I was terrified of her. She was very thin and very severe. My parents had no German friends who were their peers and neither did I. My headmaster once arranged for a few of us to go to a German primary school and meet some of the girls there. A deeply embarrassing affair, because they all spoke lovely English and we spoke no German, yet we were fêted and treated as honoured guests and we didn't know what to do with ourselves. So there were no German friendships made. When I got to boarding school I wasted no time in learning German. As far as Army friendships were concerned, I had plenty of friends at school. None of these survived my going to boarding school, though I did make one effort to keep in touch with a girl once we were back in Catterick Camp. More recently I saw a girl I had known who was also sent to boarding school. It was interesting, reminiscing about our growing up in the British Army; neither of us had found it very easy.

'On weekends and on holidays in the winter we went tobogganing. There was a hill at the back of the flats and all the Army kids and the German kids lined up there in the snowy weather and tobogganed down the hill. It was great fun. Then there were a couple of big outdoor swimming pools to choose from in the summer and I'd go to those with my Canadian friends. School friends would sometimes come and stay and I'd go to stay with them. On occasion this was tricky – I remember my favourite friend, Carol, had a dad who was "another rank". He always saluted my dad when he handed Carol over or came to collect her and I always found that embarrassing. I used to go for walks in the great pine woods around Hemer with my friend Andrea, where we would scare ourselves silly with stories of bears and getting lost. In the evenings I played out in our back garden, on my own or with the Canadian children. We would climb over the fences between each garden and go right down the row like that.

'My parents liked going out to eat and we often went to a place – I think it was an American social club – called Zoest. For Sunday lunch I always ate *Wiener Schnitzel* followed by *Eis Krem mit Zahn* (ice cream with cream). In the holidays, my parents liked to travel and we visited towns along the Rhein and Moselle, the "*Romantische Weg*" (romantic way), as well as driving to the Netherlands, France, Austria, Switzerland and Italy.

'I'm not sure how my mother took to being in Germany. She didn't work. She complained about Klara a lot, but the truth is she couldn't have managed without her as Klara did all the talking with tradesmen etc. She did "good works" by visiting wives of the other ranks when the husbands were posted off to a war or on manoeuvres or to somewhere the wives couldn't go. These visits sounded ghastly and I don't think she enjoyed making them, but she had to go – it was some kind of Army officers' wives' etiquette. She attended the officers-only wives' club, and entertained quite a lot. She got on with the Canadian Army wives and they did coffee mornings with each other and helped each other in looking after the pre-school-age kids. She also did a book round in the hospital once a week, which she enjoyed. She read a lot and took me to other kids' parties and entertained my friends, playing canasta and monopoly with us.

'When I eventually got to boarding school, I found it exceedingly strange. Although I spent eight years there, that feeling never quite wore off. I think this was partly because there were hardly any other girls there who had Army backgrounds. I only recall two and they were in different houses so I never saw them. As far as Catterick Camp was concerned . . . well – there was still no central heating in our first Army house. The camp was a dump, far more so than Iserlohn, but by that time my life was primarily centred around surviving boarding school.

'I have never thought of my time in Germany as important; not until fairly recently, when I began to think how extraordinary it was that in the 1960s I had spent time in this country as part of something called the British Army of the Rhine . . . what an imperialist notion. I began to realise just how "imperial" my experience had been – that whole thing of not really *seeing* Germans, let alone talking to them, living in this little English world, with English food shops, clothes shops, bookshops, all courtesy of the NAAFI, with English friends and English concerns. I never saw one of my parents' friends read a German newspaper.'

Unlike their parents, not having the typical formative experience of schoolchildren back home, many of these children appear to have enjoyed their Army-based education and, judging by their memories and subsequent lives back in the UK, they seem to be none the worse for their slightly different upbringing. There are also a significant number who came away with nothing but bad memories of their German sojourn. Much of this stems from the fact that even within Germany, the Army was always on the move. Speaking as one who attended a dozen schools between the ages of five to fifteen, I can testify that the regular uprooting from your home, friends and schoolmates every few months can add more than a few miserable memories to your formative years. For those who seemed to be bounced from base to base in Germany, the idea of ex-pupils' associations and reunions are an anathema.

However, there is a special, enduring bond between service children. Many of the base schools throughout BAOR still have well-run ex-pupil networks, regularly updated websites and message boards. Annual reunions are commonplace and there appears to be a particular camaraderie and distinct sense of humour one might not find in UK-based schools.

Sydney Turnbull was a pupil in Germany in 1951. His father was a major in the REME. Sydney joined the Royal Signals in 1959, was transferred to Royal Artillery in 1968 and left with the rank of sergeant in 1976. Today he lives in Canada, where he drives trains for the Canadian Pacific Railroad.

'In the spring of 1951 my mother received notification from my father, who was a major at the time, to join him in BAOR and move into quarters with him in Hanover. He had already arrived in Germany and had to sort out quite a few things before we could go over. I had just turned seven years old.

'We took the train to Harwich and sailed on a troopship. Because of my dad's rank, we were berthed in officers' cabins. When we arrived at the Hook of Holland, there were numerous military trains. We boarded the one for Hanover, and eventually arrived at the *Haupt Bahnhof* [main railway station] after many stops on a journey of nearly two days. My father was there to meet us with a military staff car with a German driver.

'Our quarters were in the Herrenhausen area of Hanover. The place was just huge and very, very opulent – what a shock for my mother and me. All or most of the officers' quarters at this time had been requisitioned. They were all executive-style homes. Ours was a German banker's house, with six bedrooms, two huge bathrooms, a scullery and pantry, enormous kitchen, living room, drawing room, study, plus a huge cellar with a double garage. There was a very large garden which was surrounded by a six-foot stone wall, with a very large patio to the rear of the house. My mother hated the place right from the start as it seemed so vast and impersonal. In fact, for a family of just three this was much too big, but my father told us that within six months we would most likely be moving to a smaller house. The next big shock came when we were introduced to our live-in maid! Apparently, all officers had live-in maids, for cooking, housework, etc. Our maid's name was Chrystal, a really pleasant young girl of about 20. My mother took an instant liking to her and they became really good friends. Chrystal was more than simply "the maid".

'At this time all able-bodied German citizens were required by the West German government to perform two hours, five days per week, of some kind of labour in order to help rebuild the German economy. Be it construction, bomb damage, clearing up, Chrystal was required to put in her two hours, over five days for about three months, when this particular regulation was relaxed. The three of us got used to our huge house and I started my first stint at a BFES school, namely Hanover Primary. Also probably requisitioned, it was a beautiful, grand old building in spectacular grounds. As it was not on the regular school bus route, I would be picked up every day by an Army staff car. Most Sundays my father would take us to his officers' mess, which was not too far from our quarter, for lunch. During the war this mess (there were many officers' mess establishments in all major German cities) had been an officers' club for some branch of the Wehrmacht. It was a luxurious place, with superb grounds and a full-size swimming pool. We always had sumptuous Sunday lunches and then high tea, followed by a film show, as the place even had a small theatre.

'Even at my young age I quickly realised that our style of living in Germany was going to be very much a different prospect to the Army quarters we had in the UK, such as Catterick Camp, for instance – a cold, draughty place with no central heating! This was the first thing that impressed everyone who moved to Germany – central heating, double-glazed windows, private maids, duty-free purchases, and a very thriving black-market economy, all of which combined to make BAOR, in its infancy, an instant "must-have" posting.'

'Hanover Primary was my first school in BAOR, and I found it very different from my school days in UK in that all pupils were from military families with a few exceptions. So as youngsters we had at least something in common.

'My next school was at Bielefeld as my father was now posted to a base workshop at a place called Kunsebeck. By now I was settled in to life here in Germany and my parents had moved from Hanover to Bielefeld and had a much nicer quarter – it was big, with an orchard.

'The school here was very well managed and our teachers were all first class and very professional, with one or two exceptions. It was here that I found I was eligible to attend a three-week summer camp at the BAOR resort at Winterberg. I was fortunate to be accepted and could not wait for the day of departure.

'We were given a booklet of instructions on how to live in tents and to manage under these type of conditions. We also found out that we would be integrated with children from German schools, and this did not go down too well with many parents and children, as there was a very apparent "We won the war, and all Germans are no good" attitude at the time in BAOR. This did not bother me as by now I had made friends with many local German children. The great day came and we all departed in coaches from Bielefeld, and each coach was a 50/50 mix of British and German children.

'Even on the coaches us British kids soon found out that the German kids were very friendly and more to the point, much better prepared than any of us for a couple of weeks in tents. They had torches, sewing kits, backpacks, hiking boots, etc., and this was just the beginning!

'We arrived at Winterberg – a very scenic resort with a beautiful hotel, tennis courts and swimming pools, set in lovely rolling country with alpine surroundings. Our tented area was all set up and very well organised. We settled in and our daily programme was full of interesting and fun things to do.

'I could go on about this three-week period, but in a nutshell we all had a wonderful time, and got along really well with the German kids, who seemed much more worldly than us. We were often entertained during the evenings by them as many were very accomplished musicians on the accordion, harmonica, piano and other instruments. The highlight for us British kids were two movies, *The Conquest of Everest* and the *Coronation of Queen Elizabeth*. As we were here at Winterberg during the Coronation, we all received our Coronation souvenirs of a nice pen and pencil set, a special commemoration book and a small model of the state coach and horses.'

'My father was posted from Bielefeld to Wetter-am-Ruhr, and by then I was old enough to go to one of the three BFES boarding schools, so from my father's point of view, Windsor School, Hamm, was the choice.

'A lot of preparation was needed – new school uniforms, and everything else required for life at a boarding school – and I was quite looking forward to the idea. Windsor School was a mixed boarding school, situated on the outskirts of Hamm, and in an extensively refurbished barracks. We were all divided into houses; I was in Hillsborough boys, and the next block to us was Hillsborough girls. The other houses were Balmoral, Sandringham and Caernarvon.

'The school ages ranged from around 11 to 18 years of age for the students, and my first term was a little intimidating for all of us new to boarding school, but we all got used to it, and learned to live together and get along. We shared in just about everything except our accommodations with the girl pupils, and I always remember that we dined together, six to a table, three boys and three girls, with white linen tablecloths. The food, surprisingly, was pretty good.

'The school would have been the envy of many schools in the UK. It had a full-size outdoor swimming pool, huge science labs, a full-size theatre, agriculture block, metal and woodwork block, and hobbies centre, and was set in acres and acres of grounds, coupled with a full athletic facility and numerous cricket and football pitches. We had really good teachers and German house matrons. On reflection, I really enjoyed myself there and we all got along with each other and behaved like young ladies and gentlemen. That it not to say that we did not get up to a great deal of mischief and typical boarding-school pranks.

'My time there came to an end and my father was posted from BAOR back to the UK. What a come-down from a posting of living in luxury to the reality and harshness of soldiering in the UK.

'I was accepted into the Army Apprentice college at Harrogate, which was the beginning of an 18-year career in the Army. I will not dwell on my time in the Army, suffice to say that much of it was spent in BAOR, and I did visit many of the places where I spent a great deal of my childhood years. I did have the fortune as a serving soldier to be in Germany during the Cuban Missile Crisis (we were all put on a war-time footing), visited the wall in Berlin and did a tour of East Berlin. I also became a reasonably accomplished off-shore sailor with the British Kiel Yacht club, and visited many places all over Europe. I did a tour of duty on HMS *Fearless* and was on duty in Londonderry during Bloody Sunday. Last, but not least, for my final assignment, I was privileged to command a battlefield tactical nuclear missile detachment.'

If you're an Army child, then of course you don't have a say in the matter. Children grow and adapt to their environment, as many have on German bases. The schools there are run on a similar basis to their UK civilian counterparts and the teachers are civilians. The BFES was established by the Foreign Office just after the war in 1946. It fulfilled the need to provide schools for British children who were stationed in Germany. During the winter of 1951–2, the Army took the service over, and it became known as Service Children's Education (SCE). By 1967 an association had been formed: the British Forces Education Service Association. This was eventually merged in the 1980s with the Service Children's Association to become the BFES/SCE Association. This enables teachers to maintain contact, and annual reunions are organised.

SCE has always provided a reasonable curriculum based on Britain's educational policy, and today there are many thousands of service children in fulfilling careers throughout the UK who enjoyed a totally different childhood from that of their working colleagues. Inside the confines of the base everything was as British as could be. The difference lay beyond the perimeter – Germany. For most, it seemed to have been an enjoyable part of their upbringing.

Susan Cullen was born in 1955 and educated as a child on bases in Detmold, Osnabrück, and in 1966 at boarding school in Rheindahlen. She also worked as a waitress in Germany. Her father was in the 12th Royal Lancers.

'My father had joined the Army in 1948 and served 25 years until 1973. He met my mother in her native Scotland and they have now been married for 50 years. I was born in 1955 and I'm the eldest of five children. We were always on the move with the Army. We lived in Detmold for a few years then moved every two years all over the place: Ireland, Buckinghamshire, Berwick-upon-Tweed, Osnabrück, Rheindahlen.

'When my father was sent to Aden, I had to go to boarding school at Rheindahlen in Germany. It was called Kent School, based at Chatham House. My family was living in Osnabrück at the time. There are two things I remember about being the age of 11, at school for the first time in Rheindahlen: one was the great food we had, and the other was the bullying we had to put up with from the boys. It was also very disorientating at first, too, being away from my parents in this strange place. We only went home for Easter, summer or Christmas – and when I say "home", that, for me, was Osnabrück. We had no concept of life in England. Yes, we were surrounded by our own British schoolfriends, but England to us was just another place. In fact most of us had spent most of our lives outside England.'

'Looking back, it was a very odd "school" building, because it had been a German hospital during the war. We used to get changed in the old operating theatres! The classes were actually held in what used to be the wards – great long places that seemed all echoing, with tall ceilings. But we didn't have to put up with big dormitories. We had rooms and in each one two or three shared. Our school days began with us being called up at about 7 a.m., and then we had to see who could make it first to the washrooms. If you got there late all the sinks were taken up. Breakfast was at around 7.45 a.m. It was always pretty substantial. We had German cooks and I recall that we were actually served at table. Classes started at 9 a.m. My favourite teacher was a stocky old woman called Miss Galbraith who taught us English. The most awful teacher – and I can't remember his name – was the maths master. He was a real terror. We also learned German. I can still speak it a little, although I haven't been back for years and I've forgotten a lot. Sometimes they would take us out on a trip. I remember touring German places like castles and old buildings, learning about how people lived there in medieval times. And we were once taken to see the Mohne Dam, which was quite impressive. But we never ever touched upon the subject of the war. I can't say that I encountered any bitterness from the German civilians. The only serious occasion I recall was in Detmold, when one of my friend's mothers had had a baby and was pushing the pram along the pavement in the town. Two middle-aged German women were coming the other way and they refused to move, causing her to have to push the pram off the kerb and into the road to get by as these two women bellowed abuse at her. I suppose it was some old bitterness they had to get off their chests, but it was a little frightening. Makes you think what they might have been saying about us all behind closed doors.'

'Our accommodation and sleeping blocks were not near the school, but about ten minutes away. They were three long single-storey buildings joined along one end by a long corridor. The kitchen and dining area was housed in the middle block. The rooms had big windows that you could actually climb through, and some of the older girls did sneak off sometimes at night, as there was no security, which is surprising for something connected with the Army. I always thought it was foolhardy having those big windows, and the buildings were surrounded by trees. It wasn't unusual for us to be warned that there was a pervert in the grounds looking for a bit of peeping Tom activity! We had plenty of entertainment. We had our record players, and we watched both German and Dutch TV. We could buy records from the NAAFI. We would go to the cinema in the town, and on Saturdays we could go swimming in the local pool. Sundays was always church in the morning, then after lunch we'd spend time making sure that all our uniform and kit was ready for the coming week. Yes, we had to wear a uniform; grey blazer and skirt, white blouse and the Kent School tie. And just like in the Army we had inspections, and we had to clean our rooms and keep things spick and span. My worst subject at school was maths and my best were needlework and art. My parents only ever visited me once during term to see how I was. I was called to the Head's office and was wondering what I'd done. Then I saw my mum and dad.

'I don't recall the day we left very much, but soon we were in England, which seemed just as strange to me as Germany would be to an English girl. We moved to Catterick and I was then nearly 14. I left school in Catterick at 15 and off we all went again to Germany, back to Rheindahlen.

'My dad found me work in Rheindahlen, where my first job was washing up in an Army–Airforce café called The Blue Pool. I then worked as a waitress in a civilian mess until 1972 in Rheindahlen. The civilians were Brits who had come over to do all kinds of work – plumbing, electrical, that kind of stuff. My mother was a cleaner for General Howe, who was C-in-C for the area. He lived off-camp in a big house somewhere. There wasn't a lot of social life for me as a young teenager – I remember that most of the time I seemed to be babysitting for army couples who wanted to go out for the night. But I did have a happy time with a boyfriend called Chris, a Greek Cypriot who worked with me. I can't say I had an unhappy childhood because although we never had much to do with the Germans themselves, I did like the country and I'm planning to go back. I still have a friend over there from those days who got married and lives in Germany. There is one thing I got into over there, though; we always had British rock bands touring and we would go and see them if they were in the area. I went to see a band called Uriah Heep and they're still playing, still on the road, and me and my husband John are great fans and get to meet them backstage. So I suppose Uriah Heep are a direct link back to my German teenage years, and when I think of that time it always makes me smile.'

Germany always seems to have been quite an adventure. Today we may have become more complacent about foreign travel, so it is hard to imagine what a sudden change of country must have felt like for small children just after the war.

Rosalee Meehan (née Blake) of Exeter moved to Lüneberg in Germany in 1946.

Rosalie was aged seven, with her brother Robert, aged eight, when their father, a regular (who eventually served for thirty-four years), then serving with the Devonshire Regiment (later the Devon & Dorset) was posted to Germany.

'During the war years, my brother and I and our mother lived in the wilds of Suffolk, and, like thousands of other men at the time, my father was someone who visited sometimes.

'In 1946, Dad was posted to Germany and we were all able to go with him. It was a great adventure to us, sailing on the troopship on the way to our eventual destination, Lüneberg.

'We didn't live in barracks, but in a married quarter on the outskirts of the town. My dad was a sergeant-major at the time. The family who owned the house, Herr and Frau Marker, with their two small sons, had to move into two rooms and a kitchenette. In addition to the four Markers, in that same cramped two-room apartment, lived two of their grandparents.

'My mother was always a kind and caring person and was very sorry for the family and allowed Frau Marker to come and do her washing in our basement, and to grow vegetables and pick fruit when it was in season from the garden.

'Considering what had just occurred – the war – this was of course frowned upon by the authorities. I remember visiting their apartment and not being able to understand why they had to put up with such cramped conditions whilst we lived in the rest of their five-bedroomed home. One day my brother and I discovered some bowls of what looked like blood in the basement. We were too terrified to ask Mother why it was there, but the mystery was solved; Frau Marker had made some red jelly for their boy's birthday party and had left it in the basement to set!

'We went to British Services' School in the town. We were picked up each morning by a three-ton truck to take us there. Although the lorry was covered over at the back with canvas, it was open at the rear, so we got the terrible fumes gushing into the area where we sat. I guess they picked up about 12 of us each day for the school run.

Our dog "Spotted" Dick often followed the lorry – he hated to see us leave. He'd follow us for quite a distance, with all the kids shouting and telling him to go home. He always did in the end. Dick was not the first dog our father brought home. Before Dick he'd brought a small brown dachshund, which we immediately fell in love with. But we had him such a short time – just a few days – that I don't recall his name. One day my dad took him to the barracks. The CO spotted the dog and pulled rank so my father had to let the officer have our little "dachsie". We were heartbroken until Dick came into our lives.

'In addition to my dad's batman, Cousins (we never knew if he had a Christian name), we had a nanny/housemaid, called Frida. We loved Frida. She was about 25. She taught us German – some of which I remember to this day. She took us on picnics and played with us when we weren't at school. Frida had very long hair which was always tied up in plaits. I remember that when she had several inches cut off her hair, she used some of it to fashion a head of hair for my doll. She was also a good needle-woman, and made my doll an outfit – I remember it was white with red spots. She would take us to see an elderly gentleman friend of hers who lived on a houseboat. That was a novelty, and although our parents were quite happy about those visits, they weren't too keen on the harmonica he gave us, which we insisted on playing all day long.

'Winter was great, with snow, wonderful for small children. Our mother, ever resourceful and also a skilled needle-woman, made us snowsuits from grey blankets, which she dyed brown. Very warm and smart they were. In those days of clothing and rationing coupons, these were the best clothes we could have. They weren't so great when we got wet; falling off sledges was frequent and the coarse blanket material on a small kid's skin gave us very sore and chapped inner thighs! I also remember being driven along on the thick ice of the frozen Rhine one winter. I recall that we would put our shoes out on the windowsill on Christmas Eve to find the next morning that Santa Claus had put sweets in them overnight! That was a common practice in Germany at Christmas.

'We were in Germany for two years altogether. I guess I remember it as idyllic – and it probably was for us children. Mother didn't have it so good. She was ostracised for being kind to the Marker family. We enjoyed playing with their sons, Wilhelm and Horst-Dieter. I have some very pretty china cups, plates and saucers from

1. Corporal Doney serving German children at their Christmas party, Düsseldorf 1946 (R.H. Doney)

2. RASC Soldiers on the Rhine in 1947 (R.H. Doney)

3. Bombed bridge on the Rhine, Cologne 1946 (R.H. Doney)

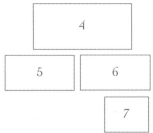

4. Ripon Barracks, Bielefeld 1958: Doug (checked shirt) is second from the right (Doug Palfreyman)

5. Exercise 'Ground Zero', 1958 (Doug Palfreyman)

6. Post card from Sennelager, 1958 (Doug Palfreyman)

7. Lieutenant 'Paddy' McGinty on the autobahn, Easter 1956 (Norman Baldwin)

| 8 | 9 |
| 10 | 11 |

8. Royal Signals on manoeuvres in the Moselle Valley in 1956 (Norman Baldwin)

9. Field kitchen on exercise with Royal Artillery and Royal Signals in 1956 – with young German in attendance! (Norman Baldwin)

10. 'A bunch of Posers': Royal Signals troop, Easter 1956 (Norman Baldwin)

11. Norman Baldwin, leaning on elbow, in a bar in Delmenhorst circa 1955 (Norman Baldwin)

12. End of Service party, 1949
(Jed Cressy)

13. Coming off Railway duty,
Detmold 1949 (Jed Cressy)

14. Allied (British) military
parade in Hitler's Olympic
Stadium, 1957 (Andrew Burns)

15. Dr Hugh Thomas, Rudolph Hess's surgeon in Spandau, Berlin (Graham Harrison)

16. Carole Isaacs, Military Policewoman, Rheindahlen 1982 (Carole Gladman)

17. Carole Isaacs RMP on leave in Cyprus in 1982 (Carole Gladman)

18. Carole Isaacs' German friends, the Brösche family, Sennelager (Carole Gladman)

19. Hamburg 1949 (Unknown)

20. RMP Carole Isaacs enjoys a drink with Lady Scotter, wife of Commander-in-Chief General Scotter, Rheindahlen 1981 (Carole Gladman)

21. A fine body of men, BAOR 1947 (Geoff Gilbert)

22. Rheinburg Convent, Home of the Sherwood Foresters Regiment, 1945 (Geoff Gilbert)

23. Spey Barracks, Buxtehude, Hamburg 1949 (John Applebey)

24. Major Reg Jones, Royal Tank Regiment (Major W.R. Jones)

25. Janine Soyer WRAC on rigorous adventure training, Bavaria 1973 (Janine Soyer)

26. Janine Soyer WRAC, with Land-Rover, Lübbecke 1973 (Janine Soyer)

27. Lieutenant-Colonel Robin Greenham, British Forces Liaison Officer, Berlin (Roy Bainton)

28. The original hut from the border crossing at Checkpoint Charlie in Berlin (Roy Bainton)

Bavaria. My mother had swapped these for coffee and other goods on the black market. We were lucky enough to get chocolate but my brother and I were always told to share it with the Marker boys.

'I remember being taken to Hamburg and Hanover and seeing the devastation of those cities, due to the bombing. Even as a small child I remember how shocking this was to see. Even today I can still see the flattened streets of Hanover. I could never understand how people could be so bad to each other.

'When we returned to England we were posted to Plymouth, another devastated place to which I was almost able to equate the damage I'd seen in Germany.'

One positive aspect of being an Army child was that it broadened your horizons and exposed you to a much wider world than you could have experienced during your UK schooldays. There were opportunities for travel around Europe and, of course, as one grew older, if your parent's military career seemed inspiring, then at least you had a foot in the door and would understand more about what life in the services meant than the average curious civilian recruit.

Brian Airey of Weston-super-Mare moved to Germany with his family in the 1960s. He attended the Queen's School, Rheindahlen.
'In 1960 we were an ordinary family living in a bungalow near the Gibraltar Barracks at Bury St Edmunds. The only connection we had with the military was that Dad worked with them as a civilian, but doing what I had no idea.

'I had just started at the local grammar school and my sister was at the junior school. One day my father came home and told us we were moving to Germany. Unless one counted a week's holiday in Jersey, we had never been abroad before.

'In what seemed like next to no time we found ourselves in Krefeld, being placed in a *gasthof* because our quarters were not ready to move into.

'We moved out the next day on the insistence of my mother as she found the place "dirty and inhospitable", so we spent the dark days of winter in another *gasthof* on Hubertusstrasse. None of us could speak the language and I felt sorry for my mother who now found herself in a strange country, living in a single room and finding difficulty in occupying herself all day, whilst Dad was working and we children were at school. My sister and I attended Queen's School,

HQ Rheindahlen, which was about an hour's bus ride away. Within a couple of days I had met a girl who had lived only 100 yards along the road from us in Bury St Edmunds, and we became lifelong friends. Soon after starting school I attended a party and I was still in school uniform because our clothes had not yet caught up with us. I felt a real idiot and I was soon taken to one side and loaned a different shirt and tie.

'After a couple of months we moved into officers' quarters on Kempener Allee. Everything was there to enable us to move straight in. We now lived in spacious rooms and had a reasonable-sized garden and a small number of British neighbours. We could not get used to the cost of living! Cut-price petrol was obtained by producing coupons at the local garage, there were very cheap drinks in the mess, and if anything was accidentally broken it was replaced.

'Weekends were spent in shopping and thereby learning a little of the language. I found it a bore that, as I was learning Latin at the grammar school, I was not permitted to drop it and learn German when I arrived at Queen's. The funny thing is that I also took French to A-level standard – and failed – and have not used the language in the last 40 years. I picked up German from living there and can make myself understood and actually translated for my wife when we returned to Germany 20 years later!

'Living so near the border with Holland, we frequently went to Venlo or Roermond to shop and see the sights. We also visited Walcheren, where Dad had helped to rebuild the dykes towards the end of the war. It was embarrassing when we approached the frontier with Germany again to be waved straight through, whilst German nationals had their cars thoroughly searched for excess butter and other contraband.

'We also spent our holidays touring various countries – Switzerland, Austria, as well as southern Germany. It was easy to get there on the autobahns. The opportunities for travel whilst at school were also good. I joined the Army Cadet Force and went to Hohne and a few other places on the Lüneberg Heath to learn the art of patrolling and digging trenches as well as jumping out of armed personnel carriers and riding on tanks. The school had a very dynamic vicar, the Reverend Sellars, who had forged links with a certain Father Borrelli who ran a shelter for the street kids of Naples. One year Reverend Sellars took a party of 12 boys – of which I was one – to Italy to meet those kids and entertain them for a week. We travelled there in a very old Army bus that we ended up abandoning as it tried to negotiate the Alpine passes. We camped on an extinct volcano near Pozzuoli and visited Mount Vesuvius, as well as the ruins of Pompeii, and on the way back we visited Venice.

'The same gentleman also arranged visits to Berlin and Poland that I did not go on. But the real trip of a lifetime was an overland visit to Jerusalem and the Red Sea. We recorded our adventures in the school newspaper and they have remained with me. We were followed by secret police in Bulgaria, strip-searched at the border and had several punctures whilst travelling towards Istanbul. We visited the Topkapi Museum and Florence Nightingale's hospital at Scutari. In Tarsus we camped unknowingly in the grounds of a mosque and were awoken to the sounds of the Mullah calling the faithful to prayers, only to find slugs all around us. We disturbed snakes in the boulders when relieving ourselves near Jerash and went on horseback through the narrow defile to Petra. Jerusalem was as dangerous a place then as it is now. Any thoughts of sunbathing on the roof of the school we stayed in there were short-lived as the border with the Israeli sector was very close. On the way to Bethlehem we found machine-gun nests at most intersections. I found the desert of southern Jordan fascinating and the small village (as it was then) of Aqaba dirty and depressing when we were camped in the grounds of a luxurious hotel on the sea front. The colours of the surrounding landscape at dusk were beautiful.'

'Friends were hard to make and keep. The turnover at schools was great. A few families were on three-year tours, but many more only stayed a term or two. Somehow Dad managed to get a double tour so we stayed for six years. It's only in the last three years that one of my ex-colleagues and I started a Queen's School (Rheindahlen) Association and have now found some 150 ex-pupils and staff. We've held three reunions, which have been quite successful.

'I enjoyed my time in Germany, although some of those we have contacted of late said they hated it. Yet I certainly broadened my horizons and I saw many lands, people and ways of life that I may not have seen in later years.'

As Brian Airey's experiences show, being an Army child in Germany certainly had the potential for adventures undreamed of by the ordinary comprehensive-school pupil back home. Some of the German-based children, now adults, have suggested that in some ways they felt distanced from their peers in England, not always in a beneficial way. As Brian Airey mentions, 'friends were hard to make and keep', yet this doesn't seem to have been an obstacle to the setting up of a very active ex-pupils network on the Internet. Almost every BFES school seems to have one and their archives often contain fascinating insights into a totally different school life to the one they would have experienced back home. They fondly refer to themselves today as 'Army Brats' and judging by the message boards they have developed a language of their own with which to exchange reminiscences. Some schools have wisely posted up articles from their school magazines. The following, by Marguerite Frost, comes from the excellent website run by the Gloucester School Hohne Association.

Marguerite Frost describes the visit to Gatow School, Berlin in May 1975.

'On Friday, 7 May, at about 3.20 p.m., we all loaded onto the military train at Brunswick Station. We were on the train for about an hour when we reached Helmstedt, the last station in West Germany. Here the engine was changed and an East German guard boarded the train. We passed through the frontier, which was interesting, being made up of mainly concrete posts, barbed wire, minefields and look-out posts. It was quite frightening to know that you were now trapped inside the corridor.[1] We travelled on to Marienborn, where we stopped and were called for our meal. It was a very interesting place as there was an impressive shop with bicycles in the window, but we were told that it was just for show and was never open.

'It was lovely being served by waiters with soup, hamburgers, vegetables and fruit. It was a good meal but it was difficult to enjoy with wild, fierce Alsatians probably walking up and down beneath you, hunting to kill stowaways, but I think we all managed to force the food down. The rest of the journey was uneventful except when we passed over the wide River Elbe, and then passed a large rock which we were told marked the foundation of the German Socialist State. It was known locally as *Biederiz Busch*. We carried on for several hours until we reached Potsdam, where the engine was searched and the guard left the train. We then came out of the corridor, and saw the Wall, with guards and watchtowers on either side. We then arrived at Charlottenburg Station.

'We left the train and were met by our hosts, and taken to our various homes. The next morning we went to Gatow School. Luck was not with us at all, as we lost at rounders 9–5, and the boys lost at football, 1–0. Next was swimming, which we all knew we'd be pretty hopeless at; in fact they absolutely slaughtered us, so I won't say any more.

'We had a great lunch at Gatow School. At 2 p.m. we all went off to the athletics track. Our results were pretty disastrous again but we tried our hardest and we weren't too put out by our losses during the whole day.

'That evening my host and I met up with some friends at the cinema. After seeing the film *Under Ten Flags* we spent the rest of the evening at a girl's house enjoying ourselves until about 11.30 p.m.

'The next morning we caught the bus and travelled through the West to Checkpoint Charlie. Here we passed through barriers just wide enough to let the coach go through. We saw other cars being thoroughly searched inside and underneath with mirrors to check for people hanging on. Luckily we were military and didn't have to go through all this. We passed through without any fuss. The first thing we saw was the Brandenburg Gate, which was far more impressive than we had expected; it was especially more interesting from the East than from the West. We then moved into the main street where we saw the main shops, including the shoe shop, which was only open for a few hours a week. We passed the Fernsehturm TV Tower. At the top of this tower is a glass orb and when the sun shines, a cross forms on the orb. This cross is said to have annoyed the East Germans and is nicknamed "the Pope's Curse". The main hotel was apparently the same style as the one in Moscow, but slightly smaller. We carried on and then stopped outside a large statue of a man that stood out from various other monuments. It was the most impressive. We walked back to Checkpoint Charlie, went through and back home.

'That afternoon we went swimming with one of my host's friends to the BIB unheated open-air pool. It was a lovely sunny afternoon and we really enjoyed ourselves. That evening I gloomily prepared to go back to lovely old Hohne.

'At 5.45 a.m. the next morning I said my goodbyes and thanks to my hosts and reluctantly went off to catch the "Berliner" back to Brunswick. It was the same journey as coming to Berlin, but it was interesting and we had two meals, breakfast and lunch, which were both delicious.

'It suddenly struck us all on the way back that we were on our way back to Gloucester School. What a depressing thought after a busy, and although unsuccessful, enjoyable weekend that was probably a once-in-a-lifetime visit to Berlin. Everyone enjoyed the trip, and I'd like to thank all the teachers who accompanied us for helping to make it successful.'

No doubt as you read this, British children's voices are still ringing out along the corridors and across the playgrounds of schools in Sennelager, Gütersloh and Rheindahlen, as they have done for over 50 years. Perhaps the twenty-first-century Army children are much wiser about the wider world, but the memory of living in Germany will stay with them for the rest of their lives.

6

Berlin I: City of Ghosts

In 1994 I watched the Allies leave. Part of me longed for them to stay; part of me was overcome with joy. All those fine, marching soldiers, all those years, and now we faced the future on our own.

Erwin Gotthald, Berliner, November 2002

They say that the writer John Le Carré can still occasionally be seen in Berlin. During those four decades of Cold War, this was the tinder box, the focal point of East–West relations. Yet for all the tension, real or imaginary, the Berlin experience is one which most British servicemen and their families remember with some affection. The city has a certain feel; it's big, brash, confident, a place which buzzes with life.

This was once Le Carré's metropolis of microfilm, dead-letter drops, border exchanges and mysterious phone calls. It was the place where MI5 discovered that their top man, George Blake, was a double agent, and the city that was the launch pad for Le Carré's glittering career as a spy writer, the location for his intricately crafted novels, such as *The Spy who came in from the Cold*.

As a posting, it seems to be remembered with more fondness among soldiers and their families than many other German locations.

Rosemary Blackwood of Corby, Northants was stationed with the WRAC of the 1st (British) Corps at Bielefeld from 1979 to '82 and in West Berlin between 1985 and '87.

'I met my husband in Bielefeld. We married in 1981 and our first son was born in 1982. In those days women were discharged from

135

the service when they became pregnant. How different it is today. So then I followed my husband around many postings both in the UK and in West Germany.

'At the time we were in Berlin the Cold War was still very cold. Having always been interested in history, particularly military history, I was enthralled to be living in a city of such historical importance. At the earliest opportunity I booked myself on a guided tour with all the sights of interest pointed out. I was able to select places that I would visit at a later time.

'My adventures were limited, though, with having a toddler and then having another baby on the way. Since a soldier stationed in Berlin had many duties, my husband, being a junior NCO, seemed to be always required.

'Some memories are still very clear. I remember the annual 17 June parade when all the Allied forces – French, British and American – paraded their troops and military hardware down the 17 Juni Strasse. I remember particularly in 1985 watching the parade next to an elderly German gentleman who engaged me in conversation. His first words were about my son and his blonde hair, and how, with his blue eyes, he was very "Germanic, Aryan".

'I found the Berliners were always ready to talk and the conversation usually started with comments about how "German" my son looked. The German people are not exactly world renowned for being open and friendly, but my son always came home with a pocket full of *bon-bons* given to him on the buses or the U-Bahn. My second son was born in Berlin. When he was perhaps about one year old I dressed him in *lederhosen* and we went on a boat trip on the Havel Lake. He was the star of the boat with all the old ladies admiring him, commenting on his *lederhosen* and, inevitably, his blond hair and blue eyes. The fact that his parents were British seemed irrelevant. We were spoken to as Germans and not treated as strangers in their country.'

'The most memorable part of my time in Berlin was our visits through Checkpoint Charlie into the Eastern Sector. This was like taking a step back in time and it was easy to imagine what the city had looked like perhaps 40 years earlier.

'The first visit was very nerve-wracking. I wondered what would the people be like, the different currency – and would we be allowed back? I was not allowed to go on my own; my husband had to accompany me. He was to wear his number two uniform, which, being of a Scottish regiment, involved the wearing of tartan trews and his Glengarry cap.

'We negotiated Checkpoint Charlie without any problems and parked near the main square, Alexanderplatz, which was dominated by the city's only department store, Centrum. However, to get to the store we had to make our way through a mass of football supporters from Magdeburg who were in the city for a local derby with Brandenburg. They caught sight of my husband – not exactly easy to miss – and surrounded us. I must admit to being a little frightened. However, my fears were groundless as the fans were all very friendly and kept shouting "Glasgow Rangers! Glasgow Celtic!" After much back-slapping and handshaking we managed to get into the store.

'Later experiences, however, made me realise that the reaction of these East Germans that day was not typical. They must have felt safe being in such a crowd to be able to show open friendship towards us.

'All over the eastern part of the city there were reminders of the benevolent Soviet soldiers who had liberated the Germans from the Fascists, and of how they were protecting them still. Statues or posters depicting a Soviet soldier carrying a small – presumably German – child were everywhere. It must have been very confusing to the Easterners seeing "the enemy" walking amongst them. My husband frequently lifted our small son up into his arms to negotiate stairs or escalators and I once heard two girls say in a very surprised tone of voice what I translated to be: "Look! A Scotsman with a child!"

'Apart from the occasion when we encountered the football fans, no individuals openly engaged us in conversation. Sometimes the Germans would talk to us through our son. On one occasion we were leaving a restaurant and a man quickly approached and shook my husband's hand, saying "Scottish?", and then rushed through the exit door. On another occasion, my husband was trying on a pair of shoes in a shop. As he bent forward to tie his shoelace, the man sitting next to him also leaned forward and whispered to him, "I was in the free Czech forces in the war. God bless you." He then got up and walked away without another word or a backward glance.

'Sometimes it was quite amusing; I would walk some paces behind my husband, and as people walked past him they never even glanced in his direction. But once they had walked a few paces past, they would quickly glance over their shoulders and nudge each other.

'On another warm day in the Eastern Sector my husband bought us all a tub of ice cream from a street vendor. There were no tables to sit at, only a wall surrounding a flowerbed. Sat on this wall and also enjoying their ice creams were a Soviet soldier and an East German soldier, both in uniform. Without thinking my husband sat down next to them. What a sight that was; three different soldiers all sitting eating ice cream. I would have loved to have taken a photograph but was frightened in case that would land us, and indeed our enemies, in trouble with the authorities.

'I hadn't realised just how much I've remembered of my Berlin days: travelling through the Berlin corridor by car, and the military train, the Queen's Birthday Parade on the Maifeld. I remember the unforgettable concert in the Waldbuhne when the military bands played Tchaikovsky's 1812 Overture, with real artillery pieces and the bell of the Glockenturm replacing Russian cannons and the victory bells of St Basil's. There was also the poignant site of the old Gestapo headquarters, the graves of those who died attempting to escape from the East, and the cemetery for the British servicemen who we remember in our two minutes' silence today – those who, unlike us, did not return home. All these years on I am surprised how much has stayed in my memory.'

A flash of tartan wasn't anything new to Berliners. With the numerous regiments stationed there, and, indeed, with both the French and the Americans dominating the city, the Germans even by the early 1950s had grown quite familiar with a wide range of uniforms, habits and accents. This was the true front line of the Cold War, and being ringed around by Soviet territory gave the city a compressed feeling, like some huge urban pressure cooker. Long after the original wheeling and dealing of the immediate post-war black market, there were still some odd military transactions taking place in Berlin.

Private Bob McLaughlin of Glasgow was a national serviceman with the Black Watch. He was stationed in Berlin between 1955 and '56.

'I was a private, the deputy regimental tailor – we had two tailors in our workshop – but I was more in the tailor's shop then than the regimental tailor was, as he had a habit of being in the wrong place at the wrong time.

'I remember a deficiency of kilts being reported and the lads short of a kilt having to pay the full price of a new one, which, of course, if not a perfect fit, had to be adjusted by our staff to fit the measurements of the person concerned. At the time a kilt cost quite a lot and a lot of sympathy was extended if you "lost" one. Sympathy started evaporating when a number of American GIs started turning up at the NAAFI in central Berlin in sports jackets made of Black Watch tartan. Apparently, so I was informed, the kilt could be sold to an American serviceman for more than it cost "the loser" to purchase a new one. Enterprise indeed!

'Also, being deputy regimental tailor held me in good stead on one occasion. My mates decided to take me out for my 20th birthday. We travelled down town, seeing the sights, and eventually reached the Brandenburg Gate – the border with East Berlin. It was a beautiful sight. Quite near the gate was a café (or the German equivalent) and the boys decided to take me for a drink. I had a couple of small beers with a lot of froth on top and a glass of local spirits. I'm afraid I became the worse for wear and threw up several times in the café. I think you would term my condition as one of intoxication. I was half carried, half pushed on to a local tram (and I threw up again before I got on) and as that tram reached the area where the NAAFI was located, the lads tried to remove me, the idea being to indulge in even further revelry. However, although slightly inebriated, and knowing that the NAAFI would be crawling with MPs (who were less than charitable in Berlin), I held my ground, so the lads decided they would take me back to the barracks.

'There was no way past the guard room. With each of my arms over the shoulder of two "friends" I was taken – reluctantly – into the guard room. The guard commander, recognising who I was, booked me in as "sober and properly dressed" – as I collapsed on the guard room floor. I was, after all, the deputy regimental tailor.'

Andrew Burns of Glasgow was a lance corporal with the Royal Military Police. He was stationed in Berlin and Buxtehude, Hamburg between 1950 and '52.

'My duties comprised of foot patrolling in all areas in Berlin's British Sector, along with some escort duties. Army exercises were held quite frequently in the woods which abound in Berlin.

'I expected to find the city absolutely demolished, but the Spandau district in particular was relatively intact; even Kurfürstendamm seemed only lightly touched by bombs, except for the famous church. The people were obedient but not servile, not particularly welcoming, yet polite with no bitterness.

'My duties were not particularly arduous and at times we patrolled with American MPs in the evenings to keep the soldiers in check. It was not long before I was transferred to a detachment in an office building off the K'damm, a unit I did not know existed. This was a small unit comprising only a handful of MPs. The duties differed somewhat; escorting high officials, guarding inter-zonal conferences and, more importantly, attending to all accidents and incidents involving troops of all nations, and civilians if required. I operated frequently on my own with a German interpreter. I felt quite important on my own, sitting in the rear of the jeep as we raced through the streets. As we passed civilian police officers, who still wore the old-style coal-scuttle helmet, they came to attention and saluted. The Berlin Wall had not been built then, though barriers were operated across the streets leading to the Russian sector. It was strange that it was possible to travel on the U-Bahn that entered the Russian sector and to another sector without any Russian soldiers stopping passengers. There were incidents I recall. I was sent to a railway station on my own, where two armed East German police officers had been discovered. I was apprehensive as I did not know their intention, and although I carried a .38 revolver I had to obey the unbelievable order of not loading my own gun until I was actually fired upon!

'I walked along the platform. The two East Germans were facing me with a sneer on their faces which turned into a supercilious grin when I asked them for their weapons. They both stared at me for some seconds and then obliged. I escorted them to our office where they were placed in cells. I was then told to take them to an address in the city. I had no previous knowledge of the place but found a uniformed company sergeant-major (CSM) who placed them in cells. He seemed quite amused when I asked for a receipt. It had been a nerve-wracking encounter for me – I was just 18 years old and inexperienced. There was also a number of French deserters who had placed themselves in a former Nazi building. They began shooting when they were discovered. I was again sent but on this occasion there wouldn't be any long negotiation procedure. I told them that the building would be stormed unless they surrendered. They did and were removed.

'My off-duty periods were not spent in the nearest bar, but travelling throughout the city and swimming in the 1936 Olympic pool. I even managed a few water-polo matches (that's my sport). The pool and the stadium formed part of an Army base.

'I was also sent to an incident in a bar involving an American sergeant. He was a huge man, 6 ft 6 in., who was throwing the American MPs aside when they tried to arrest him. I spoke to him but I don't remember what was said, only his reply: "You're a Scotsman and I'm not going to tangle with you!"

'He promptly gave up. I took him to our office in the British Sector, during which time he never spoke another word.

'There were road accidents which occurred between our troops, civilians, foreign troops and so on. All these had to be accurately measured, sketched and reported.

'I spent my free evenings visiting a particular jazz bar where many American players sat in with the band. Some were professional musicians and very good to listen to.

'I felt confident in my job and that I was performing it well. I believe it was an important job and, best of all, there were no drills and no bawling sergeants, and I was trusted to use my initiative. So I was shattered to be told that I was being transferred to the Black Watch. So one chapter ended.

'The Black Watch's barracks were a former German Army camp. They were far superior to any barracks in Britain at that time. It was situated outside town alongside Lake Havel, in a small village in a country setting, well away from my other unit. We were at the rear of the camp overlooking the Russian Zone.

'At the entrance there was a gatehouse with armed sentries and opposite this another gatehouse with Regimental Policemen (RP). They wore kilts and instead of the usual drab khaki hose wore light blue and matching leggings. An armband was worn with a large "RP" in brass, and each man carried a stick similar to an RSM's. I was told that day I was to become an RP. The other ex-Military Policeman who had joined the Black Watch with me was sent to an infantry company.

'The cells were almost always full with soldiers serving seven to twenty-eight days detention. Discipline was strict, so consequently I had to become a disciplinarian.

'At no time did I ever receive any infantry training. I took part in exercises and was irked by the situation. We were never told the object of our part in the procedure, we were just shifted here and there like cattle – obviously too dumb to understand. The battle plan would surely have been more successful if even a little knowledge of what we were supposed to be doing was imparted to us.'

Before writing this book I had never been to Berlin. It was an exciting prospect, and lived up to all my expectations. It was a bitter, frosty November day when I pulled off the autobahn and found myself driving along the impressively wide Bismarckstrasse. In the distance I could see the lofty finger of the Siegelssäule, the victory column, its gilded angel kissing the icy blue sky.

This is a city built for military parades. With up to eight lanes of traffic, it's easy to imagine the troops out on a show of force, complete with tanks and other hardware. It must have looked really grand on that day of the final goodbye parade in 1994.

The man in the bar cradles his beer and looks through the window. In the crisp, cold city night a thousand coloured lights twinkle. Along Bismarckstrasse the BMWs and Mercedes purr past. Erwin, my drinking companion, puts his beer down and lights another cigarette. He has obviously grown tired of my questions. He sighs wearily.

'They were the *bad* old days. Yet you people – British, American – I think you remember them as the *good* old days . . .'

Few places in the Western world possess such an ambience of sinister mystery. Berlin is an eternal vault of memories of war, tragedy and espionage, the last great front line of two monolithic political systems, facing each other across a once abominable divide – the infamous Wall. I'm here to see what, if anything, still hangs in the air from Erwin's 'bad old days'.

Today, Berlin's skyline is studded with tower cranes, as builders work around the clock, creating a futuristic steel and glass landscape punctuated with Germany's great historical monuments, like the giant edifice of the Reichstag, now crowned with an amazing glass dome designed by the British architect Norman Foster. Not far away stands the mighty Brandenburg Gate and the lofty Protestant cathedral, the Berliner Dom, completed in 1750.

~ Berlin I: City of Ghosts ~

The beautiful, wide avenue of trees, each illuminated with a thousand tiny lights, Unter den Linden, once only visible over the Wall as part of the forbidden Soviet sector, is now a showcase of twenty-first-century capitalism.

But those with a zest for the darker side of history wander the streets of Berlin for other reasons. Where have all the spies and political spooks gone? What happened to Checkpoint Charlie? What became of all those East German Stasi agents? Like Harry Lime's Vienna, the ruins of post-war Berlin possessed their own spectres of a past filled with subterfuge and double-dealing. Study the city for long enough and you'll find that the ghosts are still there.

After the war the city was divided into four sectors. To the East of the Brandenburg Gate, the Red Army ruled. Britain, France and the USA stationed their troops in their own Western sectors. Back in the 1980s, Ronald Reagan had stood on a podium facing the Brandenburg and exclaimed, 'Mr Gorbachov – open this gate!'

Oddly enough, Mikhail was listening. In November 1989, the Wall crumbled, and in 1994, amid pomp and ceremony, and a great deal of sadness on behalf of Berliners, the Allies marched out of Berlin for the last time. The Cold War was over.

I was surprised to discover that only one man remained in the city to represent the British Army. I decided to seek him out.

Out in the city's leafy suburbs in the late afternoon there seemed to be an ominous silence filled with echoes of another time. The shady avenues were empty, the low winter sun slicing through the trees. I reached a large, high, square house with a broad exterior staircase. A gardener eyed me curiously. In my faltering German I asked him if the 'Englishman' was at home. He nodded, still watching suspiciously as I rang the bell.

Lieutenant-Colonel Robin Greenham was everything I expected him to be: tall, fit, square-jawed. His very presence was commanding, the handshake firm and positive. I was warmly welcomed into his palatial lounge and served coffee by his vivacious wife, Barbara, a Berliner from Charlottenburg. They had married in 1975.

He was a part of Brixmis, the official name given to The British Mission to the Russian forces in Germany. It was to provide an open channel of communication between the British forces and the Russians. Up until 1958 the Mission was accommodated in the first

Mission House near the Potsdam Wildpark railway station. It was attacked and burned by a mob on 18 July 1958. A new Mission House was provided, also in Potsdam, which remained the Brixmis headquarters until the end of the Cold War.

What did he do in Berlin now that the Army had gone?

'My job here is with the British Forces Liaison Organisation. This was founded after the war to negotiate on behalf of the British forces in Germany with the German Civil and Military Authorities. The organisation was set up specifically to look after our interests and also to make sure that our troops stationed in Germany under the NATO-stationed forces agreement are doing their thing. After the war the organisation had a major-general in charge. Today it still does, but he doesn't exclusively do that (from his base in Rheindahlen), he also has other responsibilities. Each garrison town also has its own Service Liaison Officer. They look after such things as the Anglo-German relations. I am part of the headquarters of the organisation stationed here in Berlin responsible for liaising with the other "sending states" – the countries which send NATO forces, such as the Americans, and the Dutch, which have the most significant number of troops here. The French, the Belgians and the Canadians have virtually gone now. We still have to apply for anything the British Army wishes to do in East Germany – we don't do much there – following the agreement at the end of the Cold War between Kohl and Gorbachov that there were to be no foreign troops stationed in the East. We have no troops now in Berlin – I'm the only man here. I came here from my last job, which was as military attaché in Moscow in 1998.

'I've had three stations in Berlin, which is unusual. I was here in 1973–5, when I was a captain with the British Mission to the Soviet Forces in Germany. I came back for a year as a company commander in 1980 when I was stationed in Montgomery Barracks, which are now occupied by the Bundeswehr, then I came back in the late '80s to Brixmis as 1st Senior Officer and witnessed the fall of the Wall from both sides.

'That was probably the most interesting tour of the three. I was only once in the Berlin Brigade station, when I was in Berlin as a company commander. I was part of that brigade but only at company level. Life was quite routine by the 1980s; it was just a question of guarding the prison at Spandau, namely Rudolf Hess. I recall seeing this long tall figure in his greatcoat on his daily walk in the gardens. We took our turn in all the routine tasks, such as acting as escorts for the military train that used to go through the Helmstedt and Braunschweig, and standing guard at the Tiergarten.

'The military train started from Charlottenburg in the middle of the British Sector of Berlin, it went out through Potsdam to the first stop in West Germany, which was Helmstedt. That central road and rail corridor ran east–west, and ran on to Hanover. It was used for duty travel but families would use it for excursions to go to Braunschweig for a nice day out shopping. It was always a very luxurious existence. As you cleared Berlin you would be being served in the dining car with a cooked breakfast, and there was a cooked lunch and dinner when you came back. It was quite a unique way to travel. We were quite spoiled. The last train probably ran in the 1990s when the last station troops left.

'During the Soviet period I know that the Soviets had a pretty efficient apparatus for keeping track of any particular individual and recording any movements we were making in the West. And of course that was our job, too – to watch out for anything unusual.

'Things went reasonably well, although there was the odd crisis, such as the tension which arose when the Soviet invasion of Afghanistan happened, although anything otherwise unusual would have been picked up by the mission. That was our purpose – to look for signs of the unusual going on. The mission would have picked up early on any odd movements; we had satellite intelligence, of course, and MI6 were here, because as you know this was the place where all the spies were. And there was signals intelligence, for instance, which was run from quite near my home here in Berlin – from our radar station known as the *Teufelsburg* (Devil's Mountain). This is a radar station actually built on the mountain of the ruins of Berlin, a shared British and American facility, which would pick up any unusual surface movements. Teufelsburg is now under German Environmental protection and, would you believe, is being developed as a hotel and a restaurant by a private company.

'One odd incident which involved me was during my first tour with Brixmis. There was a Russian officer who approached me at Checkpoint Alpha and this guy chatted with me, realising I was with Brixmis. He was very friendly – as we were in many ways – but any such conversation was to be reported. I reported it and our people were quite alarmed. "If this guy is who we think he is," they said, "then this could be a problem." Of course, the Russian had seen my papers and details and knew where I was based. One day at the Mission House I got a phone call from him. He seemed quite friendly and at one point asked me if I was able to get some medicine for his wife. Were you not aware of the intelligence implications, this would have seemed quite ordinary. But I had to tell him that I was unable to help him. Of course, this was all part of a method of striking up a relationship which could lead to compromise and could be very dangerous if you took it up. I didn't hear from him again, fortunately.

'From '74–5 the one thing which is imprinted on my memory is the huge Soviet exercises that we saw – literally huge movements of troops and tanks through villages and across land, the kind of exercises one would never see in the West. We had our own training exercises, of course, but nothing on the scale of the Soviet ones, which were quite astonishing. Even after the Wall came down and the Bundeswehr took over the East German bases, they found that all their military vehicles and tanks were still at the ready, all "bombed up" and primed for action. Did they "mean it"? Well, I suppose they did. I think the East Germans maintained something like an 85 per cent presence of all their soldiers – and they always maintained that percentage at weekends and holidays. For anyone who knew the Bundeswehr, they would tell you that by midday on a Friday or a holiday weekend their barracks would be virtually empty – so if the Russians were coming, that's when they'd make their move. Although we had our Berlin Brigade, there was a Russian Brigade stationed in East Berlin and troops and many divisions stationed in places such as Potsdam, so it wouldn't have taken them too long to take over. They wouldn't have wasted much time on street-to-street fighting. Our garrison would have been fighting a rearguard action. We were well spread out; it was a division which didn't have the normal logistics of a division. It was essentially three brigades. The advantage we had with the Mission, Brixmis, was that there were around 80 of us and we lived here, and managed to get out and about quite a lot. For the ordinary soldier, I think I can say that they probably found it all a bit boring. They were busy guarding this or that, and when they weren't they were probably training. Although Berlin is a big city, in those days they couldn't get out of it other than by the Military corridor. To get out one had to apply in advance; that sometimes made Berlin feel like a prison; not physically so, but it became a closed environment. It was perhaps an ideal place for a married family with kids, but it was a long way from the UK and it did at times feel restrictive, especially for the single soldier. Yet, as with most soldiers, once they'd left this city, in retrospect it became the best place in the world.

'My time in Moscow was very interesting. It was a fascinating experience and I wouldn't have missed it for the world. Yet I found being there in '96 to '98 that I'd missed the "bad old days". Being a Brixmis hand, and after having that training for looking out to see if I was being followed, I'd missed out on that old atmosphere, because by then the Russian intelligence services had been cut back and things had been somewhat "normalised". It was a bit tame compared to what it must have been like five or ten years before, when really the attachés had to watch their p's and q's as they were gathering military intelligence. The time I was there was mainly involved with setting up cooperation programmes with the Russian Army. That was quite a difficult task as the Russian Army was then a very demoralised force. I felt sorry for them – especially when they left Berlin, because they were going home to an uncertain future. They were completely shocked by what had happened, as indeed we were, because no one really expected this great continuing confrontation could suddenly end like this.

'But the mood on the street among the people in East Germany had changed. Even though the Stasi were still arresting people up to a couple of weeks before the Wall came down, the people knew that, providing they did it in moderation, they could now express themselves without getting locked up. And there were enough of them doing it because they knew now that the regime was under pressure. That was one of the main characteristics of the movement, the fact that they could now get away with it. This provided a major upswell – they were trying their luck – and the authorities became unsure of themselves. They felt they were unsure of what to do to handle the situation, not certain of what was to happen. When a correspondent asked a Soviet official if it was true that East Germans were going to be allowed free travel into the West, he said, "Of course . . ." The man was recalled, as he'd probably spoken out of turn, but it was too late – it was the signal for the East Berliners to flood the checkpoints. Many had already fled through Czechoslovakia, but the fall of the Wall came quite unexpectedly.

'What has been fascinating for me is that all this happened whilst

I was part of Brixmis. My wife is a Berliner and we have both been involved in the reunification of Germany. I have been fascinated by the speed of development in the Eastern sector, although there is still a lot to be done – roads, communications, etc. There used to be such a difference behind the Wall; you could smell it the minute you went into the East, from the two-stroke fuel they used in their Trabant cars to the huge quantities of coal used in the Eastern industries. What remains unresolved is the hearts and minds problem – there is still today a clear difference in the thinking of East and West Berliners. Everything is not quite as rosy as the Easterners expected and there is a general train of thought there which would like to turn back the clock. The hope lies in the younger generation overturning some of the old misconceptions – both in the East and West – to overcome the misunderstandings. Many of the Westerners feel that all this has cost Germany too much and that it hasn't been appreciated by "the other side". But they haven't had to go through what the East Germans have gone through, having their lives virtually ruined by the Communist system. A lot of Berliners were very worried by the Allied departure. They were concerned about the future and the return of the Bundeswehr. But the Bundeswehr have gone to great efforts to reassure them. Like us, the German Army has suffered cutbacks, however.

'Have I enjoyed my time in Berlin? Yes – this is a great city with a great history and a bright future. And I have been lucky to be here during what has been a most fascinating period.'

I felt that, with further probing, Lieutenant-Colonel Greenham would have told more stories, but I had to leave. I had become obsessed with this Devil's Mountain he had mentioned. I simply had to see it.

I found my way into the darkening woods. Everywhere there seemed to be tall barbed-wire fences. I already felt as if I was being watched, and as I progressed ever deeper into the mass of beech and fir trees a slight paranoia overcame me . . . *must get out of here before the light goes.* I could see the news report now: 'British writer vanishes in German forest . . .'

It was dusk now and the silence was eerie. An old lady walking her dog stepped on a twig and startled me. She seemed to have appeared from nowhere. Like the gardener before, she eyed me with some suspicion. I asked her where the Teufelsburg was. She pointed through the trees. I walked a few more yards, parted some branches, and then I saw it; a mini-mountain topped with a bulbous-headed tower, flanked by two white spheres. Robin Greenham was right to call it 'phallic'. It must be one of the rudest-looking buildings in Europe.

Once converted, it will no doubt be the strangest hotel in the world.

The history of this bizarre hill is remarkable.

It rises sharply out of the *Grünewald*. This is 40 square kilometres (15.5 square miles) of forest land. Teufelsburg is easily the highest piece of land in the region at 120 metres (394 feet). I never managed to ascend the peak but I understand that from that vantage point one can view the entire city of Berlin. Thousands of trees stretch down the slopes, and there is a vineyard, which locals claim to be the most northerly situated vineyard in Europe, but now that we're growing grapes in England, that could be open to argument. Teufelsburg is a very popular spot for Berliners in their cars during the summer, and in winter it makes a fine toboggan run. New Year's Eve sees this mini-mountain as a centre for festivities, where a massive fireworks display takes place. Yet beneath these happy Berliners' feet lies a mountain of tragic history. This isn't really a natural hill at all, but a *Trümmerberg* – a mountain made of rubble. This is the funeral pile of old Berlin, a giant heap covered in a thin layer of soil beneath which lies 18 million cubic metres of the once-magnificent but now shattered detritus of a great city. Deep in the core of this lofty heap lie tons of shattered, exquisitely carved masonry, the doors and window frames of houses both grand and humble, their ceilings, their walls, their bathrooms, roofs, gable ends and mangled plumbing. Teufelsburg is not the only such poignant outcrop in Berlin. In Friedrichshain in the East lies another, there are two at Schöneberg in the south-west area and others, less impressive, dotted around the city.

Berlin was already in an extreme state of destruction, courtesy of Allied bombing, when the Red Army arrived in 1945. Now the Soviet war machine completed the task with tanks, guns and rockets.

Twenty-eight square kilometres (11 square miles) became a dusty wasteland where a fine baroque city had once stood: 612,000 out of

1,500,000 homes had been razed to the ground.[1] A further 100,000 were almost uninhabitable. Around what remained of the city the water supply had been severely damaged, raw sewage gushed from shattered drains, whilst beneath the rubble thousands of rotting corpses turned this hellish metropolis into a rat's heaven. The results were inevitable, as dysentery, typhoid, diphtheria and a host of other deadly illnesses spread like wildfire throughout the surviving population. With most hospitals and the medical infrastructure destroyed, within a short time the daily death rate reached 4,000. Accompanying this apocalyptic scenario the spectre of starvation now stalked, making the Soviet conquerors realise that their victory had been granted with a high price – the responsibility of halting this all-engulfing human disaster. Colonel-General Nikolai Bersarin of the Red Army, now appointed as military commander of Berlin, faced a gargantuan task. Although the population of the city was now 2.3 million, as compared to its 4.3 million pre-war figure, he somehow had to feed this starving mass. Living like pale, skeletal ghosts in the shattered ruins were 53,000 children, orphans of the war. Of the surviving population, 25 per cent were over 60 years of age, and due to military service – and the capture and removal of many thousands of German POWs into the Soviet Union – only 1 in 10 people were under the age of 30. Thus it was that the only labour force large enough – and available – to clear away the millions of tons of Berlin's ruins would be the city's women. And so these female legions, paid a pittance, yet classed high in the Soviet grading for food rations, earned a new name: the *Trümmerfrauen* ('Rubble Women'). Their task was huge and heavy; they salvaged building materials, cleaned bricks for rebuilding, worked with hammers, picks, shovels and trowels ceaselessly, loading ton after ton of rubble onto fleets of trucks. That rubble today makes up the Teufelsburg and its sad sister mountains around the city. Their achievement is remembered at Berlin's Rixdorf Heights, another rubble mountain, 70 metres (230 feet) high where a massive statue of a *Trümmerfrau* stands, reminding young Berliners of the bitter, backbreaking and hand-splitting sacrifice their grandmothers made in their city's darkest hours.

Back in the bar on Bismarckstrasse, Erwin is sinking his daily ration. I ask him what became of Checkpoint Charlie.

My question seems to depress him. He shakes his head. 'They've moved it. The Allies took it to their museum on Clayallee.'

I rose early the next morning. It was bitterly cold but at least the sun was out. The avuncular desk clerk at the Tiergarten Hotel launched into another of his jokey intrusions when he discovered that I had abandoned the idea of travelling to Clayallee and the Allied Museum by Berlin's excellent public transport. With three legs to the journey – one U-Bahn, an S-Bahn and a bus service to face – I figured I'd be warmer and quicker in the car.

The desk clerk smiled awkwardly. '*What?* You will drive all that way – *and on the wrong side of the road?*'

I reminded him that I'd driven all the way from Rotterdam 'on the wrong side' and topped the response off with a vaguely jingoistic 'We British are not as dumb as we look . . .' Of course, to another Englishman such a comment would be a joke. To the desk clerk it seemed like a rebuttal for some kind of impudence on his part. From then on he treated me like some visiting potentate.

Needless to say, for an hour I was hopelessly lost, driving along the banks of the glittering, blue Wannsee. But eventually I spotted through the trees the incongruity of a massive twin-engined plane from the Berlin Airlift. I had found the Allied Forces Museum.

It seemed odd to find the huts through which so much subterfuge and bitterness had passed now standing serenely in bright sunlight, encircled by trees in a Berlin suburb.

The Allied Forces Museum, which stands next door to the old US Army cinema, The Outpost, seems to contain every possible piece of memorabilia from Berlin's Cold War. Outside stands the last remaining carriage from that legendary military train. On the walls are messages from Tony Blair, Helmut Kohl and Bill Clinton. Here you get the full horror of what it was like attempting to breach the Berlin Wall.

The stories are poignant, often bizarre, like that of Mr W. Stoermer, an East Berliner who bought a ticket to fly from Tempelhof Airport to Hamburg on 14 August 1961. He was a day too late: on the 13th the Wall went up. He couldn't leave. Twenty-eight years later, in January 1990, Herr Stoermer presented his ticket to British Airways and asked if it was still valid. In return he received a voucher for any domestic flight of his choice. BA presented his 1961 ticket to the Allied Museum, but their attempts to track down the would-be traveller since have been fruitless.

On the day Herr Stoermer had hoped to leave the East, 14 August

1961, the erection of the barrier that was to become the disgrace known as the Berlin Wall had begun in earnest. Too many escapees had fled to the West since 1954. Now the division of the city of Berlin had become a reality. On 18 August the outraged West German press protested loudly at what East German leader Walter Ulbricht had proclaimed to be his 'success':

> When, after 48 hours of the division of the city, no counter-measures had been taken or opposition appeared, it could be concluded that – no matter how drastic the answer would now be – 'nothing is more successful than success' just as had been the case during the phenomenon of National Socialism. What raises diplomacy over politics is the knowledge of the moral strength of promptly accepting a challenge. When the city commandants, who were responsible for the security of and compliance with the Four-Power Agreement did not promptly appear at the sector-border to protest and fix a deadline for the removal of the barbed wire, when it became apparent that the Federal government – in spite of assurances that it was prepared for all eventualities – had to (and still has to) first investigate, review, and decide on the appropriate measures, it was not surprising that Herr Ulbricht then dared to leave his tank-protected residence to demonstrate by his appearance his fait accompli to the outraged population.[2]

Ulbricht's decision to physically partition the city is hardly surprising considering the economic needs of the Soviet zone. By 1961, 3.5 million had escaped, many of them craftsmen, doctors, dentists, pharmacists, teachers, university lecturers and others, who were creating a serious skill vacuum in the Eastern sector.[3] 75 per cent of the escapees who registered at the Federal emergency reception centre were under the age of 45, leaving a situation in the Soviet zone where over 28 per cent of employees were now aged 60 or over.[4] What is surprising is that the Western powers appeared to do little in response to the challenge. Despite the escalating seriousness of the situation there still seemed to be an attitude of inertia and bemusement in the West. Conversely, the German Democratic Republic immediately reviewed the situation and proclaimed that 'the enemy' had been too surprised to take any counter-measures.

~ Berlin I: City of Ghosts ~

At 11.45 p.m. on 14 August, one Corporal Michael Moore of the 4th Royal Tank Regiment had driven his tank up to the border close to a railway station and settled down to what he imagined would be another dull night of clock-watching and yawning in boredom. He got through the night, but as dawn broke he looked through his episcope (optical projector) and discovered a Soviet T-34-35 tank facing him, only yards away. He contacted his HQ, who asked him the distance between him and the Soviet tank. His reply must have been startling: 'Our gun barrels are less than five yards apart.'

The British 'tankie's' breakfast of egg butties and a mug of tea was in preparation, courtesy of Moore's Radio Operator. Moore decided to take his mug of tea and open the hatch to greet his Red counterpart only yards away. He placed his tea on the open hatch flap and was surprised when the Soviet hatch also flew open.

'I nearly spilled my tea – the commander's hatch opened and a head appeared wearing one of those super Soviet helmets and a pair of binoculars. All I could see was him looking at me and me looking at him . . .' Corporal Moore's comradely wave to his opponent resulted in the Soviet tankie vanishing back into his tank beneath a slammed-shut hatch.[5]

Yet despite this new stand-off, the masses of barbed wire, and the more ominous eventual appearance of the concrete wall itself, people still made every effort to get into the Western sector. On 15 August 1961 an East German border guard, Conrad Schumann, boldly vaulted over the barbed wire to freedom. One has to remember that these people, on both sides of this political divide, were not foreign to one another – they were all Germans. To be sure, the Russians, in the form of the Red Army, were ready to enter any major conflict and roll across the border at any time. But the visible presence to West Berliners of young Germans in Soviet guards' uniforms presented more heartache and longing for unity than fear. The National People's Army (NVA), of the Communist sector, strove hard to convince their Western relations that they were 'people just like you'.

Those who had fled to the West entered their reasons for doing so in a poll, which also outlined the general dissatisfaction with their life in the East: 'We had ninety-nine duties and only one right; one never feels safe. I don't want to have to shoot at any of my own countrymen.' The attraction of the West was only occasionally a motive for fleeing. One said, 'A cousin of mine has already been in Italy three times; I would also like to see some parts of the world.'[6]

At the site of the original Checkpoint Charlie on Friedrichstrasse there now stands a fascinating exhibition. Evidence of human ingenuity reaches new heights here. Crossing the border illegally was a desperate act. Yet the Easterners dug tunnels, curled up in suitcases, hid in sealed compartments under car chassis and, in one case, crammed themselves into a cavity inside a large welding machine. Those who risked a run at the wire often ended up hanging there, riddled with bullets.

Looking at the short, colourfully decorated yet poignant stretches of the Wall that still exist in modern Berlin, you are apt to forget that this tragic episode only came to an end less than 15 years ago.

And the 'spooks'? They're still around. A life in Berlin with MI5 can leave one addicted to the German way of life. Many ex-agents – who naturally don't want to be named – are still here. Today they work in industry and commerce, where 'office politics' might seem a mild extension to their former activities.

Intelligence in Berlin had many servants, from the shady spooks who crossed the border by night and day, to those ordinary soldiers further down the tree of ranks who, nonetheless, contributed in no small way to our knowledge of what went on in the East. Iain Leggatt has appeared earlier in this book, when he first discovered Germany as a private with the RAOC in 1957. Almost a decade of Army service later, he was back, this time in Berlin.

Iain Leggatt of Carnoustie, Angus was a sergeant with the RAOC Intelligence & Security. His HQ was Berlin between 1966 and '69.

'I was an RAOC sergeant, serving very happily as NCO in charge at HQ Land Forces, Hong Kong, when I was reassigned to G (Intelligence & Security) HQ Berlin (British Sector) at the Olympic Stadium, Berlin-Charlottenburg.

'Following Far East leave, on 20 October 1966 I flew from Gatwick into Tempelhof Flughafen, West Berlin's main airport, which was then located in the American Sector.

'I was met by my predecessor, Tom Hogan, a man as left-wing Labour oriented as I was right-wing Conservative. Our handover was mercifully brief and we concluded it almost on speaking terms. I had mistaken the balmy weather in southern England as being representative of greater Europe, so I wore a Hong Kong-made lightweight suit.

~ Berlin I: City of Ghosts ~

'Tom said, "Right, Iain, take a minute to get a pullover, scarf and overcoat out of your suitcase – and a furry hat if you have one."

'He was right. Outside the terminal an icy north-east wind peeled my fingernails back, chiselled the skin off my ears and enamel from my teeth, and it stayed like that every year until 1 May.

'My duties at Interrogation and Security included tasking the office's two vehicles, an Opel Kapitan and a VW Variant, and two civilian drivers, running the clerical effort, with two military clerks, a male and a female. I was also overseeing the photographic section with one RAOC photographer, coordinating the Intelligence Corps (a corporal and two sergeants), information production and managing the office equipment. This included typewriters, a duplicator, photocopiers, a display-collection of Kalashnikov Assault Rifles, ammunition, handguns of various makes and calibre, East German uniforms, boots, webbing and steel helmets . . . and a coffee maker.

'Within a fortnight, due to illness, postings and marriages, my need for the coffee-making machine became quite desperate as first the photographer, then the clerks, then two of the Intelligence Corps members left, leaving me to fulfil all their various roles. My trial-by-desertion lasted almost three weeks and my coffee consumption acquired (unrecognised) *Guinness Book of Records* proportions.

'Four days after I arrived, having sampled three days and nights of what West Berlin had to offer, I went on my official "flag tour" of East Berlin. This was a duty trip in a military vehicle with a military crew, the purpose of which was to overtly gather intelligence, plus any covert intelligence, which was available. It was the only flag tour I did during my two and a half years in the divided city and it was culturally very important to me, as I could see, right at the very beginning, the vast differences between East and West. The West shone, hummed and strutted; it was smart, coherent and proud. The East provided a frontage for the benefit of the West of tall, pristine and grand-looking buildings which, as one was being driven past them, revealed themselves to be only a couple of metres wide and not just unoccupied but totally unsuitable for occupation. They were just a dressing. The rest, hidden behind, were shoddy.

'There were plenty of military to be seen in the East, both Russian and East German. In barracks they were cleaning tanks, guns or trucks, or just marching; on the streets, they were moving smartly from one duty to the next over the large, irregular cobblestones. The civilian population in the East also went about their business, wearing shoddy coats and hats, and stout yet inferior footwear, unsmiling, carrying a string bag or a badly made briefcase, never looking to one side or the other. You could always tell when there was a shop, because there would be a queue of hopefuls snaking out of it and waiting patiently outside.

'As we rounded a corner, I saw a man walking towards us. Quite distinctly he gave me a small, low-down wave as he ambled in our direction. Then came another; a woman this time. Then another man faced us, stood still and took his hat off. There are many kinds of bravery, but that displayed by these folk was very special.

'Our four-man flag tour entered and exited via Checkpoint Charlie. Whereas much of the tour had taken place in a nervous silence, as the US Army Military Policeman waved us through the barrier and back into West Berlin, all four of us erupted into conflicting and very animated conversations, yet none of us listened to the others. In any case, I'm sure we were all spouting garbage.

'I made several friends amongst the British Military, one of whom, A.E. 'Len' Leonard, I am still in touch with. Len worked in A/Q Branch, HQ Berlin Infantry Brigade, and he and I had "a few" nights out in Stuttgarter Platz and some slightly more salubrious spots. Len was best man at my military wedding in 1968. At the reception in the Brigade Sergeants' Mess, he sent a tray of the best lead-crystal champagne flutes and the top table flying. Thanks, Len. I could be really awful and pay him back by saying that his "A.E." stood for Albert Edward, but I couldn't be that vindictive.

'The three Western powers – Britain, the USA and France – in West Berlin each had their own combat force on the ground, and political/military representation in the running of West Berlin, which all came together upstairs and at the back of the building in which I worked, in the Allied Staff Berlin (ASB). I got to know some of the Americans and the French who worked in ASB, although the only one who has lingered in my memory is Monsieur Claude, a gendarme on detachment from Paris, who performed some security function. He maintained he was the equivalent of a sergeant so insisted on the right of access to our Sergeants' Mess for his lunch, which he accompanied with a heady red liquid he poured into the Army tumbler at his place-setting. He never once offered me a drop of this *vin-ordinaire*. A French captain worked in Intelligence and was as short and as insignificant as his accompanying Great Dane was huge. The captain's jacket was always unbuttoned and he made sure we all saw the magnificent red silk lining! Making friends amongst the German population wasn't really an option. Not for me, anyway.'

During Iain Leggatt's stay in Berlin the tension between East and West continued to provide the military on both sides – especially intelligence operatives – with more than enough incidents to keep them busy. Apart from the constant tit-for-tat military face-offs along the border, heroic escape attempts to breach the Wall continued. Many were successful, others ended in tragedy. Capture could mean imprisonment or execution. As it was during the Nazi regime, the relatives of escapees left behind in the East became instant targets for the dreaded East German Ministry of State Security and the KGB.

In the life of that grim edifice, the Berlin Wall, from August 1961 until its final breach in 1989, 238 people died attempting to cross into the West.[7] Escapees showed great courage and innovation in their efforts. Tunnels, balloons, cramped secret compartments in cars, in fact any item of industrial usage that was large enough to conceal a human being, from machinery to, in one case, a large cable reel which held up to four people was utilised. In the Checkpoint Charlie Museum in Berlin this inventiveness can be seen in all its forms. On 9 September 1968 one refugee escaped across the Baltic Sea to Denmark on a contraption constructed from an auxiliary bicycle motor from which was built a mini-submarine with handle bars. This towed the escapee 25 kilometres in 5 hours, beneath the waves to freedom. So successful was this device that in 1973 a West German company went into mass production with it, to the enduring benefit of thousands of divers and sportsmen since.

All this continuing anguish, effort and misery had been the result of the Soviet perception of the West's intentions – to undermine the GDR, weaken its workforce and prevent any economic development. Of course, contemporary archives and documents reveal that this perception was more or less correct. Berlin was, after all, the ultimate ideological battleground in post-war Europe. Prior to the erection of the Wall, up to 60,000 East Berliners – known as the 'International Commuters' – were allowed to work in the West.[8] But from 4 August 1961 these workers were required to register with the authorities. Many would not, and sought to stay in the West. Thus the haemorrhaging of the Eastern Sector's already-weakened workforce led to a massive propaganda campaign by the GDR, with a barrage of accusations aimed at the Allied powers. Western politicians did respond to this and made some efforts to deter the exodus from the East, but already the plans for the building of the Wall had been completed. Many Easterners, without prior knowledge of the new barrier going up, felt betrayed by the West. They felt that that they ought to have at least been warned, but after August 1961 it was too late. As the tension reached new heights following the Cuban Missile Crisis in 1962, the intelligence community went into overdrive.

The West had MI5, MI6, the CIA and a host of connected organisations all monitoring Soviet activity. In the East, the KGB frequently demonstrated its renowned efficiency and as early as 1952 could boast a vast penetration of agents into Western Germany. In 1956 the *Hauptverwaltung XV* (main department of the East German Ministry of State Security) was re-named the *Hauptverwaltung Aufklärung* (main department of Reconnaissance – the HVA). At its head, where he was to remain until 1987, was Markus Johannes (Mischa) Wolf. Wolf's father had been a prominent Communist writer. When the Nazis took power in 1933, Wolf senior had no other choice than to flee from Germany to Moscow. Markus Wolf therefore grew up not only under his father's influence, but in Soviet Russia during Stalin's heyday.

He was an intelligence 'natural', and soon established himself as an undisputed master of his shadowy craft, during a long career as one of the Soviet Bloc's most efficient practitioners in espionage. In the year after the HVA was set up, a defector claimed that Wolf already had up to 3,000 agents working in the West, with many more trained and ready for action awaiting their call in East Germany.[9] With moles, double agents, 'sleepers', dead-letter drops and constant surveillance, it seems that everyone knew what everyone else was doing. Yet on the military front, there was still progress to be made, and men in Berlin like Iain Leggatt were there to make it.

'On 17 July 1967, an East German Lance Corporal, of 45 Berlin Border Brigade, defected to the West at Potsdammer Platz. As he had landed in the British Sector, he was interrogated by British security personnel and his uniform, equipment etc., landed in G

(Int. & Sy. – my department) that night and my presence was requested.

'The Kalashnikov (AK-47) had been the standard weapon of the Soviets since 1951. But what our East German chum had brought over was different from the standard-model AK-47 in that it had a plastic instead of a wooden stock, and in addition to the usual pistol-grip handle, there was a second steadying handle further forward, also made of plastic. The long and short of this tale is that a manual was written into the wee small hours on this weapon during which the new designation "Assault Rifle Kalashnikov 1947, Modified 1967" was created.

'This was abbreviated to AK-47 (M67), a nomenclature which appeared 100 or so times in the manual. Since I was the only person on the plot with access to paper and the ability to type, and with an eye to achieving some bed-rest that night, I took it upon myself to further abbreviate the abbreviation to AKM, which is how the weapon became known in military and civilian documents. My possibly most-treasured possession is still the real, very old, leather belt from that deserter, with its metal buckle bearing the impressed logo of the DDR – an upright hammer with superimposed protractor enclosed in a laurel wreath. It's a moveable buckle, designed to suit the girth of the wearer and, when I first acquired it 36 years ago, I could wear it at the smallest setting. Now, of course, it's at the other end of the scale. G equipment also included a wood-encased hand-operated shredder for use in the emergency situation of a USSR/DDR invasion of West Berlin. Practice use of the handle in anything approaching a hurry inevitably shredded the skin of the operator, with little effect on the documents supposedly being shredded. I also had a fall-back. This consisted of an empty 50-gallon drum, open at one end, a 6-foot-long metal pole (stirring, for the use of, presumably), a couple of bags of saltpetre and a bottle of vinegar. There were no instructions regarding the employment of this kit.'

Such are the seemingly small historical cogs which make up the military machine. Iain Leggatt went on to marry his first wife, Christine Bilson, in Berlin on 3 February 1968, and on 23 August the following year their first child, Alison Belinda, was born in Berlin's Military Hospital. Next door to the maternity ward in the hospital, also receiving military medical attention, was the sole remaining prisoner of Spandau Prison, Rudolf Hess. Nowhere in Europe would a soldier make so many connections with history than in Berlin.

Despite the restrictions and the politics, a number of British soldiers found that the eastern sector held more cultural attractions than the west.

Dr Hugh Thomas was a colonel with the RAMC in Berlin between 1972 and '74.

'I enjoyed East Berlin far more than West Berlin. The atmosphere was far more pleasant. It was less capitalistic and, as far as I could see, the people there were far more honest. The theatres, the opera there, the museums – once you got used to visiting you found the atmosphere very agreeable. I visited so much that I was actually investigated.

'The Chief of Police on our side said to me, "Hugh, I have to tell you that you are being investigated because you've been over 39 times – what are you bringing back?"

'I said, "Apart from a couple of pieces of Meissen porcelain I've mainly been to the opera and the theatre."

'I'd also visited a famous clock museum, far out on the outer limits of East Berlin where our chaps didn't go. To me it didn't matter – there was so much to see and discover. The trouble with the British officers was that they were so timid about it all. We were instructed: "Don't speak to the East Germans." Why, for God's sake? They were people just like us. So I spoke to them. Then there was "Don't converse with Russian officers." Frankly, it was all rubbish. I used to go to the opera and enjoy it. We'd see some of the finest singers and orchestras in the world with audiences who weren't stuck-up snobs; just ordinary East Germans from all walks of life who loved their culture. I'd then go over to the Stadt Hotel and have a meal. It wasn't "posh" – just very good and enjoyable. These days the same place will cost you an arm and a leg. There was one occasion, a bitter winter night, when I was at the opera. I was all dressed up in my greatcoat. In those days the opera in East Berlin had two tiers. I was in the top tier and from that level you could go and look down into the courtyard below. I knew that night I was being investigated. I looked down at where my car was parked and there was a man – a spook – obviously from the intelligence branch, waiting by my car. I asked the waiter to send him down a bottle of Sekt and a hot rum on a tray. The waiter eventually appeared in the street below and approached the agent. A sheepish grin broke out on his face and he looked up to the window where I was standing. He took the hot rum and drank it, but he wouldn't accept the wine. So, when they eventually asked me, "What *is* it that you're bringing back?", I just replied, "Culture."

'That year I was president of the Sub-Aqua Club. I was a good swimmer. Being responsible for the sub-aqua team, I was told by some members – who were all members of the intelligence branch – that they would be following me to this place or the other. It was ridiculous. I recall being in the East one night when I was called back – my locum (deputy surgeon) had a problem in the operating theatre and I was required. I made one call back and said, "Thomas here . . ." but that was the wrong thing to do for the intelligence boys – you had to use the name "Sunbeam" when communicating. Why? Because "they may discover your rank, etc." Bloody stupid – "Sunbeam!" In any case, Thomas is a surname in Germany and if they did know my rank – which was easy – so what? It was all schoolboy stuff.

'To them I was an oddball because I enjoyed culture. I'd been a Research Fellow at Yale and in Berlin I knew – and worked with – a lot of eminent surgeons. Another thing was that I learnt German and I liked to speak it. The intelligence people could only think in one blinkered way.'

There are darker memories of what was once 'the most frightening street in Berlin'. On Wilhemstrasse the East Germans sensibly demolished the old Gestapo HQ, and Himmler's SS office, leaving a symbolic mound of rubble. Along the side of this eerie site there still stands a long section of the Wall. Beneath it is an open-air exhibition, 'The Topography of Terror', cataloguing the rise and fall of the Nazis. Next door, now an art college, the neo-classical headquarters of the feared Reich Security Service run by Reinhard Heydrich still stands, ornate and beautiful despite the horrors once planned within its walls.

I called into the bar on my last night to ask Erwin one final question. Whatever happened to the Head of the East German espionage department, Markus Wolf? I knew this master-agent had been Le Carré's model for his fictional Soviet spy-master, 'Karla'.

As the barmaid pulled more beers Erwin chuckled. 'Wolf? Crafty, lucky old dog. Once we caught him we sentenced him to six years in jail. But the sentence – for treason – was never confirmed, so he's still out there. Did you know he's 82 now – looks about 60 and still going strong? Can you believe he's become a personality for his *cooking* ability?'

I laughed. 'From master spy to master chef?'

'Yes! He wrote a bestselling cookery book in 1995, *Secrets of the Russian Kitchen*. Talk about "secrets" – he had a few. Still has a holiday home in Russia, where he was educated, so reunification's done him no harm at all . . . but I bet your James Bond couldn't cook up a pan of *borscht*!'

A thought crossed my mind: what a sinister guest presenter Markus Wolf would make for one of our many 'celebrity chef' TV shows.

'Can't cook . . . *won't* cook? We'll see about *that* – release the dogs!'

Holding on to the image of the dreaded Stasi head rustling up a tasty omelette, I climbed into the car for the long drive to Rotterdam. As I watched the lights of Berlin fading away in the rear-view mirror, I knew I would be back. John Le Carré is right. This is an addictive city.

7

Berlin II: Spandau

May 5th 1955: In previous years the British officers, in spite of their aloofness, would give us friendly greetings as they made their rounds in the garden. For the past three days they have been treating us frigidly. Today we heard that last week they were shown a film on the Nuremberg trial.

Albert Speer, *Spandau: The Secret Diaries*[1]

Everyone who served with the British Army in Germany seems to have a memory of Berlin, if only of a sightseeing visit there. It remains without doubt the single most potent focal point in the Allied adventure. This is hardly surprising. Apart from being a very beautiful place, steeped in history, it possesses a haunting ambience which stays with you for ever. With the French, the Americans, the Russians and the British all stationed there for such a long, tense time, it became a city where military might and face-to-face politics combined to make this the frontline of modern history. With such continuing unease in the air – far more dangerous in the long term for overall safety of the world than anything experienced in, for instance, Belfast, we can look back with wonder and relief that the wire didn't snap. The Cold War, thankfully, never became too hot to handle, although it did simmer just below boiling point on more than one occasion. Berlin was a city of gesture and posture. The great powers sat like two heavyweight boxers in their respective corners, waiting for the bell.

In the end, everyone simply packed up and went home.

Many regiments came and went in Berlin, where duties were varied, and the 'enemy' was always visible just across the wire and over the Wall. Getting to and from this island of Western policy in the middle of a red Soviet sea seems to have been an experience in itself on the daily military train, with all its luxuries and intricate, time-consuming cross-border bureaucracy. Duties in Berlin revolved around a real military display of power and intention. This was the hub of European intelligence activity and the place where the beacon of memory of the Second World War would be kept flickering – on both sides of the Iron Curtain – long after the rest of Germany had laid that spectre to rest.

Hilary Plews was a schoolgirl with RAMC in Germany during the 1960s.

'One memorable incident was when my dad was called upon to take out Rudolf Hess's tonsils. He had to spend about a week in Berlin as all the arrangements were made at the British Military Hospital in Berlin. Dad told me he quite liked Hess but couldn't be doing with Albert Speer. He visited all the prisoners at Spandau. I'm not sure why. It may have been because he had to act as the CO for the hospital there for a while. The Russians, Americans, French and Brits provided an armed escort for Hess in the hospital – as well as in the operating theatre!'

The Hess conundrum is just one of the many morose memories surrounding Spandau. The very name of the place conjures up an ambience of dungeons, dark stone walls, lone prisoners, turning keys and echoing corridors. All kinds of political and military attitudes, influenced on both sides by the tensions of the Cold War, and the presence of real, live Nazi prisoners, seemed to get distilled here into a series of highly visual martial rituals. You can't resist calling it a 'Spandau ballet': the changing of the guards, the four powers all straining for their own particular show of intricate protocol and uniformed discipline. If ever there was a place in international military history where things were done 'by the book', then Spandau was it – and judging by the evidence, it was a thick book indeed.

Andrew Burns of Glasgow was a lance corporal in the Royal Military Police. He served in Germany from 1950 to '52.

'I was first stationed in Bielefeld for only a few weeks to attend lectures on Germany, our future role and regulations governing the conduct of troops etc. It was only on our final day in Bielefeld that we were given our final destination – or so I thought. I was given Berlin. The posting was considered an elite one where "bull" was the by-word. We travelled by train during the night. This was a compulsory order of the Russians. Blinds had to be drawn and so no one was allowed to look out.

'The barracks in Berlin (Spandau), were situated next to the famous prison where the remaining Nazi leaders were situated. The MPs had no duties connected to the prison and, though only a dividing wall separated us, I never saw into the grounds. The uniform supplied to me differed from other units in the Army in that instead of khaki it was green and of a better cut. The vehicles comprised motorbikes, jeeps and armoured cars and again they all differed – all black with white seats, which of course had to be spotless at all times.'

Black jeeps, white seats, green MP uniforms. This, plus the elite strutting of the Americans, French and Russians all seemed to set this political showcase, Spandau, apart – as it seems to have been throughout its long existence. This was where the four military nationalities could see for themselves how they compared to one another. As usual, the British Army was determined to set the pace.

Gordon Cox of Woodthorpe, Nottinghamshire was stationed in the RAMC in Germany from 1946 to '49.

'The British ran a local leave centre in the Olympic Stadium. It was on the outskirts of Berlin, and just about the only building left standing in what was a massive, total ruin. It was demolished bit by bit by the RAF and USAAF, the coup de grâce being administered in the last few weeks of the war by the Red Army, who fought for it street by street.

'Normally, at the other leave centres in BAOR it was possible to relax a bit, for example, by not having to wear a hat, no saluting, having your hands in your pockets, etc. But in Berlin you were temporarily part of the British garrison, who were determined to show the Germans who were the smartest troops in town. It was no contest, as we were up against the slobby Yanks, the scruffy French and the Mongolians who seemed to predominate in the Red Army garrison. The Russians wore rough battledress, but their officers dressed in all sorts of finery, looking like they had escaped from a palace garden party in an Ivor Novello musical set in Ruritania. The gap between officers and ordinary recruits in the Red Army seemed far greater than that in the British Army. It surprised me – I thought Communism was different.'

It was in 1232 AD that the Spandau district was first given a charter, or city rights. Back then it was known as 'Spandoh', and had appeared as a recognised place of dwelling as early as 1197. The citadel was a fortified castle, standing on the juncture of the Spree and Havel rivers in the northern sector of Berlin. Spandau was already a place of great historical importance centuries before the British arrived, and a well-used military outpost. Caesar's legions had built their roads nearby, by-ways which down the centuries would become important trade routes.

The building had begun in 928 and continued to be added to and re-modelled after the numerous European wars of the second millennium. Such a heavily fortified edifice would be the perfect place to store Germany's gold – as the Allies discovered when they arrived there in 1945. At one time the King of Prussia made Spandau his home. Plague, war and other disasters such as fire all took their toll, so much so that in the year 1240 Spandau was exempt from paying any taxes.

Since 1945 over 30,000 new homes have been built in the Spandau district, and industries have grown there, such as Siemens and the British American Tobacco Company. But it is the prison at Spandau, separate from the citadel in the region, which will forever be remembered by the Allied forces.

Spandau Prison was designed as a nineteenth-century penitentiary. The buildings had the appearance of a pseudo-medieval, red-brick fortress. Built in 1876, it was to act as a military detention centre to house between 500 and 600 prisoners.

The Nuremberg Trials of prominent Nazis lasted from November 1945 through to the end of August 1946. The greater criminals, those with the most murderous records, such as Chief of Staff Wilhelm Keitel, Security Chief Ernst Kaltenbrunner and the loathsome and corrupt anti-Semite Julius Streicher, were all executed, with Hermann Göring cheating the hangman the night before by taking cyanide. Three lesser Nazis were acquitted – Hans Fritsche (radio propaganda chief), Franz von Papen (vice-chancellor in Hitler's first government) and Hjalmar Schacht (economics minister in the 1930s).

~ Berlin II: Spandau ~

The remaining seven, however, would all become familiar to British soldiers in Berlin's Spandau gaol. They were sentenced to imprisonment for their various roles in the Third Reich:[2]

- *Prisoner No. 1: Baldur von Schirach*, 1907–74. Youth leader and Gauleiter of Vienna. Sentenced to 20 years. Released in 1966. Died in Kröv, 7 August 1974.
- *Prisoner No. 2: Karl Dönitz*, 1891–1980. U-boat and navy chief, Hitler's successor. Sentenced to 10 years. Released 1 October 1956. Died Aumühle, 22 December 1980.
- *Prisoner No. 3: Konstantin von Neurath*, 1873–1956. Governor of Bohemia-Moravia. Sentenced to 15 years. Released 1954. Died in Enzweihingen, 14 August 1956.
- *Prisoner No. 4: Erich Raeder*, 1876–1960. Navy chief to 1943. Sentenced to life (commuted to 10 years). Released 6 September 1955 due to ill-health. Died Kiel, 6 November 1960.
- *Prisoner No. 5: Albert Speer*, 1905–81. Armaments Minister. Sentenced to 20 years. Released 1966. Died London, 1 September 1981.
- *Prisoner No. 6: Walther Funk*, 1890–1960. President of the Reichsbank. Sentenced to life. Released 1957 due to illness. Died in Düsseldorf, 31 May 1960.
- *Prisoner No. 7: Rudolf Hess*, 1894–1987. Hitler's secretary till 1941. Sentenced to life. Known as 'Prisoner Number Seven', he was the last remaining inmate at Spandau and committed suicide on 17 August 1987.

Many Nazis who were sentenced to imprisonment only served a small proportion of their terms. At the height of its power, Germany's National Socialist Party had eight million members. Yet many, including members of the SS, escaped punishment. For instance, of the 361 top executives who formed Germany's federation of steel manufacturers, which included the mighty Krupp Works, an industry infamous for its blatant use of slave labour, only 33 were brought to trial.[3] The remainder all carried on in their comfortable, well-paid jobs long after the war.

Speer and Hess, however, were to spend their post-war years becoming well acquainted with the grim corridors of Spandau.

After nine months of preparation at the prison, the Allies moved the seven famous inmates to Spandau from Nuremberg on 18 July 1947.

Today, following Hess's suicide in 1987, the prison building has vanished, obliterated in a bold act of demolition which seems for all the world to signify that a long, dark chapter in Europe's political history is finally closed. Hess's suicide is still the centre of a storm of controversy and the subject of conspiracy theorists around the world. The argument revolves around the fact that, at the age of 92, weak and infirm, many believe that Hess's suicide could only have been carried out with 'assistance'. We may never know the truth.

What we do know is that the strict catalogue of regulation and routine in Spandau, as operated by the four powers, seems in retrospect to be more like an outward demonstration of the enduring international disgust felt by the rest of the world towards the memory of the Third Reich. Arguably, such a demonstration could be interpreted as a warning to criminal despots in other regimes. The arrest of Slobodan Milosevic and the deliberations of the International Court of Human Rights stand in a similar light – here's what happens to you once you're caught. Sadly, the fact that so many vicious regimes have continued to proliferate since 1945 proves that murderous dictators and power-hungry political opportunists will always remain confident in their powers of survival.

Spandau Prison, already a decaying edifice when the Nuremberg Seven moved in, was a central building which formed an island set in eight acres. It was ringed by fences, the second of which was electrified, in an area bristling with mines. Nine concrete towers jutted out from the high walls, where armed guards were on duty twenty-four hours a day. Every ten minutes these guards pressed a button for an electronic time-check in the Commandant's office. There was only one entrance and exit to the prison – through the main gate. It had been agreed between the four powers that it was their mutual obligation to maintain these prisoners in the utmost close security. Each country's forces stationed in Berlin worked to a timetable, which involved a regular monthly rotation of Spandau's guards. France served in January, Great Britain in February, the USSR in March and the United States in April. In May and September this cycle would be repeated. A separate commandant, plus two doctors, catering staff and other personnel would take over each month. This was a highly expensive routine – as a supplement to the platoon-strength military guard, the prison also retained a retinue of 18 warders – and at one time in the 1960s the cost of housing the seven was estimated to be at least £100 per minute. However, the cost of maintaining the prison was footed by the federal government in Bonn and the city of Berlin itself. The strictly regulated regime was stark and simple. Serving under military law, guards were forbidden to hold conversations with the prisoners. Prisoners would rise at 6 a.m., with lights out at 10 p.m. Two thirty-minute exercise periods in the open air were allowed each day. One of their pastimes during these outdoor sessions, described by Albert Speer, involved logging how many kilometres one could walk each day. Using an atlas, they would plot an imaginary journey somewhere overland around the world, and keep a record of how long it took them to walk to their chosen destination. In Speer's diary entry for 6 August 1955, it is easy to see how both he and Rudolf Hess utilised their imaginations as they tramped around and around the Spandau garden:

> Shimmering heat waves over the *puszta* [forest] as I covered the stretch from Budapest to Belgrade, a few kilometres away from the Danube. The roads were sandy, there was seldom even a single shade tree, and the flies were a plague. From the nearby Havel I heard the sound of tugs, which I transformed into ships on the Danube. I plucked a stem of lemon balm from our herb bed and crushed the leaves between my fingers. The strong odour intensified the illusion of foreign places, tramping the roads, and freedom.[4]

For Britain's soldiers – and those of the other three powers – guard duty at Spandau remains a gloomy memory. It was, to say the least, an unusual task in peacetime. Many of the regiments who served in Berlin became familiar with this forbidding place, where, by the 1970s, the level of security surrounding its one remaining inmate, Hess, seemed at times to be out of proportion. Once again, though, Berlin was making a statement.

In the Allied Museum on Clayallee in the old American sector in Charlottenburg stands a fine, polished wall plaque which lists all the regiments who moved into and out of Britain's Brooke Barracks in Berlin over the years. If you were there, perhaps you'll spot your regiment. If there are any anomalies here, or odd spellings – blame the Army, as this is taken directly from the plaque!

Brooke Barracks

1910–1918	5th Grenadier Guards Regiment (Germany)
1918–1935	Vacant
Oct. 1935–Apr. 1945	1st.Bn. 67th Infantry Regiment (Germany)
May 1945–June 1945	Soviet Army
July 1945–June 1949	Vacant
June 1949–Nov. 1949	1st. Bn. Queen's Royal Regiment
Nov. 1949–Nov. 1950	1st. Bn. Royal Fusiliers
Nov. 1950–Mar. 1952	1st. Bn. King's Regiment
Mar. 1952–May 1952	1st. Bn. Welsh Guards
May 1952–April 1953	1st. Bn. Royal Scots
April 1953–April 1954	1st. Bn. Royal Irish Fusiliers
April 1954–April 1955	1st. Bn. Lincolnshire Regiment
April 1955–Nov. 1956	1st. Bn. Cheshire Regiment
Nov. 1956–Dec. 1957	1st. Bn. South Lancashire Regiment
Dec. 1957–Feb. 1959	1st. Bn. Royal Inniskilling Fusiliers
Feb. 1959–April 1961	1st. Bn. King's Own Scottish Borderers
April 1961–Oct. 1963	1st. Bn. Welch Regiment
Oct. 1963–Oct. 1965	1st. Bn. Somerset & Cornwall Light Infantry
Oct. 1965–Oct. 1967	1st. Bn. Royal Inniskilling Fusiliers
Oct. 1967–Oct. 1969	1st. Bn. Gloucester Regiment
Oct. 1969–July 1971	2nd Bn. Royal Regiment of Fusiliers
July 1971–May 1973	1st. Bn. Duke of Edinburgh's Royal Regiment
May 1973–May 1975	1st. Bn. King's Own Scottish Borderers
May 1975–May 1977	1st. Bn. The Royal Regiment of Wales
May 1977–June 1979	2nd Bn. The Parachute Regiment
June 1979–April 1981	1st. Bn. The Royal Irish Rangers (27th Inniskilling) 83rd and 87th
April 1981–June 1983	2nd. Bn. Royal Regiment of Fusiliers V. VI.VII.XX
June 1983–April 1985	1st. Bn. The Prince of Wales Own Regiment of Yorkshire

~ Berlin II: Spandau ~

The 1st Battalion Duke of Edinburgh's Royal Regiment were known as 'The Farmer's Boys'. They provided guards on two occasions, in 1972 and again in 1973.

Martin McIntyre was section commander of 'B' Company of the Duke of Edinburgh's Royal Regiment. He was stationed at Brooke Barracks, Spandau, between 1972 and '73.

'Strict orders were given to the guards regarding fraternisation with Hess. All sentries were searched prior to taking up their post to prohibit the use of cigarettes. Most of those who carried out this duty remember a very old man walking around the garden on a path he had trodden himself over the years.

'I was section commander at the time in "B" Company and we were detailed to provide a guard for Hess in the prison, which was very near to Brooke Barracks. As with all guard duties we considered this to be a total pain in the neck, but "orders is orders". Once we took over, even the thickest of us could feel that this was a duty apart, and something we were never likely to repeat; we were effectively living history. As a section commander it was my responsibility to post the sentries in the watchtowers. Because of the problems with the Russians, all of our procedures had to mirror what the other powers did when responsible for the prison. Because the Russians locked their men into the watchtowers (to prevent desertion, so we were told), we had to lock our own people in as well. (I must say that did give a certain amount of pleasure . . .)

'Before we posted the lads we had to read the orders over: "No smoking. No talking to Hess etc.". Before they were marched out they were searched to ensure no cameras or cigarettes found their way in. I remember unlocking the massive side gates, which opened with a creaking noise that would have done justice to a horror film. I can clearly remember Hess in his garden, hands behind his back, as if he was inspecting the troops as we marched by en route to the watchtowers. One of the watchtowers was out of view from its neighbours and the legend was that a French squaddie had thrown himself off the tower and killed himself with his rifle sling. Whether this was true or not I was never sure, but many of the lads were a bit iffy about going into that tower. I must say it was one of the more interesting places that we "stagged" on . . .'

The mysteries of Spandau are many, but some of the more unusual and controversial stories came from an ex-officer in the Royal Army Medical Corps. Dr Hugh Thomas was born in 1935. From 1970 to 1978 he was a consultant surgeon in the RAMC. He also gained exceptional experience of gunshot wounds and their effects whilst serving with the Army in Northern Ireland. He recently retired as a consultant with the NHS. Hugh Thomas used his time in Berlin during the 1970s to great effect; to understand the impact working as a doctor in Spandau had upon him, we must return to those dramatic, early post-war months.

STRANGER THAN FICTION

On 10 May 1945, with Germany in ruins, Reichsführer-SS Heinrich Himmler, shunned by Admiral Dönitz, the man who now held the reins of what was left of the Third Reich, decided to attempt an escape to southern Germany, together with a few remnants of his once-feared SS. The party left Flensburg, near the Danish border, in four large cars. Two days later they had to abandon their vehicles and continue on foot. These men, who had once held the power of life and death throughout the Reich, had gained the appearance a motley band of tramps. They were disguised in scruffy uniforms of the *Geheim Feldpolizei* (Secret Field Police), as Military Policemen. They had fresh discharge documents. Himmler had shaved off his moustache and donned a somewhat ridiculous black eye-patch. His well-worn identity card was that of a seemingly harmless cog in the defeated and demobilised German military machine, one 'Sergeant Heinrich Hitzinger'.

By 18 May the party had reached Bremervörde, a small town on the River Oste. It was there that Himmler's luck ran out. He could have waded across the river further upstream, and avoided the British military checkpoint on the bridge. But he chose to risk the checkpoint. Unknown to the party, the Geheim Feldpolizei were every bit as wanted by the Allies as the dreaded Gestapo or SS. 'Hitzinger' was arrested, and taken to a civilian internment camp at Westertinke, seven miles to the south.

In the presence of the camp commandant, Captain Thomas Selvester, 'Hitzinger' removed his eye-patch, donned a familiar pair of round spectacles and announced in a quiet voice, '*Ich bin Heinrich Himmler*'. It seemed like the greatest catch of the war. The prisoner was transferred to 31a Ülzenerstrasse in Lüneberg, where he would be interrogated by the 2nd Army's Chief of Intelligence,

Colonel Michael Murphy, and be examined by a doctor, Captain Clement Wells.

On 23 May, Himmler bit down hard on a concealed cyanide capsule and, despite the efforts of those present to keep him alive, died within 12 minutes.

In the early hours of 26 May 1945, the Reich's Black Angel was buried in a secret, unmarked location in the woods on Lüneberg Heath. In a subsequent BBC radio broadcast, Sergeant-Major Edwin Austin – a dustman in civvy street – told listeners the colourful story of disposing of Himmler's corpse. 'I put two army camouflage nets around him and tied him up with telephone wires. I put the parcel on the back of a lorry and drove off. I had to dig the grave myself – no one will ever know where he is buried.' As the body was tossed into the freshly dug grave, the only words spoken were Austin's: 'Let this worm go to the worms.' Another version has him saying 'Good riddance to bad rubbish'. It is a wholesome, satisfying end to a life of such inscrutable evil. No novelist could have produced a better dénouement.

For almost five decades, this version of Himmler's death has been the standard in every history of the war. It may have remained so had chance not taken a hand in the appointment of an inquisitive Welsh surgeon as the Prison Doctor at Spandau. His first patient was to be another high-profile Nazi – Hitler's deputy, Rudolf Hess.

The tranquil hills and leafy lanes of Brecon on a crisp late-autumn morning are a long way from the shattered hell of defeated Germany in 1945. But within a secluded, imposing stone-built house in a quiet Welsh village, a decomposing body of official Second World War 'fiction' has been under the forensic microscope for some time and the results of this autopsy are shocking and fascinating in equal measure.

Dr Hugh Thomas belies his 68 years. He is a compact, lively and erudite Welshman whose whole life has been the study of truth through his chosen profession as a surgeon.

He has recently retired from a long and auspicious career in medicine, the eminence of which has been added to over the past three decades with his emergence as a gadfly on the rump of modern history, with a series of well-researched, bestselling books on the Second World War. He is not popular with what we shall call 'the Establishment'. Using the scalpel of forensic science, his autopsies

173

on the bodies of 'evidence' surrounding the deaths of Rudolf Hess, Hitler, Eva Braun and now Himmler, have cut deep into a tissue of official myth and legend to expose some serious anomalies.

Hugh Thomas's father was a chemist. The family already had its share of doctors and physicians. After studying at London's St Mary's Medical School, his skill and enthusiasm soon gained him a Fellowship of the Royal College of Surgeons at the very young age of 26. In the 1960s, he worked at consultancy level in America where he began performing operations then unheard of in Britain: kidney transplants.

'I came back to Britain to discover I was part of the "BTA" syndrome – "Been to America? Who the hell d'you think you are? How dare you perform kidney transplants – they're not ethical!"

'I was back to kicking my heels, watching excellent surgeons still having to wait until their 50s to become consultants . . .'

In 1967 he returned to America as an academic surgeon at the prestigious Yale University School of Medicine, where he specialised in cancer research into oncology. Then came the Vietnam war.

'The Americans had this bright idea of putting foreigners in the front line. Not being an early riser, I wasn't ready to face the Vietcong in their black pyjamas. Although I was British, to work in the US I had to pledge my allegiance and it would have been perfectly legal for them to put me in a MASH unit on the front. So I left for Canada.' Eventually he returned to Britain, yet despite his experience and qualifications, he still found the 'dead men's shoes' path to promotion had not altered. But there was a fast-track through this stifling tradition. In 1970, Hugh Thomas joined the British Army as a consultant with the rank of colonel with the RAMC. He knew that when he left the Army, the civilian medical world would have to accept his consultant status.

After first working in Northern Ireland, he was moved to Berlin. It was in Germany that Dr Hugh Thomas, surgeon, became Hugh Thomas, historian.

Amongst the French, British and American surgeons in Berlin, he was the senior.

'I had no interest in Hess other than as a patient. I was called to examine him – he had a perforated ulcer. Checking his medical records, I saw that he had received a gunshot wound in the left side of his chest in the First World War. But when I examined him I was totally flabbergasted. I looked at his torso, front and back, but could find no evidence of a gunshot wound. I asked him, "What has

happened to your war wounds?" and his reaction startled me. He
began shaking, staring at me, saying, "Too late . . . too late . . ." His
X-rays showed nothing. He refused ever to speak to me again, except
through the interpretation of a Spandau guard called Whittaker.'

Colonel Thomas became curious and began delving into the
archives. To begin with, he discovered that Hess had left Germany
on his flight to Scotland on 10 May 1941 in a Series D Messerschmitt
110 with the number NJC+11. Yet the plane that landed near the
village of Eaglesham was a Series E2, with the identification VJ+OQ.
Luftwaffe radar records show that NJC+11 vanished from radar
screens just 27 miles off the Dutch coast. As Dr Thomas continued
to dig, stranger evidence emerged. By 1979 the results of his
research produced his book, *The Murder of Rudolf Hess* (which
suggests that either Göring or Himmler may have ordered Hess's
death). It caused a furore, as did the follow-up, *Hess: A Tale of Two
Murders*. The latter precipitated a six-month Scotland Yard inquiry
which saw its report immediately suppressed.

If we are to believe the evidence, the conclusion suggests that
Prisoner Number Seven in Spandau was not Rudolf Hess at all, but
possibly a double. Yet we might ask why, if this is the case, did the
hapless prisoner maintain this subterfuge for so long? If this
fantastic scenario is true, could Prisoner Number Seven's family
have been living under an enduring threat from the leader of the SS,
Heinrich Himmler?

The result of one of his conversations by proxy with 'Hess' through
the guard, Whittaker, led Dr Thomas into another mystery – the
death of Heinrich Himmler.[5]

'Whittaker said to him, "Why don't you say who you are? You
have nothing to fear – Himmler is dead . . ." but he turned on his
heels and snapped, "*Really*?! – and how do you *know* that?" This
seemed very odd. I eventually made contact with the doctor who
had looked after Himmler, Captain Clement Wells. The story he
told me of Himmler's suicide was vastly different to the official
one.'

The most compelling evidence, which leads to the conclusion
that Heinrich Himmler did not die on 23 May 1945, comes from the
hasty removal of the corpse and Dr Thomas's own analysis of the
photographic and archive evidence which produced more questions
than answers. The mysteries surrounding Hess and Himmler

emanating from his time in Berlin will continue to occupy conspiracy theorists, but Dr Thomas is cautious.

'If you speculate, you're dead in the water. But there was a definite post-war SS financial network and instructions for its operations emanated from *someone*. This "network" had three centres: Vienna, Zurich and Hamburg. It involved SS men such as Himmler's personal agent, Karl-Heinz Krämer, and Klaus Barbie.'

So, did Himmler live on after the war? It remains an intriguing question. By 1945, he was one of the richest men in the Reich with several bank accounts, many of which remain undiscovered. Was he able to pull off an immunity deal through Allied intelligence? Like the Hess file, the Allied file on Himmler remains embargoed until 2045.

Hugh Thomas does not profess to be a historian. But he continues to upset history's apple-cart.

'Forensic science deals in facts. What many historians lack is cynicism. As a surgeon, you need cynicism. When I open up an abdomen I have to be ready to accept that my previous diagnosis might be wrong. My books offer evidence – what historians do with it, and how they incorporate it into their work, is up to them.'

As Colonel Thomas of the RAMC, Hugh very much enjoyed his stay in Berlin, and as an officer and a surgeon his time at Spandau did not produce the same brooding memories recalled by lesser ranks.

'At Spandau I was the senior surgeon. There were also two Americans and two French surgeons, L'Cordier and Thibedeau. L'Cordier was a keen yachtsman – and he only liked to sail in the roughest weather – he saw it as a challenge. Thibedeau was a very good tennis player. My best memories of Spandau are the meals we had there every month – especially with the French. We would go up onto the first floor and turn left into the Officers' Mess and there we would gather for some really excellent cuisine. Sometimes the Russians and the Americans would be there. I remember one of the KGB intelligence men, called Voitov. He loved his whisky and would frequently end up crying into it. He always had photographs in his wallet of his family to show us.'

The solitary Hess would remain Spandau's reason for existence until his death in 1987. Many more visitors, medical or otherwise, would gain access to the prison over the years to witness this ageing representative of the Hitler years, whose power had waned even before they were born. One man recalls his own experience not long before the old deputy führer died.

Nigel Dunkley, MBE, was based at Spandau in the mid-1980s.

'I also knew Hess well. In the mid-'80s I was a young touring captain in Brixmis and as such provided interpreter duties at the prison as a sideline to touring in the GDR. I speak Russian, German and French, and had to do duty as interpreter for one of Hess's medical examinations. He told me that his *"supensorium"* was hurting him. I hadn't the faintest idea what he was talking about. So I translated into Russian using the same word in the hope that the Russian doctor would understand. He did, straight away. I translated the same into French, using the word *"suspension"*. Lastly, the grumpy old British doctor told me off for being such a smartie and doing the translation into every other bugger's language – *but what was wrong with bloody Hess*?

'I still had no idea! It turned out to be another (Saxon) root word in English – his *"truss"* was chafing. No one had briefed me about that!

'We had a lot of fun down at the prison and I witnessed Hess on lots of occasions. When Major-General Bernard Gordon-Lennox (Bernie the Bolt), having taken over as GOC Berlin, did his initial inspection of the prison and of Hess, we duty officers were in the middle of fooling around with the two duty Russian interpreters, Valentina Anufreyeva and Natalia Grinkievicha, both of whom we knew well. We were in the middle of trying to hide behind each other like silly school kids. We had warned the two girls that Bernie was a Guards officer and very fearsome indeed. They saw him arrive through the window and shrieked in not altogether mock panic as they saw him heading straight towards us. Just as Valentina grabbed me and pretended to hide behind me, he strode in. It was very painful explaining myself afterwards – in his eyes such behaviour was tantamount to fraternising with the sworn enemy!

'I had several tours in Germany but by far the best were there in Berlin.'

No doubt many British soldiers have no problem with the fact that Spandau Prison has been removed from the Berlin landscape. There are some Germans with an interest in their history who believed that the building could well have been preserved as a monument or a museum. This seemed to be the view of some of the older people I met in Berlin. But the majority of younger Germans, those born during or after the war, are understandably keen to put the whole memory of the Third Reich behind them. The long tenure in Spandau endured by the man known as Hess had been regarded by many as an example of international vindictiveness. In those last solitary 21 years, he remained the sole living reminder of a terrible period in German history. It still seems ludicrous that so much Allied manpower was involved in maintaining one man, yet it is a fact that the governments of Britain, the United States and France repeatedly argued for his release. The Russians, however, remained unmoved by public opinion. Perhaps they had a point. It may be viewed that Hess was a living symbol of their vengeance. Despite all the privations and casualties the Allies suffered during the Second World War, they pale into insignificance alongside the devastating effect Nazi Germany had on the Soviet Union. Yet Hess's strange demise remains like a bad smell. It has also unfortunately become something of a cause célèbre for the far right and the Holocaust revisionists. Hess was a living link to that inhuman 'new order' to which they all still aspire.

Was he murdered? Many think so, including Hugh Thomas. The evidence for murder is very convincing. Hess had become the most expensive prisoner in the world. The eventual cost of maintaining the staff and the guard at Spandau was estimated at around $100 million per year. Hess is supposed to have hanged himself in the summerhouse, a building he spent time in each day in Spandau's garden, using the electrical cord from a table lamp, looped around his neck, the flex tied to a window catch. Yet there was hardly any 'drop' at 140 cm (just over 4 feet) to accommodate the force required on a man's neck for a hanging as we know it. As Hugh Thomas says, 'it was the first horizontal hanging in history'. Autopsy reports on Hess show signs of strangulation rather than suicide by hanging. The American guard with Hess at the end behaved suspiciously, and the summerhouse was burned to the ground immediately after the incident.

The final truth of what happened in Spandau's last mysterious, dark days is forever buried by history. But generations of British soldiers will recall their duty there with mixed emotions of melancholy, tinged with the occasional moment of pleasure. Like everything experienced in Berlin, the memories, still vivid in their detail, will endure.

8

'Every Night Something Awful'

Frankie Howerd, Tony Hancock, Kenneth Williams, we saw
the lot – and some good bands and musicians. But believe
me, a lot of the turns were nothing short of terrible. It's
always been easy entertaining the troops – that's why we got
so much rubbish.

Corporal Don Rowley, Royal Artillery

Driver/Mechanic 14332308 of the Royal Electrical and Mechanical
Engineers always complained that, 'I was five years in the Army and
never got a stripe.' He'd also become tired of having his sergeant
bellow at him: 'You're an 'orrible, dozy little man!'

In some ways he'd been lucky. He'd arrived in Normandy three
months after D-Day on 1 September 1944 as a searchlight operator
with the 3rd Light Anti-Aircraft Searchlight Battery. They had come
ashore via the legendary Mulberry harbour. They pressed inland past
Dunkirk through what was known as 'buzz bomb alley', but, despite
a few tragic casualties, men killed on guard duty, there wasn't much
action. This particular soldier survived the war and, as Benny Hill,
became a household name as a comic on both sides of the Atlantic,
known for his racy running around with scantily clad women. Hill
admitted that he was, in many ways, a pretty poor soldier. But like
many young men with a certain degree of talent who found
themselves transferred to Germany, his acute sense of humour saw
him through. He was once asked by a sergeant, 'Hill, what's a "fine
sight"?' to which the chubby one replied, 'Two dinners on one plate.'

Before long, once the bullets stopped, Benny was entertaining his
comrades in Germany as part of the line-up of a legendary show,
Stars in Battledress.

Stories surrounding the entertaining of troops can usually raise a smile. Soldiers, just like the rest of us, like to be entertained. The old variety show may be long dead, but showbusiness for British troops certainly isn't. Even in the NAAFI bar of today's barracks, with its big-screen TV sets, quite a few squaddies are flexing their own vocal chords, as karaoke evenings grow in popularity. Modern leisure time in Germany offers just about everything you'd expect back home, including a wide range of beers and vastly improved food. All this is part of a noble tradition which stretches back to pre-war years.

The Allies, benefiting from that rich, available mix of American, French and British showbiz, arguably had a more diverse entertainment culture than their Soviet counterparts. However, based on the recollections of those squaddies of a more cultural bent who ventured over the border to see a show, the quality in the Eastern Bloc was always high.

Due to the political partition of the city, Berlin's Deutsche Opera House was situated in the Soviet eastern sector. At some time during 1967, a Welsh male voice choir were due to perform there. The 40-plus choir members were duly placed on board two military buses and set off for Checkpoint Charlie. Once there, this cultural exchange was stalled for over two hours as the Soviet intelligence machine attempted to unravel what appeared to be an inscrutable Allied plot. Upon inspecting the choir's passports at the Checkpoint, the East Germans were baffled by the fact that a great percentage of these visiting Sons of the Valleys had the same name: Jones. An international crisis loomed as officers of higher and higher rank were summoned to the checkpoint, until some determined cultural research revealed that this genealogical phenomena was just that, and not an attempt to smuggle in two busloads of tuneful agents.

Many stars began their career in the forces. In the immediate post-war years, some of those national servicemen based in Hamburg may not have believed that they would, in years to come, see another side to the talents of one of their handsome young officers. Once demobbed, he would become a model for men's cardigans, and within two decades young Lieutenant Roger Moore would receive a celluloid promotion to become Commander James Bond.

A list of all the performers – those who remained unknown and those who made it big – who have toured Germany to entertain our forces since the war would probably fill this book.

The Entertainments National Service Association, known to all during the Second World War and the immediate post-war years as ENSA, has been immortalised for later generations by the TV series *It Ain't Half Hot, Mum*, written by Jimmy Perry and David Croft. The show still runs on some cable and satellite channels, well over two decades since it was first aired. ENSA was founded by entrepreneur Basil Dean, himself no stranger to Army life after serving as an officer in the First World War.

The organisation was essentially an off-shoot of the NAAFI, which had always had an entertainment branch whose mission was to take shows out to some of the more remote military postings around the globe. With the distinct possibility of war approaching in 1938, Basil Dean wasted no time in convincing many of his associates in the entertainment world that they should volunteer their services – specifically to entertain the troops during what seemed to be an inevitable war in Europe.

The speed and efficiency with which ENSA organised its forces is demonstrated by the fact that, only eight days after the declaration of war, the NAAFI had moved into Drury Lane's Theatre Royal, where ENSA set up its headquarters. By April 1940 ENSA shows – 1,000 per week in Britain alone – had a combined audience of three million around the world. No destination was too remote for the entertainers. Apart from Germany, these hardy footlights troupers made it to Africa, India, the Pacific, even the Shetland Islands. If live performers weren't available, they'd send a film show crew. For performing thespians, vocalists, comedians, magicians and musicians, ENSA was a proving ground – and often a baptism of fire – for many artists who would later go on to become Britain's top entertainers. By 1944, there were 4,000 performers on ENSA's books. NAAFI had a huge logistical task on its hands. Girls needed training as cinema projectionists. Hotels had to be booked, or hostel accommodation found for visiting artists. There was a variety of transport needed – apart from moving people around, many shows had props and heavy equipment. The popularity and success of this organisation reached a new peak towards the end of the war when, in the space of one month, at a cost of £450,000 around the world, ENSA put on 20,000 film shows and 13,500 stage shows.[1] When the

NAAFI picked up the bill for ENSA's efforts at the end of the Second World War, it came to some £17 million.

Very few of Britain's leading variety and musical performers missed the chance to entertain in Germany. Surprisingly, the great comic Max Miller was one who refused duty, but some stars, such as Gracie Fields and George Formby (who appeared more than anyone else) seemed to spend more than their fair share of time facing a sea of khaki.[2] Rumour has it that Joseph Stalin was quite a George Formby fan. There was always a tradition in Eastern Bloc countries that ensured that any artists appearing as the stereotypical working-class underdog would have a place in Soviet culture. This made Norman Wisdom a huge star in Albania, where he is still a pop icon today. Charles Dickens, with his speciality being stories of the downtrodden classes of Victorian Britain, often ranked in the USSR with Tolstoy and Pushkin. However, the downside of Stalin's fascination with George Formby is said to have contributed to Hitler's hatred of our own gormless hero. Still, our lads in Germany loved him, as they did in every theatre of war.

ENSA shows were a real curate's egg. The variety theatre in Britain was in its twilight in the post-war years. The constant trawl for acts – any acts – often carried out by scouts such as Derek Agutter, an officer in the Tank Regiment (whose bouncing baby, born in 1952, Jenny, would grace the silver screen), often produced a few dead fish in the net. Thus homesick squaddies and national-service draftees were frequently subjected to suspect conjurers, dud animal acts and assorted vaudeville routines, many of which ought to have hung up their tap shoes long before Hitler took power.

The Germans during the Third Reich had experienced live entertainment which had been rigidly monitored by Dr Joseph Goebbels' Ministry of Propaganda. Many of the acts which were to appear before British troops in the immediate post-war years – and, to a good number of German civilians, would have been condemned under the Nazis. When it came to radio, however, the crafty Goebbels knew that this medium, over which he was able to exercise a tight control, was a special case. Although all forms of 'race' music, including jazz and swing, were outlawed, he still knew that a diet of National Socialist ideology and Hitler's speeches could hardly unite the nation. 'Broadcasting,' he said, 'should serve to lighten the daily round . . . No one could go around continuously wearing his Sunday best. Broadcasting, a product of its time, must go with the times, and has to be up to date and modern.'[3]

Without absorbing the influences of the world beyond the Reich, German popular music remained frozen in a kind of folksy, sentimental time-warp. However, this didn't stop the occasional international runaway hit record.

Hans Leip had served in the German Infantry in the First World War. In 1915 he wrote a poem which was eventually published 22 years later in his book *Die Hafenorgel*. In 1935, in the Simplizimuss, a Munich restaurant, Leip's poem, set to music by Rudolf Link, was performed by a young cabaret singer using the name Liselott Wilke. Four years passed and with a new melody by Norbert Schultz, Fräulein Wilke made a recording of the song under her new name, Lale Andersen. With its march tempo, by 1941 'Lili Marlene' was to become one of the most popular songs of the Second World War – in fact it was the first German million-selling record. Legend has it that the record had languished, disregarded for some time, until a German officer, Karl-Heinz Reintgen, discovered it in a box and played it on the new Belgrade radio station. The response from soldiers and the public was overwhelming. In contrast to the record's overnight success, Lale Andersen at this time was banned from performing by Goebbels, as she had been 'seeing Jewish friends and other undesirable persons'. Goebbels had no choice but to lift the ban, such was Andersen's popularity with the Wehrmacht. The song was equally popular in the Allied ranks, and soon an English translation written by Tommy Connor had been recorded by Marlene Dietrich, and there was a very popular version by Britain's Anne Shelton.[4]

Many soldiers wondered if there really was a 'Lili Marlene' in real life. Over 250 women have come forward over the years claiming to be Hans Leip's inspiration. However, before he died in 1983, he revealed that there were only two girls involved: a doctor's daughter called Marlene and a girl called Lili he'd met in a greengrocer's.

The influx of new music which accompanied the Allied troops into Germany from 1945 onwards and the opening up of entertainment would influence German pop culture for a generation, producing a genre known as *Deutsche Schlager* (German pop) peculiar to that country. It began with Lale Andersen, (1913–72) and during the 1960s and '70s spawned a stable of artists, many of whom used anglicised stage names to broaden their market appeal. Thus the German Gerd Hollerbach (1943–91) became Roy Black, the Austrian Manfred Nidi-Petz (1931–) is Freddy Quinn, his countryman Peter Neumayer (1926–) is Peter Alexander. Others include Germany's Erna Strube (1944–) who is Joy Fleming, and Margaret Annemarie Batavio, born in the USA in 1948, known as Peggy March.

Goebbels and Hitler would have been horrified, but the folksy, superbly produced recordings of these artists and band leaders such as James Last and Burt Kaempfert sold in their millions and were a soothing balm that helped the German music industry to grow and prosper. Many servicemen of a certain age will remember Petula Clark singing 'Sailor'. This was originally a hit for Germany's Lolita, under the more cumbersome title *'Seemann, deine Heimat ist das Meer'* ('Sailor, your home is the sea') – the ultimate in Deutsche Schlager.

During ENSA's short life, real talent had a chance to spread its wings. Whatever bright new act we were listening to on the radio back home would turn up sooner or later in Germany. It is a remarkable fact that by 1945, ENSA (an acronym regarded by many of its khaki-clad critics to mean 'Every Night Something Awful') in conjunction with the NAAFI, was putting on a staggering 3,000 shows around the world. British forces in Germany were probably luckier than the lads in the Far East, but as one Geordie infantryman commented:

'You couldn't escape the buggers – we had all sorts. It wasn't compulsory to go to shows but you knew they were making the effort so you turned up, and for a lot of the time there was sod all else to do. Mind you, if a turn was rubbish, we'd soon let 'em know!'

A lot of the 'turns' were far from rubbish. Tony Hancock was popular, and at the height of their fame in the 1950s, the Goons – Spike Milligan, Harry Secombe and Peter Sellers being no strangers to service life – often travelled from base to base in Germany. American harmonica star Larry Adler, having been spurned by his own countrymen during the McCarthy witch hunts, was nevertheless accepted and welcomed as an ENSA artist. All the stars who would find lasting fame in the *Carry On* movies, including Kenneth Williams, Sid James and Barbara Windsor, were regular attractions in Germany.

~ Every Night Something Awful ~

Stan Roberts, from the Wirral, was a staff sergeant with REME in Hamburg in 1946.

'It wasn't all work. There was a small open-air swimming pool nearby, and we could visit Hamburg. There was the occasional film show put on locally by the Army Kinema Service and later on we were able to organise dances. In September 1945, Sadler's Wells Opera came to the Garrison Theatre in Hamburg and I was able to see *Madame Butterfly*, *Cosi Fan Tutte* and *La Bohème*. Thanks to the NAAFI and ENSA I was thus able to see my very first operas. In the cast of *Cosi Fan Tutte* I note that the part of the maid was played by Rose Hill, who probably had a far greater audience in the TV show, *'Allo, 'Allo*. The Hamburg Opera House had been burned out in the bombing, but the safety curtain had saved the vast stage area. This stage area was so huge that it was still possible to build a reasonable-sized auditorium on it and still retain a stage area. In May and June 1946 I saw *La Traviata* and *The Marriage of Figaro*, both performed by the Hamburg State Opera Company. We had a concert at our Gasthaus where one of the singers was a fine bass called Karl Otto; however, in *Figaro* he only had the non-singing part of the gardener! The Old Vic Company also visited Hamburg and I saw Ralph Richardson, Laurence Olivier and Sybil Thorndyke in *Richard III*, *Peer Gynt*, and *The Chocolate Soldier*, with all three appearing in each production.

'Radio entertainment was provided by the British Forces Network [BFN] from studios set up in a grand Hamburg concert hall. Here they also gave concerts for the troops. One of the announcers at BFN was Trooper Bob Boyle who went on to become Robin Boyle, a BBC presenter, who eventually presented his own Saturday-afternoon show on BBC Radio 2.'

There was much more to all this itinerant showbusiness than comedy and music hall. Drama was also on the menu. Many shows and plays that had succeeded in the West End often toured Germany. Actors such as John Gielgud and Ralph Richardson did their bit. As for classical music, this was the cultural hub of the genre, the land of Beethoven and Bach. After the rigours and restrictions of war, the great orchestras of Germany began to regroup to shake off the shame of the Nazi era. For the majority of working-class boys from Britain, the thought of attending a symphony concert at home may never have crossed their minds. For Alec Kingsmill in Hamburg, it was all quite an experience:

'There were seven cinemas for British troops, besides the State Opera, the garrison theatre and the concert hall of the BFN. It was in Hamburg that I went to my first symphony concert. On Remembrance Sunday in 1948, I was among the congregation of the BBC's *Sunday Half Hour*, which was broadcast from the Garrison Church. Above all stood the NAAFI – Victory House – reputed to be the best NAAFI in the world. Saturday-afternoon tea, accompanied by a string ensemble, was really rather fine.'

To some, such as Corporal Allen Parker, RASC, of Grimsby, the cinema was a favourite: 'The AKC cinema in Düsseldorf was a favourite trip. We also went to the Düsseldorf Operahaus. I remember seeing Frankie Howerd there – and *Madam Butterfly* (which was boring).'

For Staff Officer Reg Jones, serving with the Royal Armoured Corps, the cultural experience on offer in Germany was both enjoyable and revealing:

'Through the good offices of ENSA we enjoyed a week of the Lydia Kyasht Ballet. On the feast of St Nicholas, the officers and sergeants gave Christmas parties to the local children. It was interesting to see how the German custom differed from ours. St Nicholas arrived with his black pageboy. As each child approached the saint in eager anticipation or in fear and trembling, according to his or her conscience, the good man, who had been briefed by confidential reports by the parents, gave his blessing and a few words of praise or a severe wigging. This was followed by a Christmas dinner very much off the ration, and cartoon films, which the children did not seem to find very funny – except for the violent bits!'

As an organisation, ENSA's life was cut short when it was disbanded shortly after the war, to be replaced by the Combined Services Entertainment Unit (CSE). As we shall see, a lot of talent was still lying dormant in the barracks, where many young men with a variety of skills to offer the entertainment industry would soon realise their potential. Private Adrian Cooper, an 18 year old in the Royal Engineers, soon found a new dimension to his national service:

'Fortunately I did not have to stay at the barracks much longer. A notice went up on the Daily Orders board that the CSE was holding auditions for parts in a forthcoming play. I applied and was given time off to attend at the Hamburg theatre. The play was called *White Cargo* (a drama set in Africa involving a sultry native girl and an English officer who falls for her, thus causing a scandal) and the producer was a civilian, Mac Picton. His job was to produce dramas and comedies with actors and actresses from England, supported by forces personnel. More often than not the West End show would be adapted or tailored to fit the minimal stages on offer at camps in the British Sector of occupied Germany. Military personnel were employed as tour minders, for walk-on parts and stage management duties. The play or show started from Hamburg and toured for three or four weeks. I landed the part of an idiotic new settler who appears in the play's final four minutes, and to my delight the offer included elevation to corporal and escort for the play's tour. In effect, I joined a little group of national servicemen plucked from a diversity of regiments, and we lived in a small hotel beside the Hamburg theatre. It was a fine old building close to the city centre. Our time was spent preparing props and scenery (built and painted by the German theatre staff), rehearsals and arrangements as well as getting to know the cast. They were accommodated in a better hotel on the other side of the theatre. One never knew what shows were coming from London until they arrived. Sometimes it was a West End comedy, a drama, a popular band or a cobbled-together variety show. One, in particular, consisted of two middle-aged Scots comedians, three girl dancers, a female singer, a magician and a contortionist with four musicians to bounce things along. None of the acts knew each other and temperament often overflowed. The order of performance and who had the best dressing room at the theatres or the camps, were bones of contention and we tried to keep the peace. All performers noticeably changed soon after arrival. Their lives transformed from a drab London, with its ever-present rationing, to comfortable accommodation, a free supply of cigarettes, cheap drink and a military escort.'

The contrasting way of life for a performer first visiting Germany must have had a liberating effect. Here was a country that had been devastated by war and where the population was suffering all the grim vicissitudes of a conquered people. Back in Blighty things might not have been quite as harsh, but as history has shown, despite their bitter defeat, the Germans would regain their equilibrium long before Britain's last bombsite was cleared. Rationing in Britain, the country's remaining military and colonial commitments around the globe and a huge financial debt to America made the decade after the war a grey period of struggle and sacrifice. It wasn't a good time to be an actor, musician or performer. Yet here in Germany was an insulated world, ring-fenced by our forces, where the imagined, expected fruits of one's vocation could, for the duration of a tour, become reality. However, as the newly promoted Corporal Cooper goes on to tell us, too much reality could sometimes be a dangerous thing:

'And they were also *paid*. Small wonder that some became difficult, with arrogant behaviour, and worse – that they drank too much or went out looking for young male or female Germans. We even had to cope with transvestites. But there was a certain caution about causing the Entertainments Unit too much trouble – it could mean an immediate return to England. Our concern was the habit of jaunts after dark, which could mean being mugged or even killed, apart from the complaints of affronted Germans to the military authorities. It was a worry and we were only 18 years old and in charge of these worldly-wise artists. My troubles really began when Eric Winstone and his band came out for a tour. One of the saxophone players picked up a woman on his first night in Hamburg and contracted venereal disease. I had to arrange penicillin injections for him at military hospitals for much of the tour and that meant facing the wrath of medical officers and sergeant-majors. They were obliged to give assistance but regarded me with extreme dislike. By the time the Eric Winstone tour ended I was thoroughly fed up but the sax player was cured. By chance I bumped into him many years later at Oxford Circus Underground entrance. He was quite taken aback and begged me not to tell his wife – which was absurd because by then I had forgotten his name and in any case had no idea where he lived. The rest of the band were reasonably well behaved – if one overlooked the heavy drinking and smoking of marijuana. I tried a puff or two, and felt dizzy and nauseous, so that was the end of my incursion into the drugs scene. The music and the songs still linger in my head. If ever I hear "Sabre Dance" being played today I am whisked back to 1948 – I listened to it seven nights a week for three weeks then.'

In many ways, as the post-war years progressed, the quality of the acts improved to reflect the rise of television, the mass marketing of sport and the grip of rock 'n' roll on popular culture. Even today, stars such as Geri Halliwell, Frank Bruno and that arch patriot – the *bête noir* of the politically correct – Jim Davidson, have all combined to keep the worthy tradition of 'entertaining the troops' alive. But the biggest entertainment success in Germany was achieved over the airwaves.

Back in 1945 the pocket-sized transistor radio was still over a decade away from invention. But radio, a powerful weapon in war, was to be just as important in peace. In those frantic months covering the early post-war occupation, the BBC broadcast to the troops in Germany through the Allied Expeditionary Forces Programme (AEFP).

However, following the Allied victory, a decision was taken that this service would be closed down at midnight on 28 July 1945. As the military audience had grown rapidly, something was badly needed to replace it. Fortunately, there was a role model already in existence.

As ever, the Americans, leaders in popular entertainment, had got their own forces' radio act together a couple of years earlier. From their first arrival in Britain in 1942, the numbers of American servicemen grew steadily until, just prior to D-Day in 1944, an estimated 1,700,000 US Airforce and Army personnel were camped throughout the UK. The culture shock for most of them was enormous. Their own country, although conscious of the war, had only experienced it prior to Pearl Harbor through newsreels, radio and newspaper reports.

A massive network of local commercial radio stations covered the USA, all offering a wide variety of music, drama and comedy. Even television, the domain of the rich and the upper-middle classes in the UK, was already common across the Atlantic.

Britain had struggled, battered and bruised, under a punishing war economy, and entertainment, although important for morale, had been way down the nation's list of priorities. To GIs, the British public house was a mysterious, antiquated experience, and the legend of its 'warm beer' has persisted to this day. Standing around the piano singing 'The Old Bull and Bush' may well have been a novelty at first, but to say we were two nations divided by a common language was, in 1942, an understatement. Without a radio service of their own, GIs had to rely on news from home to catch up on baseball and football results. These boys were from the world's entertainment epicentre. They had grown up with the movies, with jazz, the blues, swing, country and bluegrass music. Our sports were a mystery: cricket, soccer and rugby had the poor young Americans scratching their heads. We drank tea, they had coffee. We had odd licensing hours. Our shops were quaint establishments which actually closed early, and on Sundays didn't open at all. All in all, Britain was a pretty place, but it was a far cry from the USA, and the resulting fun to be had via a bar of chocolate, a pack of chewing gum or a pair of nylons would soon lose its exotic appeal.

As morale sank under a tough regime of constant training and the looming thought that death, as it already had done for thousands of Britons, might lie just across the Channel, General Dwight D. Eisenhower, supreme commander, decided to take action.

At 5.45 p.m. on Independence Day 1943, the American Forces Network (AFN), burst onto the airwaves with 'The Star-Spangled Banner'. This was followed by a speech by station chief Brewster Morgan and five hours of material recorded in the US, including the *Bing Crosby Music Hall, The Dinah Shore Show* and *The Edgar Bergen and Charlie McCarthy Show*.[5] The whole broadcast was sent out via telephone lines to five fifty-watt transmitters around the UK from premises loaned by the BBC at 11 Carlos Place, just off London's Grosvenor Square. By D-Day, those five hours of daily radio had increased to nineteen, with the addition of another forty-five transmitters, five of which were installed in Northern Ireland.

For any keen adventurer in popular music, especially in Europe and the UK throughout the 1945–65 period, AFN would prove to be a beacon. But the Brits were not to be outdone.

It was a tall order for the British Army. With just over two months before AEFP went off the air, the commanding officer of the Mobile Teams of 1 Field Broadcasting Unit, Major John McMillan, had to put something in its place. From his base in Lower Saxony at Liebenau he began his mission, accompanied by Lieutenant-Colonel Eric Maschwitz of the Welfare Branch of 21st Army Group, to find a suitable building which would act as a permanent base for a new broadcasting service.[6]

When they arrived in Hamburg, things didn't look promising. The devastation seemed to stretch as far as the eye could see. Maps of the city were studied, and one building seemed to fit the bill: the *Musikhalle*. Maschwitz and McMillan were amazed to discover when they arrived at the Musikhalle that, externally at least, it seemed to have escaped any major damage. Their first task was to get inside and take a look around, yet the caretaker, who had been hiding himself away in the boiler room, was far from keen to open the doors. Eventually, no doubt convinced that he was not about to be hauled off for some form of military interrogation, the frightened old man let the insistent soldiers in.

The Musikhalle was perfect for a studio complex, and the officers immediately 'requisitioned' it in that wonderfully bizarre British fashion, by simply jotting on an army form the legend 'Requisitioned for Army Broadcasting', and signing it 'Bernard L. Montgomery'.[7] With this flimsy piece of paper pinned to the Musikhalle door, the Army now had its very own German version of Broadcasting House. The next problem was finding a suitable transmitter, and converting the interior of the building to make suitable studios available by 29 July – the day they planned to start transmitting.

The transmitter needed to be very powerful if it was to cover the entire British Zone, but there was one suitable for the job in East Frisia: the Norden transmitter. Eleven men were sent to requisition the machine. Unfortunately, Berlin, still geographically and politically out 'in the sticks' would have to wait until the following year before having its own transmitter. Even then the Russians would not agree to allow the installation of land lines to carry the broadcast signal between Hamburg and Berlin, so the Americans helped out by providing an FM link.[8]

McMillan scoured Army units in and around Berlin to find men with the right civvy-street skills to press on with the conversion. Joiners, builders, plumbers and electricians were badly needed. After weeks of hard work, the job was completed with only hours to spare, and seven hours after the last AEFP broadcast at midnight on 28 July 1945, courtesy of the BBC in London, the new service, the BFN, went on air from the Musikhalle.

In those days before television was commonplace, radio was king. It is impossible to overestimate the impact BFN would have over the years in Germany, not only for British servicemen, but for millions of Germans to whom radio, under the Nazis, had been little more than a duplicitous propaganda tool. Now the airwaves had been opened up to an exotic new mix of previously forbidden sounds, and the German civilian population loved it. For the next four decades, along with its American counterpart, AFN, BFN would become an important cultural listening post for generations of post-war Germans, and be remembered by them with some affection as a source of enlightenment. BFN was the place many gained their first grasp of English – and it opened up the golden age of international pop music.

John Saville of Wallasey was a lance corporal in the RASC at Sennelager and Itzehoe between 1952 and '54.

'The radio set in our room at Itzehoe really was "wire-less" and could receive all manner of stations, albeit through a great deal of interference and with a lot of necessary retuning. The main attraction of one station, Radio Luxembourg, was the Top 20 (which would bring Pete Murray to fame) at midnight on Sundays and through that I followed the changing favourites, from January 1953 to July 1954. Hits included Nat King Cole's "Smile Though Your Heart Is Breaking", Lita Rosa singing "How Much Is That Doggy In The Window" (which was soon to appear locally as "*Was Kostet Das Hund In Der Fenster*"), Charlie Chaplin's "Eternally" – the theme from his film *Limelight* and, redolent of Whitsuntide 1954, Doris Day's hits from *Calamity Jane*. Another favourite was the serial, *Dan Dare, Pilot of The Future*, presented, I think, by Ovaltine. In those days, BFN Hamburg's main presenter was Chris Howland, who was a friend of one of our soldiers, Peter Rawlinson, both of them coming from a more rarified background than most of us.

'Chris was succeeded by the radio show *Your Old Uncle Bill*. Re-transmissions to Germany of BBC Light Programme shows included Peter Brough's *Educating Archie* with early appearances by Max Bygraves. *Riders of The Range* was a Western adventure serial with music from The Sons of the Pioneers. We listened a lot to the American's AFN station, the main attraction being the genuine country and western music featuring such giants as Hank Williams. Even today, real country and western takes me back to Itzehoe. When it came to baseball and American football commentaries, however, we hastily retuned.

'Cinema choice was limited, but I recall seeing *Shane* and as getting transport was no problem, we would sometimes visit Hamburg, calling at the Church Army opposite the Hauptbahnhof (the same building is now a top-class hotel) and the AKC Cinema in the Marienstrasse. Today, to see *The Glenn Miller Story* on TV transports me back to Hamburg's AKC, as does Joan Collins' early film where she was shipwrecked on a desert island, with the old song "If You Were The Only Girl In The World" featuring as the soundtrack.'

John Saville's other memories of how he spent his leisure time include the camp library, which included a popular raunchy selection of Hank Jansen novels, a book by Richard Dimbleby entitled *Storm At The Hook*, and an illicit copy of *Lady Chatterley's Lover* – banned in England but printed in English in Denmark – of which 'certain pages were very well-thumbed'.

Apparently, after a two-week stay at the camp by a team from the Royal Navy, *Lady Chatterley* mysteriously vanished. John also recalls rather glumly the eclectic cinematic fare on offer from the Danish Army's cinema, the *Biografen*. 'On one occasion they presented a whole evening of *Mr Magoo* cartoons. We sat through this but I actually felt physically nauseous at the end. As someone commented much later on a similar experience, it was like eating six Curly Wurlies.'

On the broadcasting front, although pop music was to gain a keen following, cultural standards were high. Major McMillan's policy for BFN was every bit as impressive as the BBC's. It included drama, features, light entertainment and music 'of the highest standards'.

The first voice on the air at 7 a.m. on the morning of Sunday, 29 July 1945 was Sergeant Bob Crier. The news followed, and then a music show called *Sunrise Serenade*. It was a bright start to a promising autumn.

One of the cultural fortunes of war is that it places men and women with talent in the path of opportunity. The services have never been strangers to a broad selection of musicians, actors, singers and dancers. Many of the twentieth century's greatest stars, both British and American, had their start in uniform.

Yet Major McMillan knew that many of the soldiers and airmen in Germany would soon be demobbed. Finding good radio announcers, performers and disc jockeys in battle dress would prove more difficult once the troops began marching home. With this in mind he issued a notice that went up on each unit's bulletin board:

> To men who are interested in radio: BFN invites you to write for an audition. Demobilisations have created vacancies on our staff and if you have the necessary qualifications, you stand a very good chance of getting in provided you apply at once. Essential qualities are a sound educational standard, good voice, clear diction, intelligence, initiative and a capacity for work. There is no point applying if you have less than six months' service to run.

This notice was probably the springboard that brought many talented announcers and performers under the BFN umbrella, some of whom went on to become household names. One of the first responses to Major McMillan's plea became in later years one of Britain's finest opera singers, Geraint Evans. Presenters such as Keith Fordyce, Cliff Michelmore and the man who will always be associated with the rise of The Beatles via radio, Brian Matthews, served their early broadcasting apprenticeship with BFN. Amazingly, Brian Matthews can still be heard every Saturday morning on BBC Radio 2, where he presents the ever-popular *Sounds of the '60s*.

Over the decades, BFN's output and quality would rise steadily to match anything put out at home. As public tastes in music, drama and comedy changed, the service reflected these and thus kept servicemen in Germany culturally abreast of every aspect of entertainment, and supplied a broad range of news, sports and live broadcasts that kept them in touch with what was happening in the Army throughout Germany. Today, with the British Forces Broadcasting Service (BFBS), service personnel have a radio and TV network which can match anything modern media has to offer.

As with every major advance for troops abroad, however, broadcasting has its roots in an era of make-do-and-mend innovation where keen and dedicated men and women, often learning as they went, had to contend with more than their fair share of difficulties. If poor young Corporal Cooper had his difficulties with wayward saxophonists, imagine having to tackle the world's finest orchestra – the Berlin Philharmonic. In his excellent history of BFN, Alan Grace, a veteran broadcaster who served with BFN and BFBS around the world for 36 years, tells the story of the first time the great orchestra graced BFN's Musikhalle in Hamburg in 1948 under their conductor Sergiu Celibidache.[9] At a

~ Every Night Something Awful ~

Sunday-morning rehearsal, Corporal Bryan Hodgson of the music department was asked by the orchestra's spokesman to check on catering arrangements for the musicians. Corporal Hodgson had a problem: the Musikhalle canteen could only provide light snacks. The Philharmonic were expecting something far more substantial – a full Sunday lunch in generous German style. Hodgson was then given an ultimatum to 'Feed us or we will not play'.

As the concert was already sold out, this must have raised a real atmosphere of panic. However, the canteen staff went into overdrive and cooked and prepared as much food as they could. The orchestra seemed placated by this, but not maestro Celibidache. He proclaimed that, as his musicians 'weren't getting enough to eat', he would change the running order of the programme. He would bring Tchaikovsky's *Pathétique* forward to before the interval, 'while they still have the physical strength for it'. The live radio broadcast wasn't a problem, as this could be adapted, but programmes for the live audience had already been printed. Such occasions would form part of a steep learning curve for budding battledress broadcasters.

If there was a slightly aloof cultural ambience to BFN's early output, it would soon alter to accommodate the growing demand for popular music. There were always musical temptations on the airwaves as AFN's output of jazz, swing and popular music was, as usual, well ahead of Britain's. So eventually, apart from the afore-mentioned Eric Winstone, more jazz heavyweights were soon gracing the airwaves. Duke Ellington and Tommy Dorsey, as well as Stan Kenton and the great British bandleader, Ted Heath, all gained massive audiences not only among British troops but with the German civilians who simply couldn't get enough of this new and exotic music.

Spend some time in a record shop today in Berlin or Hanover, and you'll find the musical fare available covers every aspect of world music. Everything is on offer, from Romanian gypsy bands to African groups, French chanson and country and western, all rubbing shoulders with the usual international output of Sting, Simply Red and U2.

Browsing in the jazz and blues section in a shop in Bielefeld, I stood next to an elderly man who was avidly studying the works of Count Basie and Duke Ellington. With the jump and jive of Louis Jordan throbbing through the store's hi-fi system, it was impossible not to strike up a conversation. The jazz fan was Erich Kessler, who, as a teenager in Cologne, was one of the many young Germans who had longed for an outlet for his enthusiasms.

'We always knew that one day we could hear jazz and not have to do it in secret. With BFN and AFN playing so much great music we soon caught up on our musical education and before long some of us began to form our own little jazz clubs. It was difficult to afford records, so those of us who had bought something new would bring it along and we'd have a fine session over a few beers. It was also great when rock 'n' roll came out. The Americans played lots of stuff in the '50s by Louis Jordan and we often heard Cab Calloway. Eventually we heard Chuck Berry and Little Richard and by that time there was no turning back!'

Music has charms to soothe the savage breast and, occasionally, ruffle it. One of BFN's contributions to this burgeoning scene was a regular show presented by Derek Jones, *1600 Club*.[10]

Jones once received a postcard from a trio of Army clerks requesting a favourite by Peggy Lee, 'Don't Smoke In Bed', which they asked to be dedicated to a certain Charlie 'Fuzzy Bristle' Britton. The request was duly played, and the dedication made – but with significant repercussions. The following day, the phone lines from BAOR went into meltdown. Apparently, 'Fuzzy Bristle' was a BAOR CO, who had banned smoking in bed following a fire in a barracks. BFN's station director had no option but to issue the statement: 'Unfortunate repercussions in official circles mean that, in future, no requests can be played unless a rank is given.'

For some soldiers, the Army was to be a launch pad for an even better career. Today one of country and western's most popular artists, voted three times the nation's favourite by the British Country And Western Association, Birkenhead's Charlie Landsborough owes much to his time spent in Germany.

In the mid '50s Charlie was bored with his life on Merseyside and envied the travels enjoyed by his brothers in the merchant navy. He thought the Royal Navy might be a good choice, but things turned out differently when he went to join up.

'Finding the Navy office closed, I joined the Army without informing any of my family. My sisters were in tears, but armed with my guitar and a DA hairstyle I set off to Wales to do my training. I then applied for a posting in Hong Kong and with typical Army logic I found myself in West Germany. I made many great friends (some of whom I meet up with on my travels) and started to play in bands with such exotic names as the Rockavons and The Onions.

'One abiding memory of my Army days was the Cuban Missile Crisis. Being only 30 miles from the border, I was convinced that within a short space of time I would be dead. After going into NATO camps I found there, the scene was one of frenzied activity. When I got back to our camp, what did I find? Our lads were padding around polishing floors and locker knobs for an inspection the next day. Was I relieved when those Russian vessels turned around!

'After four enjoyable years I grew a little bored and bought myself out. My Army record states that I am "intelligent, reliable and a good runner"! Not a very distinguished career, eh? Still I had learned German and how to drink with the Scottish, the Irish and the Geordies, without falling over.'

Before the birth of rock 'n' roll there was no such animal as a 'teenager'. The 'age of maturity' was 21 and during those years between leaving school and maturing, the young were simply expected to be well-behaved, scaled-down versions of their elders. The idea of the teenager grew in the late 1950s out of the new marketing science that would become known as consumerism. As ever in the Army, youthfulness was not of singular importance. If one was old enough to volunteer or be called up, and had passed the medical, then you were a soldier and that was that, and at 18, you could legally sink a few pints in the NAAFI. In general, young men are fit men and fitness is the first requirement of any fighting force.

Apart from the defence of the Realm, for soldiers in Germany and elsewhere the whole Army experience had an additional bonus: it would 'make a man of you'. So for the older population in the 1950s, those who had fought a war to a soothing background of Vera Lynn, Glenn Miller and George Formby, the arrival of rock 'n' roll music, with its new, seemingly impenetrable 'youth' culture and rebellious stance, was an unprecedented break with tradition. With the war almost a decade and a half behind them, young national service conscripts, still babes in arms when their fathers had struggled home from Dunkirk, often found their enforced two years of military discipline hard to take in those two crucial years before official maturity. When it came to this new cultural sedition, no doubt the older British population had the Yanks to blame. The unifying power in wartime of Glenn Miller and the Andrews Sisters was one thing, but as AFN Europe continued to broadcast America's bestselling records during the 1950s, an infectious, more raucous new sound was being picked up on radios throughout Germany, and, indeed, being received by the more adventurous dial-twiddler in the UK. It is interesting to compare the ten most requested records on the AFN in 1944, just a year following the station's founding, with those on BFN a decade later. The ten most requested songs on AFN's 1st anniversary, July 1944, were:[11]

1. 'Long Ago And Far Away' by Dick Haymes and Helen Forrest
2. 'I'll Be Seeing You' by Bing Crosby
3. 'I Love You' by Bing Crosby
4. 'I'll Get By' by Harry James Orchestra
5. 'Amor' by Bing Crosby
6. 'I'll Walk Alone' by Dinah Shore
7. 'It Had To Be You' by Dick Haymes and Helen Forrest
8. 'San Fernando Valley' by Bing Crosby
9. 'Besame Mucho' by Jimmy Dorsey Orchestra
10. 'Trolley Song' by Judy Garland

In the immediate aftermath of the D-Day landings, the AFN broadcasting crews had moved with the troops and theirs was a task far removed from the potential showbiz glamour one could expect as a disc jockey in later years. In fact, this was a dangerous job. Broadcasting close to the front from mobile units, they were bombarded daily. The US 7th Army's Sergeant Jim McNally lost his life in a raid, to become AFN's first casualty, a tragedy repeated a short while after when Sergeant Pete Parrish, an AFN correspondent, was killed as he accompanied paratroopers into France. One will notice a certain poignancy in these Top 10 songs, too. This has much to do with war. The homesick men who made those tunes their favourites often had little hope of survival, so titles such as 'I'll Be Seeing You', 'I'll Get By' and 'I'll Walk Alone' come as no surprise.

Just over a decade later, in October 1955, the Top 10 records the British Army were listening to in Germany tell a different story:[12]

1. 'The Man from Laramie' by Jimmy Young
2. 'Blue Star (The "Medic" Theme)' by Cyril Stapleton

3. 'Yellow Rose Of Texas' by Mitch Miller
4. 'Everywhere' by David Whitfield
5. 'Rose Marie' by Slim Whitman
6. 'Cool Water' by Frankie Laine
7. 'The Breeze and I' by Caterina Valente
8. 'Rock Around the Clock' by Bill Haley & The Comets
9. 'Hey There' by Johnnie Ray
10. 'Hernando's Hideaway' by The Johnson Brothers

The rude intruder and harbinger of a new age of loose living, Bill Haley, is there at No. 8. Like the British Army in Germany, Jimmy Young would still be performing a service to the nation as a broadcaster four decades later, and David Whitfield would continue to inflict his strained tenor onto BAOR audiences until his career fizzled out in the mid-'60s.

As a new kind of popular culture took over the music world, it fortunately coincided with the approach of the end of national service. Some of the young men who managed not to get caught up in the net of conscription could still find themselves in Germany on a totally different mission. Quite a number of BAOR soldiers seeking an illicit thrill as the decade of peace and love opened up donned their civvies and headed into Hamburg. It was there, not far from the infamous Reeperbahn, that something was about to happen which would change the face of pop music. John Lennon and Paul McCartney, with drummer Pete Best and Stu Sutcliffe on bass, arrived in Hamburg in August 1960 to begin their first residency in the Indra Club. The area around the Indra was infamous for its sex clubs, but it was in this concentrated patchwork of streets that the Germans were absorbing the new phenomenon called rock 'n' roll. Following Stu Sutcliffe's death in April 1962, with the young George Harrison in the line-up, still under contract to the German entrepreneur Bruno Koschmider, they moved to a different venue, the Top Ten Club. At this stage in their career in Germany The Beatles were known as 'The Beat Brothers'. (The word 'Beatles' didn't translate well into German – it referred to the male sex organ.) The rest, of course, is history, but those early days serve to remind us of how our cultural landscape was influenced by the German connection.

It would be easy to simply wallow in the early nostalgia

surrounding all the legendary performers who have done their bit for our troops in Germany, but over the years, especially in the field of broadcasting, this sterling work has continued and the quality and content of radio broadcasts has been scrupulously maintained. The German element in the careers of many famous BBC names has always figured largely. To personalities such as Raymond Baxter, Keith Fordyce, Jean Metcalfe, Nigel Davenport, Bill Crozier, David Hamilton and many others, the highways and by-ways of Germany were as familiar as they were to our Army. BFN provided a varied and often adventurous mirror service to the BBC we all know and love. Many of the popular radio shows we were listening to back home were equally available in Germany. Apart from topical output such as *Does The Team Think*, the British squaddie was also treated to *The Archers* and the stars, such as Frankie Howerd, Frankie Vaughan and Cliff Richard kept on coming. In addition, such giants as Orson Welles, who at the height of his fame following his film *The Third Man*, still found time to talk to BFN listeners about movie-making. Welles had another treat in store for listeners when his own radio repertory company starred in BFN's *Radio Playhouse* series with some stirring Shakespeare.

But perhaps one of the most memorable innovations of this time was the establishment of *Two Way Family Favourites*. This was a show which became as traditional on Sundays as roast beef and Yorkshire pudding. At its peak it had an audience of 16 million, and the opening announcement by Jean Metcalfe: 'The time in Britain is twelve noon, in Germany it's one o'clock, but home and away it's time for *Two Way Family Favourites*,' followed by the Andre Kostalanetz signature tune, 'With A Song In My Heart', always promised a unifying hour of reasonable records, messages to and from servicemen far away, plus some light-hearted banter.

The show had its genesis during wartime when it was known as *Forces Favourites*. Once it became *Family Favourites*, the BBC, in true 'Auntie' style, decided that the moral content might be raised a little. So out went the jazz records, and there was to be no mention of fiancées or girlfriends. This was a mums', dads', sons' and daughters' event. Eventually, over the years, as society became less straitlaced, the programme loosened up a little, even to the point where the odd rock 'n' roll record or the nasal twang of Lonnie Donegan was allowed to creep in. For two presenters in particular, *Family Favourites* was to do far more than bring families together.

Jean Metcalfe was already engaged, but when her co-presenter Derek Jones was replaced one week in Hamburg by a man called Cliff Michelmore, the cross-channel telephone banter took on a flirtatious note. When Michelmore came to London to meet Jean Metcalfe, the chemistry they'd experienced over the airwaves proved to be just as electric in a face-to-face situation. Jean's engagement fizzled out and, although any suggestion of an on-air romance was taboo during broadcasts, in 1950 Cliff Michelmore married Jean Metcalfe.

With an estimated weekly audience of around 12 million, Jean had a huge army of fans in Britain and Germany. To her surprise, when one of them passed away, the grateful listener left Jean the then princely sum of £3,000. This came in very handy for the Michelmores when buying their family home.

Family Favourites probably did more to familiarise the British public with the geography of Germany than any atlas. With Hamburg, Bremen, Hanover, Berlin, Sennelager and Mönchengladbach being mentioned every week, we soon began to accept that Germany wasn't as far away as we'd thought.

By the 1970s BFN had become BFBS – the British Forces Broadcasting Service. Television was now part of the output, and in 1977 the decision was made to continue broadcasting through the night. New presenters passed through, for instance, Sarah Kennedy, who had come from BFBS in Singapore to join the team now based in Cologne. Perhaps many old soldiers will be reminded of their time in Germany when they tune in to Sarah's early morning show on Radio 2 from Monday to Friday each week.

The days of ENSA were perhaps short, but their legacy is a huge one. Today, the Services Sound and Vision Corporation (SSVC) is a registered charity set up to entertain and inform Britain's armed forces around the globe. It encompasses radio, television, live entertainment, retailing and cinemas, and has a huge film archive of training material held by the British Defence Film Library, containing military footage going back over three decades.

BFBS Radio offers a service today that Major McMillan, back at the old Musikhalle in Hamburg, could have only dreamed of. The old 'Auntie' stuffiness of the BBC is long gone. Forces radio in Germany today offers its own version of Radio 1, especially tailored to entertain the younger soldier, and a broad mix of topical discussion, sport and classical music through BFBS Radio 2. BFBS TV broadcasts the best of UK television around the clock. The old Army Kinema Corporation has come a long way, too. SSVC now has 12 state-of-the-art cinemas in Germany alone. As for the CSE arm of SSVC, the show still goes on. Today the military have a new forces' sweetheart. Once it was Vera Lynn – now it's the vivacious and glamorous actress, dancer and singer Claire Sweeney. CSE puts on around 125 shows per year, covering everything from stand-up comedy to the Bee Gees and girl groups like Liberty X and ex-Spice Girl Geri Halliwell.

The old Musikhalle still stands, but in a modern, bustling Hamburg and a vastly changed Germany than that shattered landscape of 1945. For the men, women and children who found themselves stationed in the land of their erstwhile enemy, those early strains of music and laughter were all part of the healing process. Alongside the grief, war produces some odd consequences. To paraphrase the old saying, in Army terms, there's certainly no business like military showbusiness.

9

Off-Duty

> There was always the good old NAAFI to help out when you
> were feeling down. It was the centre of everything. There's
> nothing like a cup of tea and a wad to clear your head after
> an exercise, or a day being bawled at by some uncouth RSM.
> Private George Enderby, Royal Artillery

It's an official Army fact that on average, each British soldier
stationed in Germany gets through one pack of Tesco sausages every
week.

But that's not all – there are 2,000 Tesco brands alone on sale there
to British troops in a range of shops, from small Express stores to the
Max stores that stock a huge range of foods and goods, all available
at a fraction of the price you would pay at home. You can get a cool
pint of Guinness or a sausage buttie at any NAAFI Junior Ranks
Club throughout Germany. And if you don't want to mix it with the
Germans, you need go no further than your own barracks to have a
good social night in.

Three organisations were often both a spiritual and a practical
refuge for the young soldier far away from home in a strange
country.

The NAAFI has a proud tradition going back to its founding in
1921, although its roots can be traced to the trenches of the Great
War. Soldiers continue to hold the NAAFI in affection. This
dedicated body of men and women were always on hand during
some of the toughest campaigns of the twentieth century, providing
Britain's armed forces around the world with rest, refreshment and,
through their excellent shops, comforting retail reminders of life
back home. At the height of the Second World War the NAAFI

employed 110,000 people; by 1955 that figure was down to 30,000, but the organisation was no less efficient and still turned in a profit.

The Women's Voluntary Service (WVS, later to be graced with the appellation 'Royal' to become the WRVS), often worked closely around the clock with the NAAFI to provide a broad range of services, including various entertainments and libraries.

Another fine establishment, TOC H, came into being during the strife of the First World War. It began in a house in a Belgian town called Poperinge, not far from the front-line trenches, an oasis of peace for weary soldiers that became known as Talbot House, the initials of the building, in Army telephone jargon, giving TOC H its distinctive name. In this house a young Army chaplain, the Reverend 'Tubby' Clayton, set up a rest-care centre for soldiers. Unusually for that time, it was open to all ranks. Many who visited gained a deeper understanding of other people, and of their own faith. In Germany, especially in the early post-war years, TOC H, like the NAAFI, provided many happy occasions and memorable periods of leave for soldiers.

These organisations come up regularly in memoirs and conversations and are remembered fondly.

TOC H's 'Four Points Of The Compass' were:

1. Friendship: to love widely.
2. Service: to build bravely.
3. Fair-mindedness: to think fairly.
4. The Kingdom of God: to witness humbly.

TOC H's universal symbol has always been a burning lamp, so it is hardly surprising that one of the best insults a sergeant-major could make against a hapless squaddie whose intelligence was in question was 'You're as dim as a TOC H lamp!', a statement any worker of a certain age might be familiar with from the past few decades.

Every soldier, wife or child contributing to this book has something to say about the NAAFI. In a foreign setting this 'service to the services' provided a comforting bond to our home culture, where that beverage which built an empire – tea – was brewed by the gallon and corned-beef sandwiches, sticky buns and that stalwart traditional favourite, the full English breakfast, brought back memories of the kitchen or parlour at home. As British Railways were to civilians before privatisation (and looking back, the old BR years seem a halcyon age now), the NAAFI was often the brunt of a multitude of jokes among servicemen. Yet for its morale-boosting properties alone, one could argue that it has been just as important a factor in campaigning as any tank, rifle or artillery piece.

Feeding the troops in Germany was a challenge the NAAFI took on with all its customary confidence. In those immediate post-war years no one could have predicted that half a century later Britain would still have its armed forces stationed throughout the country, or that the NAAFI would need to expand its range of services so widely to encompass the broad changes in British society and the growth of consumerism. But expand it did, and today it has been transformed into a sophisticated marketing operation that can match anything on the UK's high streets.

In the early nineteenth century, the feeding of soldiers was a somewhat shoddy affair, prone to all kinds of corruption. In Wellington's time a soldier had two meals per day. Breakfast was at 7.30 a.m. and dinner at 12.30 p.m. After that midday meal the soldier had a long wait of 19 hours before his next official meal. The food was, to say the least, rubbish. Meat was often rotten and what bread there was would be literally alive with weevils. With such hunger stalking the ranks, it was hardly surprising that the majority of soldiers indulged in looting. Living off the land became common practice, providing, of course, an army was progressing over territory where foraging was possible. Anything that moved or grew became eligible for the soldier's cooking pot. As ever, commercial opportunism entered the field in the form of the Sutlers.

The Sutler could be vaguely deemed to be the early precursor of the NAAFI, although these avaricious tradesmen who followed the Army's campaigns with their wagons, selling a variety of over-priced and suspect food and drink, hardly had the fighting prowess of the British Army at heart.[1] The Sutlers sold far more alcohol than they did food, the effect of which, on an empty stomach, leaves one wondering how our Army managed to be as successful as it was during its historic campaigns throughout Europe. It would be wrong to tar all Sutlers with the same brush, as without them things could have been much worse. Theirs was an age before cold storage and refrigeration, and the sheer logistics of carrying large amounts of meat and flour across continents was a challenge. It was not uncommon for a British regiment to enter the field with a herd of cattle and several wagonloads of live chickens in tow.

Our military leaders such as Nelson, Wellington and Marlborough were far from happy with the situation. Wellington and Marlborough put a stop to looting and Nelson did his best to secure a bounty for his sailors. With an average working life expectancy in those days of 45, and with the well-heeled officer class living a comparative life of luxury on private incomes, the poor foot soldier was lucky that at least someone at the top realised how grim his life was.

Even so, there were those behind the scenes in the Army's higher echelon who saw, in the Sutlers, a chance for further profit for the State. When the problem of alcohol being smuggled into barracks began to grow, canteens supplying booze were officially allowed to be set up in barracks yards. Before long, the body that oversaw the running of the barracks, the Board of Ordnance, turned these ad-hoc off-licences into a kind of franchise and put out tenders. Based on the number of soldiers in a barracks, the successful contractors then paid fees to the Board, known as 'privilege money'.

The turning point that forced the plight of the British soldier into the public's conscience was the Crimean campaign (1853–56).

Just as the Crimean War was about to break out, the government decided that, at long last, a soldier would be allowed a third meal in addition to their daily breakfast and dinner. At the time this decision was made, the soldier's official ration was one pound of bread and three quarters of a pound of meat per day. To boil the meat two copper cauldrons were provided for each barracks. But this seemingly generous act was anything but, as the soldier had to pay for his victuals with 50 per cent of his 7 shillings weekly wage.[2] He was also charged an extra 1s 10d for 'laundry and general maintenance', leaving him with the princely sum of less than 3d per day to spend.

The Crimean War was a war of staggering incompetence that was brought home by the fact that for the first time the British public could actually read about it via W.H. Russell's regular reports in *The Times*. Russell was the first man to be called a 'war correspondent' and the new craze for photography saw Roger Fenton out with the troops with his cameras, sending back many pictures of men in the field. However, few if any photographs showed men in action at the front and many of Fenton's efforts were blatantly used by the government for propaganda purposes. Yet these factors, together with the high profile of Florence Nightingale, all served to highlight the grim conditions British soldiers were experiencing. A good, stable diet is crucial in any occupation to maintain health and efficiency, and the tragic casualty figures of the Crimean War told an unavoidable truth: 4,600 men died in battle and 13,000 were wounded, while 17,500 died of disease, exposure and malnutrition.[3]

With real news arriving back in England every week the public began to sit up and take notice. The resulting publicity forced changes in military attitudes, the first of which was the transfer from the Treasury of the military department that supplied food to the troops, the Commissariat, to the War Department. This department went into action and began to set up its own bakeries and butchery departments and started to provide general groceries for British troops serving abroad.[4] By 1863 a 'canteen committee' supervised the establishment of regimental canteens, which by now had become a military responsibility.

As the twentieth century dawned, in 1900 the Canteen and Mess Society had an annual turnover of about £250,000. The canteens became known as regimental institutes, but the old mentality of making a shady profit from soldiers still engendered an atmosphere of corruption, which reached scandalous proportions during 1913 and '14. Bribery to firms approved by the War Office instigated a major inquiry. On the investigative committee sat one Mr R. Burbridge, who, during the Second World War, would figure largely in the management of the NAAFI.

It was in 1921 that the NAAFI, as we have come to know it, came into existence. Its task was to provide leisure and retail services to the British Armed Forces and their families wherever they were stationed.

Of the postings abroad, Germany was undoubtedly the best served by this comprehensive service. The Army of the Rhine owed much to the NAAFI, which supplied officers' messes, became adept at requisitioning German hotels to accommodate its staff, and at one time even ran two ships on the Rhine to provide rest and recreation for troops. With its headquarters based in Cologne, it was also to pay attention to the plight of the hard-pressed German civilian.

In the immediate post-war period, the NAAFI often supplied large quantities of food and beer to the civilian population, as well as employing many former German prisoners of war, who at one time had been interned at London's Alexandra Palace.

The end of the Second World War saw an increase in commitment by the NAAFI throughout occupied Germany. When the German prison camps were finally opened up, British prisoners going home would receive special NAAFI packs, and their staggered journey back to Britain would be pleasantly punctuated by visits to various clubs and canteens along the route. The NAAFI was also highly mobile and able to move with the troops on their exercises in Germany. With an astute eye and ear for what was happening in civilian society, they kept step with such small but crucial innovations as the installation of vending machines and even jukeboxes. The early appearance of vending machines was more to do with a shortage of suitable staff rather than adventurous retailing, but it helped to put the NAAFI in Germany way ahead of most retailing outlets in civvy street. Although popular in America, the notion of self-service, which we take for granted today in our supermarket culture, was still largely undeveloped in Britain. Yet as early as 1953, at RAF Kabritt in Egypt, the NAAFI had opened its first self-service store. They soon introduced self-service to Germany, first at Bielefeld and soon throughout the British zone.

Progressive though all this was, there were still several confusing and antiquated anomalies to overcome. One was connected with cleaning NAAFI premises. If one sometimes wonders where the Goons got their plot-lines from, then look no further than Queen's Regulations. Although the Army provided them with their canteen premises, military regulations dictated that the soldiers should clean the canteen up to the counter, with the area behind the counter becoming NAAFI staff's responsibility. If a NAAFI was housed in a tall building with walls more than twelve feet high, lunacy ruled supreme. Regulations dictated that the NAAFI staff had to clean the first eight foot of wall, and everything above twelve feet upwards was the unit's responsibility. This of course left a four-foot gap of wall between the eight-foot and twelve-foot mark – in cleaning terms, an official 'no man's land'.[5] Even as late as 1956 only officers could buy wine in the NAAFI – with junior ranks restricted to beer only. No doubt this beverage restriction wouldn't bother many soldiers. Several years earlier, in 1948, there had been a suggestion that the NAAFI might operate wine bars. One can imagine the response of male squaddies, but it was the female officer class who opposed such an urbane development. Their somewhat motherly argument was that wine bars might loosen up the behaviour of the junior female ranks and result in their parents being worried. Apparently, once the wine bars did finally get the green light to open, lewd and lascivious behaviour amongst 'the gels' did not in fact raise its ugly head and moral decline in the ranks was avoided.

A decade after the end of the Second World War, with the new West German Federal Republic government now in place, the Allied forces in Germany could no longer be regarded as an army of occupation. Since entering Germany in 1945, British soldiers had enjoyed certain financial advantages which, by small fiscal accidents of history, had given them a reasonable leeway in spending their wages. Although the old black-market days had receded, all spending by squaddies in the NAAFI had been done with baffs. In 1948 the new Deutschmark had replaced the old Reichsmark and the NAAFI, always an astute organisation in getting the best deal, was enjoying a generous preferential rate when buying in local goods and services at 40 Deutschmarks to the pound. When trading with an army of occupation perhaps such deals might seem reasonable, but by 1955 Germany had regained some political dignity and an attitude of economic independence. The French, the Americans and the British were all welcome as members of the NATO alliance. They were a valuable and necessary presence in the face of the unpredictable Soviets. But the British Army was no longer one of occupation. Other than in Berlin, the '40 Deutschmarks equals 1 pound' arrangement was withdrawn, leaving the NAAFI to wrestle with a new rate of 11.76 Deutschmarks to the pound. This transitional period was very difficult, as everything would now cost up to four times as much. Not only the goods in their stores had to go up, but all the costs of local services, rents, etc., which ultimately meant that the NAAFI's management had to increase wages. Eventually, once the British realised that Germany was a nation on the same economic footing as themselves, both the NAAFI and its customers got to grips with the new economic reality.

The NAAFI was always the place to gather and a centre for a degree of comfort. There was an added attraction in Germany, too – quite often the civilian girls behind the counter turned the meagre pleasure of having a drink or a sandwich into something more promising. You couldn't get everything in the NAAFI, but all roads seemed to lead there in the end, and all kinds of drama occurred within its walls.

Iain Leggatt of Angus, Scotland was based in the RASC in Germany from 1957 to '58.

'I had little time for girlfriends, although as I had made one Lotte Kellner rich by buying all the Frankie Laine LPs, EPs and both 78 rpm and 45 rpm singles, from the record shop she managed in the civilian shopping area of Rheindahlen, she invited me home for dinner on a number of occasions. But not only was she married, her husband was always present as well, so I don't think she counts. However, I did go out with SACW [Senior Aircraftswoman] Marsha Hunt for a week or two . . . no, a week. I made the mistake of bringing Marsha into the exclusively Army-used NAAFI Club's snack bar and restaurant for egg and chips one evening. Two toughie WRAC drivers told her in no uncertain terms to "fog off" from their pitch and return in a swift and Brylcreem style of movement back to her own rat-run. Poor Marsha was terrified into compliance mid-egg but I think I beat her to the exit.

'Sticking with the Army for safety, then, I also went out with Corporal Rita Gaffney (my Irish "older woman" – she was 24, I was a 19-year-old Lance Jack) for a few dates.

'The love of my life in Germany, however, was lovely, dark-haired Annaliese Roepke. Liese and her older sister, Magdalena, worked in the main NAAFI club and I had known them both since my arrival in Germany. The sisters had German men-friends and had never been known to associate with common soldiery, so I was quite surprised and absolutely delighted when Annaliese finally agreed to one of my almost daily requests for a date. Our work patterns conflicted more than they coincided, but we were able to get out together a fair bit. I was head over heels and besotted with *meine niedlich fräulein* (my pretty young lady).

'In late October 1957, a month or so after we had started going out together, Liese was on holiday in the American Occupied Zone, visiting her parents who lived in Würzburg.

'I casually walked into the NAAFI snack bar one afternoon for a sustaining cheese roll and a mug of tea before going to take my shift in the SMC and Liese's sister, Magda, broke the news to me that Liese had been killed in a train crash. Liese would have been 19 that Christmas. Totally disbelieving at first, I fell into a state of shellshock which gripped me for days. Hugh Smith, from the SMC's daytime staff, proved a tower of strength by getting himself temporarily attached to my shift, helping me to cope with my work and quite literally getting me going again. November may have only 30 days, but in 1957 I found it to be a very long month.'

There was far more to the NAAFI than eggs, chips, beer, bacon butties and tea. Over the years in Germany the level of sophistication in the service rose rapidly and many new marketing techniques were employed. When the Rhine Army held its annual horse show, NAAFI did the catering. By the autumn of 1954 it was capable of such logistical triumphs as keeping 137,000 NATO troops on manoeuvres fed and watered in the field from no less than 33 mobile canteens.

For the first ten years following the end of the Second World War, the organisation had its HQ at Bad Salzuflen, with its main warehousing facility for distribution based in Hamburg.

When BAOR's new HQ opened up at Rheindahlen (Mönchengladbach), the NAAFI also relocated, moving the Hamburg operation down to Waldniel. Higher management were fortunate enough to be housed in a series of requisitioned suburban dwellings, an area that soon earned the title 'NAAFI Alley'. By this time there were around 400 clubs, stores and canteens to be supplied throughout the British Zone. The German workers employed by NAAFI, numbering over 450 at Waldniel, were usually sent over to the UK for training at the NAAFI facility at Totteridge. However, they soon grew too big even for Waldniel and a further move took them to an impressive new centre of operations at Krefeld.

Krefeld was more than just 'NAAFI Alley' – it became more like a bustling, commercial British precinct, with its own bakery, mineral-water bottling plant, power station, garages, workshops and a hostel for the staff. It was also at this time that the NAAFI, long before any other businesses took the plunge, invested in an early computer system for its accounts department.

It was easy for the local Krefelders to see that this was Kleine England on their doorsteps, separated off from Germany and ringed around with an impregnable, high security fence.

Apart from self-service, flexible opening hours and vending machines, the NAAFI was one of the pioneers in offering credit terms for soldiers, which was a boon to service wives who rushed to buy washing machines and other household appliances at competitive rates.

In West Germany, as the 1960s progressed, the NAAFI's annual turnover had reached a healthy £26 million. The married portion of the British armed forces in Germany represented around 25,000 families. These families shopped regularly in the 70 NAAFI stores around Germany. In Rheindahlen alone, the NAAFI supermarket had an annual turnover of £1.5 million.

With the post-war austerity years long gone and rationing at home just a pale memory, the variety of goods and services on offer from the NAAFI covered everything a British family might need or want: cars on hire purchase, car insurance, caravans, TV sets, radios and camping equipment. Ladies' fashions were not forgotten, either. A constant convoy of trucks trundled in and out of the Krefeld base, bringing in up to 100 tons of new goods and supplies each day.

Britain's recent brush with foot-and-mouth disease had a precedent in 1968. Then, as in the 1990s, Germany placed a ban on British livestock and all meat products from the UK. For a while it seemed that one of our squaddies' favourite delicacies was under threat – the humble British sausage. Despite the perceived superiority of the traditional European sausage (which often contains real meat), the NAAFI deemed it necessary to ensure that this looming gap in military cuisine was dealt with quickly. British banger experts were brought over from the UK to brief both German and Danish sausage makers, as ever keen to do NAAFI business, on the piquant peculiarities of the Army's favourite. No doubt much rusk, seasoning and cereal crossed the Channel that year.

In the 1980s Margaret Thatcher had her eye on the NAAFI for privatisation. Due to the way the NAAFI was founded – as a kind of co-operative – she was informed that this sterling organisation didn't actually 'belong' to the government, and therefore it wasn't hers to sell.

Today's NAAFI, led by its chief executive Chris Reilly, is a big, successful business. Its profits for the year 2001–02 were £500,000. This represented a substantial improvement in the company's performance. Still, the Army is the biggest customer. Of that half-million-pound profit, £275,046 came from the Army, £132,938 from the RAF, and £92,016 from the Navy.

Perhaps modern British soldiers, with a wide choice of consumer outlets and activities available in an ultra-modern society like Germany, may take the old NAAFI a little for granted. Yet to each new generation of fighting men the canteen seems to have always been there: in Iraq, Kosovo, the Falklands, it's always been a constant fixture somewhere not far off from the action. It seems a long, long way from the grim days of foraging, looting and the old Sutler's wagons. So it's a comforting thought that in the twenty-first century, from Rheindahlen to Sennelager, should soldiers feel the need for that comforting old British institution, 'a cup of tea and a bun', then they'll know where to go.

When it comes to sporting activities, the British Army in Germany has always provided a choice second to none. Even among servicemen, who are in the main young and often very competitive, not every man is keen to get onto the pitch on a cold winter afternoon. Sport, as in civvy street, isn't everyone's cup of tea, but in general, Army life offers much more sporting opportunity than most occupations.

Corporal Mike Robinson of the Royal Artillery was based in Sennelager from 1979 to '82.

'Thank God we had television in our day in Germany – at least we could follow football. I suppose the old lads early on listened to it on the radio, but it's not the same. But we always had good facilities for sport in the Army, and I pitied the blokes who weren't sporty – all they had left was beer and women . . .'

For an adventurous, single young man, the idea of yomping around the German countryside in a Challenger or a Warrior tank might in itself satisfy all the competitive needs of the youthful spirit. Working out real battle plans in the computer room at Sennelager beats any games console ever invented. To the interested outsider, it would seem that it must be hard to be bored in the Army, but many young soldiers often feel so. Barracks life for the 'singlies' holds far fewer comforts than those of the married soldier, yet things have improved much over the years. Sport and social recreation have always been a big part of Army life. The former fits in well with the rigorous fitness regime, and the latter, in a country possessing some of the world's finest beer, is invaluable for loosening up after a tough week on the ranges or a long, involved exercise. Sports, keep-fit, mountaineering, swimming, even flower arranging and amateur dramatics (the latter two probably more subscribed to in married quarters), have all been common on German bases for years. There has always been an inventive mind somewhere in the chain of command capable of coming up with something new to while away any time deemed 'spare'. The following article appeared in the British Army's newspaper *Keynotes* in 1958:[6]

> Divisional Headquarters, no doubt having decided that its staff is becoming far too chair-bound these days, has started a series of initiative tests to be undertaken by teams of soldiers from its numbers. The plan is that every Tuesday a team of three soldiers leaves Tunis Barracks heading for some objective in the misty distance. No tricks are played on them, they have money, haversack rations and a form printed both in German and English explaining their predicament and tasks. But they are literally on their own.
>
> The first team, composed of Sapper Nicholson, RE, Trooper Retallack, 3 DG, and Craftsman Collins, REME, left at ten on the morning of Tuesday the 19th August, in search of the signature of an AFN Munich announcer, a picture postcard of the Oberammergau, and the official stamp of the Austro-German frontier. The account of their '*Selbständigkeitsprüfung*' goes as follows;
>
> 'From Minden to Rinteln we had two German cars and from there to Weser Bridge, an REME Champ. Here, as the weather was quite warm, we made a short pause for a "Coke". Then on to Kassel in a Volks Bulliwagen, where however we had to walk right through the town and past the autobahn entries. By this time it was dark, we were tired, hungry and thirsty after our 18 kilometre walk and therefore when a lonely barn loomed up, we made camp and had a good night's sleep.
>
> 'By seven o'clock the next morning we were once more on the move and reached Bad Hershfeld by 10.30 that night by way of a series of lifts. Here we met a Diesel driver who offered us a lift to Karlstadt, where he left us at about 2.30 am. We spent quite a comfortable night in a cornfield protected from the wind by two stooks. After a cold

breakfast we were once again on the move by seven o'clock. Further lifts from German civilians and an American Army three tonner took us through Wurzburg, Kitzingen, Neustadt and Fürth and on to Nürnberg. Here an American bus picked us up and took us the 20 kilometres to the autobahn, where, after a wait of perhaps an hour an Opel Olympia carried us to Ingoldstadt, a fairly large town half way between Nürnberg and Munich.

'Luck was with us now: another German civilian took us to the end of the autobahn at Munich, a short lift to the centre of town, a good deal of questioning and walking, and we were outside the American Forces Network buildings – our first objective. The staff, although a trifle worried at first in case we were some sort of security check, made us very welcome indeed. After a bath and a general clean-up we felt much better than we had for days, and joined our new friends in the cellar for a chat over a pint . . . or was it two? Anyway, after at least two hours' sleep we awoke to find the staff trying to arrange a helicopter trip for us to the border, where lay our second task. Having failed, they set us on our way in a staff car, which deposited us at the start of Route Eleven. An Opel Rekord seemed rather an anti-climax after the 25-foot-long Ford, but by means of it we comfortably reached the lovely lakeside town of Starnberg. Yet another American car pulled up and a voice, with a pronounced Polish accent, offered us a ride to Oberammergau. Luck indeed, for we had to obtain a picture post-card from this town.

'After a wonderfully exhilarating run up the hills through Schöffau, Böbing and Rottenbuch we arrived at the United States Army Special Language School. The driver stopped a moment to allow us to purchase the necessary postcard, and we were away down the hills again. Having arrived at Garmisch, we went to the main American Army barracks there.

'Seeing a person with a great deal of gold braid, eagles, medals and crests hovering near at hand, we humbly asked for transport to the border. The major – for such he turned out to be – ran us there and back to the barracks in his own car. We thanked him and pondered . . . we had our signature, our postcard, and our stamp – now all we had to do was to return to Lübbecke.

'On Friday afternoon we set off from Garmisch on the return journey with an American Sergeant who was at school in Oberammergau. He took us to the United States Highway Patrol at Macgraw Kaserne in Munich. A series of phone calls, and, before we fully realised what was happening, we had been whisked away in a black and white Chevrolet to the start of the autobahn and, what is more, were awaiting the next one.

'These cars patrol a forty-mile stretch of autobahn and after four rapid changes we found ourselves comfortably installed in the Guardhouse at MP HQ in Ulm. Immediately following breakfast we were away again in a relay of cars, through Stuttgart, Karlsruhe, Heidelberg and finally Mannheim, where, unfortunately, we had to leave our new-found friends. But we soon found a Franco-American family headed for Weisbaden, then a German truck to Limburg. But here our fortunes changed and after a discouraging three-hour wait we decided to walk to the nearest filling station and Rasthaus and "get our thumbs turned up for the night". The chilly sleep we had on the roadside did little to ease the depressing after-effects of our fifteen-mile hike down the autobahn. Another hour and a half of desperate thumbing followed before a Mercedes took pity on us and dropped us at Königswinter. An Opel took us to the beginning of the Bonn-Köln autostrade, and another Mercedes to Köln put us in high hopes of reaching Lübbecke in time – three o'clock Sunday afternoon. But our hopes were to be dashed by a three hour wait, a period of thumbing, watching heavy traffic go sailing past, smiling and sometimes swearing, before a Volkswagen took us all the way to Osnabrück.

'We left our friend at the route 65–51 junction and once more started on the old routine.

'Half an hour or so later, Mrs Kyte, the CRE's wife, came along in the Vauxhall and we completed the journey in the manner to which the American Army had accustomed us!

'All in all, we enjoyed our trip, saw some beautiful country, and met some interesting and not a few rather eccentric people. We had quite a deal of hard work, mixed with a good measure of Chevrolets, candy bars, and Coca Cola.

'The only advice we would give to any would-be "initiative testers" is – don't walk along the autobahn at night – there's no more heartbreaking form of existence. Every step you take moves your destination a kilometre further away! And, of course . . . good luck!'

Perhaps you can't exactly put initiative testing under the heading of sports, but the adventure enjoyed by Nicholson, Retallack and Collins held an unusual kind of challenge, one which they tackled well. I have been unable to track them down, so it's to be hoped that one of the hardy trio might read this and celebrate that a page from a yellowing old Army newspaper might stir their memories.

People do not get into the Army unless they are physically fit, so the importance given to sporting activities is hardly surprising. Most bases in Germany have their football teams, and inter-battalion fixtures have always been followed with all the enthusiasm you would expect for the Premier League back home. On odd occasions the Army would play a local German team. Usually these friendly matches would be just that, but there have been occasions where less-sensitive squaddies have let their emotions give way to their stereotyped view of their hosts and more than a few well-booted fouls have been the result. Sometimes, however, even an innocent game of soccer between teams on the same base could end up with a military casualty. Luckily, in this case, the victim had just about the best doctors the Army could offer waiting in the wings.

Gordon Cox of the RAMC was based at Bad Oeyenhausen from 1947 to '48.

'Wednesday afternoons were a sort of recreational period in HQ BAOR, and in order to dodge the attentions of the PT instructors, the Medicine Branch would organise a football match against the Engineers or the Ordnance or any other unit willing to have a game.

'On one such afternoon we were halfway through a match when our left-winger, a fellow Lancastrian bearing the marvellous name of Joe Sidebottom, was struck in the face by the ball and had to leave the pitch. We were about five miles from HQ and at the final whistle we climbed back into the TCV, the first stop being the MI room, where Joe went in to have his badly bruised eye examined. He returned to duty the following morning but was soon spotted by Brigadier Harsant, BAOR's top surgeon. The Brigadier took Joe into his office, examined his injury and ordered Joe's immediate admission to the nearby British Military Hospital, where Lieutenant-Colonel George, BAOR's top ophthalmologist, was based. We visited Joe regularly and I seem to remember he was transferred to Hamburg Military Hospital to await the arrival of a hospital ship which was due to arrive at the last of its many ports of call since putting to sea from Japan. He would be disembarked at Southampton and after a brief stopover at the RAMC hospital would join the RAMC ambulance train that would scatter its patients to various specialist hospitals. I would like to think that Joe made a full recovery. Thankfully, there were no waiting lists for him that day.'

If football could be considered a slight area of risk, then at other times it could be played in conditions that were memorably uncomfortable. Many soldiers were often taken aback by the severity of the German winter. This is a country which has pleasant summers, but when the cold arrives, it does so with a vengeance.

Major Reg Jones of Beverley, Yorkshire was posted to the BAOR at Osnabrück in 1945.

'We gave our German domestics the day off and the officers, warrant officers and sergeants waited on the men at their Christmas dinner, to the great amazement of the *Herrenvolk* ("toffs"). Even more amazing were the carryings-on in the afternoon of Boxing Day when the officers played the traditional game against the sergeants. They had wanted to take us on at soccer and the officers, as former public- and grammar-school boys, had opted for rugby. As a compromise the sports committee chose hockey, but using a rugby ball so that no unfair advantage might be given to those ex-Indian regulars who had played hockey before. Inevitably a certain amount of handling crept in after one of the officers, a County centre three quarter, like the immortal William Webb Ellis at Rugby School, picked up the ball and carried it.

'Two days later the final of the Brigade Sevens took place at Melle, and I was in the 53 RHU team. As we travelled to the venue in a three-ton truck we were hoping and praying that our opponents would not show up. After the game, which was played on what seemed like a concrete pitch in sub-zero temperatures, our opponents told us that they had had the same thoughts. There were no spectators and our drivers acted as linesmen. The referee disappeared after the game as suddenly as he had arrived. When we had played our game we were so glad to have got over it that I have never been able to remember who won or what the score was.'

Yet there's far more choice than football. Throughout the Army's presence in Germany both men and women with a zest for something a little more exciting have had the Harz Mountains to stretch their endurance. The mix of mountaineering, wildlife under canvas and the subsequent socialising in one of Germany's many excellent hostelries is irresistible to this day. In addition there's swimming, tennis, cricket, squash, and for the less than physically enthusiastic, the odd game of darts in the NAAFI after a game of pool always goes down well with a few pints.

Slightly up the sporting scale, the officer class have in the past taken their love of all things equestrian to new heights in Germany. The Germans are proud of their status as horse breeders, and there's nothing like the old British cavalry spirit when it comes to displaying the Army's riding skills. Many garrisons had their own saddle clubs and the annual horse show, held in Bielefeld, was always a major attraction to German civilians. There was invariably an undoubted superiority among the German-bred horses, usually owned by rather rich businessmen, but such events as Bielefeld and others, like the Polo matches between German teams and teams from the 1st Armoured Division, have all helped to foster better Anglo-German relations. The fact that the Germans won more matches than the British was accepted as a sporting fact of life, and had its compensations, as the Germans were always extremely generous hosts in the bar afterwards.

Horse-riding, however, has not been the exclusive domain of the officer. It was a leisure-time option, as was tennis, for soldiers determined enough to try it out, even in the very early years.

Alec Kingsmill of Nottingham was a Lance Corporal in REME between 1948 and '49.

'There was a swimming pool and, eventually, tennis courts associated with the Minden barracks, although it seemed our small unit provided the most active participants. Up to that time we had been using the courts in the local park, which were primarily for the use of the Control Commission for Germany (CGG); these were the British civil servants who then controlled much of the German civilian administration. We were comparable to them in the pecking order, with the Germans a lowly third. In theory we could ask the Germans to leave the courts if we wanted to play, but I can never recall that happening. There was also a chance of horse-riding. I thought that I definitely ought to have a go at this, so one afternoon, (a Wednesday no doubt, for that was always sports afternoon), some very fine horses were paraded for us. They were said to be ex-Wehrmacht animals. We had no proper gear and were only shod in plimsolls. No horse worth his salt (and certainly not one of the quality that we had) was going to kow-tow to ignorant squaddies like us. Would my horse move? It certainly would not, and I have never felt more vulnerable in all my life. After a few abortive gestures I got off, precisely where I had got on, and to this day, that remains the totality of my equine experience.'

Alec Kingsmill's BAOR experience as a national serviceman may have been short, yet he seems to have taken every opportunity his Army life offered whilst in uniform. His detailed memoir is an acutely observed window on what life was like for teenagers who faced the sudden challenge of military discipline. In the 1940s many of the activities associated with modern youth culture didn't exist. Rock 'n' roll was still a decade away. TV was simply a novelty, not to achieve any importance until after the Coronation in 1953. Music, be it dance bands or otherwise, or the cinema, wasn't a style statement; they were simply part of general entertainment that you either enjoyed or ignored. The idea of 'fashion' was a luxury few young men could aspire to; we simply dressed and looked like youthful versions of our dads. It was also a time when the Church still held some power and respect, with juvenile activities such as Scouting a major offshoot of the Diocese. From school into young adulthood, the one binding social activity had always been sport, and Alec made sure he got his share.

'At the other end of the scale was Padre's hour. An Army padre visited us in our classroom at fairly regular intervals but I cannot recall the extent of the religious content. I recall him more as an early counsellor, an activity which has been such a growth industry since those times. If we had a gripe, we shared it with him, but even the incidence of those occasions was quite rare. What we did bless

him for, and he us, was that on two occasions he arranged for us to
go on a four-day or so Christian Leadership Course held at Church
House in Preetz. I suppose you would call Church House, Preetz a
retreat. At one stage it had been a nunnery. It was situated to the
east of Kiel, an enclave of rather nice old houses set about a
fourteenth-century church in a parkland setting. Here we ate
excellent food served quite graciously, slept in comfortable beds,
and partook of religious observances, church service and
discussion. It was, I suppose, a monkish existence (of the more
relaxed variety). It was the only time that the late service of
compline, for instance, featured in my life and although in truth the
occasions didn't really resolve my doubts, I think that we were all
quite moved by the experience. Certainly, discussion was active and
positive. The resident team, along with some of the more theatrical
of our own members, put on a concert and I still recall the padre's
introduction of one character called Virginia – "virgin for short but
not for long". I really thought that was quite saucy for a vicar –
albeit an Army major with the Military Cross.

'On the second occasion we had to assemble a football team to
play a local side. We were quite taken aback when we realised that
people were paying to come and watch, a measure of esteem which
was quickly eroded when we realised that they were paying to
watch the game after ours. I think we lost 1–0, but we put on a good
show. We very much enjoyed our two visits to Preetz.

'Soon after we arrived at 22 Heavy, I started to play rugby for the
unit. I was quite a lightweight among many more beefy players
(who, surprisingly, were mainly sergeants and officers) and I was
quite surprised to hold my place – not that the competition involved
was all that intense. But it gave me the opportunity to travel a bit,
albeit in the back of some draughty three-tonner, and forces teams
were always very well treated by the home side. In my letters home
I often extolled the tea that followed the game more than I did the
game itself. It was also a leveller in respect of rank. One dark night
leaving Lübbecke after playing the Third Hussars (Huge Tanks
Everywhere) and after a very fine tea we turned the wrong way and
truly feared that we may have inadvertently strayed into the Russian
Zone, but we determined our error in time.

'Yet I was once asked to leave the field. The Army supplied the
shirts which often came in bulk to the field if you were playing at
home. On this occasion they didn't turn up. I was detailed (privates

do have their uses) to go and find them, and a vehicle was arranged. By the time I returned with them, it had been decided to start the game playing in their normal Army shirts. I joined the field, but then a bit later the referee counted the players – we had 16. As the last one to join the field I was asked to leave. I wasn't sorry – it was a messy game!

'Getting away from the camp, seeing just that little bit more of Germany, was an additional reward for playing rugby.'

The Army's sporting activity in Germany today still offers a wide variety of challenges in an environment most sporty civilians back home would have to pay dearly for. Pastimes such as skiing, parachute-jumping and sub-aqua clubs never lack for enthusiasm.

The sports motif also runs through the military exercises carried out in Germany. Although these training periods are designed to be as militarily realistic as possible, peacetime has enabled a competitive factor to add an extra element of involvement and commitment when the tanks and artillery are rolled out. Every other year, for instance, the Allied forces in Germany would compete against each other for the Canadian Army's Tank Gunnery Trophy. Winning this was the tankie's equivalent of winning the World Cup. The German Army, the Bundeswehr, held a regular competition between armoured regiments, the prize being the coveted Boeselager Trophy. The British Army had its own tournaments, such as the 1st Armoured Division's Rhino Trophy. There was a shooting competition for Military Police at Hohne, and at Sennelager, dog handlers and their canine charges took part in an international biathlon.

Sport is one activity that, apart from slight changes in the rules over time, remains constant in its form, planning and participation. The recollections in this chapter come from that early post-war period, when everything about Army life seems to have been more meticulously catalogued by young men who were suddenly presented with a range of recreational and athletic opportunities, many of which they may not have been offered in civvy street. Yet these little vignettes about football, rugby and horse-riding would, if written in later years, read just the same. As countless soldiers in BAOR and other armies around the world have discovered, sport is the leveller, an extra area in which to shine, and is often a valuable method of bridging the culture gap between officers and men.

10

The Brass

As for being a general, well at the age of four with paper hats
and wooden swords we're all generals. Only some of us never
grow out of it.

Peter Ustinov, *Romanoff & Juliet* (1956)

There is always, in all occupations, a certain advantage in being at
the bottom of the pile. Life is less complicated.

From private to sergeant is about as far as some soldiers would
want to go. In that short range of rank you are still dealing with
'your own'. Those above dish out the orders – you make sure they
are carried out. The officers, however cushy a modern squaddie may
think their lives are, have their own responsibilities. Based upon his
or her military education, an officer must take crucial decisions,
inspire high morale and maintain strong discipline. Such
accountability carries a heavy price. It is one of the fruits of
ambition. Unlike civilian management, running the Army adds a
very real, sobering dimension to leadership and the obligations
which accompany it – if you mess up the job, people could die.
Perhaps the last great age of the blundering, puffed-up military
poltroon was during the Great War. Then class was never
questioned. Either you had it, or you didn't. Chances were you were
going to die in any case. With the advent of the Second World War,
things were about to improve.

As recently as the Second World War the selection of officers still
passed through this old-fashioned class filter. Regimental selection
interviews often paid little attention to an applicant's ability.
Everything hinged on the applicant having 'the right background'.
That said, despite the system, there have been some fine, brave and

efficient officers of whom the nation can be truly proud. Yet as the war ground mercilessly on, by the early 1940s the stark realisation dawned that the officer corps were running out of people who had received the 'right' education, those with private means or a well-established military parentage. In any case, even with all the desired, archaic parameters satisfied, the Army had to accept the grim truth that class background was no guarantee of quality. A cut-glass accent, schooldays spent in the cadets at Eton and Harrow, combined with a well-tailored uniform do not necessarily add up to make a leader of men. Many such martinets would have an easy ride in peacetime, but faced with the fanatical ranks of the Waffen SS such phrases as 'You absolute bounder, Fritz – this isn't cricket!' wouldn't keep you alive for long.

A change was in the air, brought about by sheer military necessity.

In 1948, a different method was brought into the officer-selection process and one much despised by the old guard: psychology testing.

Of course, selection by pedigree has still not been entirely stamped out. Certain regiments, which will remain nameless (although horses are usually involved), are still as keen as ever to keep the common 'oiks' out of their ranks. Sadly, there are still a few old class warriors in the upper ranks to whom the drastic changes in British society have remained completely out of sight.

> A British Army tradition of banning sauce bottles from the officers' dining table has come under fire after objections erupted at 9th Regiment Army Air Corps in Dishforth, North Yorkshire, where the commanding officer has described the sight of tomato sauce bottles on the table as 'ungentlemanly and unseemly'. Under dining rules, all types of sauces, whether tomato ketchup or the dark brown variety, have to be kept on a side table for all meals, including breakfast, and were normally in silver dishes, not in bottles, an Army spokesman said.[1]

Thankfully, today the Regular Commissions Board gives paramount importance to a wide range of crucial abilities which help to sort out the men from the gung-ho public schoolboys. Fitness, endurance initiative; fast, clear and creative thinking; all these qualities and more now go towards a commission. An officer in the Army should not be measured against a management candidate in civilian life. The Army means, above all, devotion to duty. It does not welcome the unorthodox in either thought or method. Officers have to spot the potential in their troops, develop that potential, inspire and lead. Officers have no time for intellectual argument. Modern war may be more technology-driven, but the social structure and expected behaviour of the chain of command is a constant not to be tampered with.

Many of these new procedures have been developed and utilised in Germany over the past four decades. But they need not concern us. It is refreshing to go back in time to a simpler age, where a man could write: 'Bread is the staff of life but the life of the staff is a long loaf.'

'Corollary: a regimental officer knows a little about a great many things, but in the passage of time he learns less and less about more and more until he knows nothing about everything; whereas a staff officer knows a great deal about a few things, but in time he learns more and more about less and less until in the end he knows everything about nothing.'

These are the words of the ebullient Major Reginald Jones, of Beverley, East Yorkshire.

Major Jones's career is worth looking at as an example of just where dedication and a real taste for Army life could get a young man in the Army in just over two decades.

Pre-Second World War	46th Liverpool Welsh RTR	sergeant
1939–40	Regular	
1940	Westminster Dragoons	officer cadet
1941–2	Sandhurst (Instructor)	staff captain
1942–5	Royal Armoured Corps	staff officer
1945–6	Regular Army Reserve	captain
1947–9	Cheshire Regiment, TA	lieutenant
1950–5	HQ 23rd Armoured Brigade	major
1955–7	Royal Naval Vol. Reserve	lieutenant commander (Hon.)
1957–64	TA Reserve of Officers	major
1981	Awarded Territorian Decoration (TD)	

Degrees and Distinctions: TD, MA (Oxon) Inter Laws, London FRSA

As you can see, apart from a brief flirtation with the Royal Navy, Major Jones knuckled down over the years and made something of his Army life. Starting as he did before the war as a sergeant, it seems obvious that Reg is made of 'the right stuff'. But for every keen officer like Reg Jones, back in those early days there were probably a dozen officers who were in the British Army simply because they'd been to a recognised school and had the right parentage. Today, as a prominent member of the Hull and East Riding Branch of the Royal Tank Regiment Association, Reg has assembled a fond, fine and erudite recollection of his time in Germany. The following is an extract from his unpublished memoirs. As a man designated to enforce the Army's rules and regulations, Major Jones offers a different perspective on the life of the ordinary soldier – that as seen from the higher ground of a serving officer.

We pick up the story not long after Reg has passed a written examination in Military Law with a mark of 98 per cent.

My predecessor handed over his office and his files with the remark 'This is where they all forgather when the NAAFI is closed and the bogs are all occupied!'.

There were plenty of scrimshankers and wasters and quite a few would-be dodgers of overseas postings on medical and pseudo-compassionate grounds. It was easy to put on my other hat and dispose of the latter by consigning them to the Far East theatre of operations. Any genuine cases that called for welfare attention were conscientiously dealt with by marriage guidance, legal advice and compassionate leave where appropriate. My experience of work in courts martial was extended by the opportunity to sit as a member of the court and to make several briefs as defending officer, which like dock briefs in a civil court could not be refused. The majority of these cases involved absence without leave. Absence being usually proved without doubt, I normally advised my client to plead guilty and leave me to put in the best plea in mitigation I could think of without putting his character in issue. There was an interesting variety of cases and consultations.

When the lady who commanded our detachment of ATS asked if anything could be done about the Lothario who had put no less than three of her girls in the family way, I pointed out that it was a serious offence under the Army Act 'to render a comrade unfit for duty'. But the best I could do in the short term was to post him to the Far East. Then there was the villain who had compounded his absence with various breaches of the peace and adulterous activities in his home town, leading to his being beaten up by his lady friend's husband, and his brothers thrown onto a railway line – the comment of the local police being that 'he richly deserved it'. He asked me to be counsel for the defence. When I asked him whether he wished to bring medical evidence of amnesia caused by his injuries, I informed him that he was entitled to civilian-qualified legal assistance.

Another case was that of a corporal of communist tendencies who had insinuated himself into the education classes and preached his peculiar Gospel according to Saint Marx. Co-operating with the Special Branch we managed to catch him red-handed and commit him for trial at assizes on the charge of treason and incitement of His Majesty's forces to neglect their duty. Bypassing the usual Squadron Orders and CO's charges, he was not court martialled, and received a sentence of imprisonment with no return to the Army envisaged.

DIE WACHT AM RHEIN

Eventually with the disregard for previous planning I had come to expect from the Military Secretary, my movement order arrived, not for the Far East but for north-west Europe. I was instructed to report to the British Army of the Rhine in the area of the 21st Army group, my duties being unspecified. My first unit was stationed in a former barracks of the dreaded SS at Bielefeld. It was a quiet area where we were made more welcome than the previous incumbents, whose mark could still be seen in the mess hall with a large Gothic graffito which proclaimed *'Du bist nichts, das Volk is alles'* (You are nothing, the people are everything).

The local population was very respectful and co-operative and went about their business with little apparent aggravation and observed the curfew. I once heard an old man say that when the country was reorganised the province of Hanover should be restored to direct rule by the English, whose sovereigns were of German descent and local magnates, from George I to Queen Victoria and her descendants. About this time an elderly German was picked up after curfew by a patrol and arrested. He was put in the guard room overnight, and early in the morning his tearful spouse presented herself before the provost warrant officer. The adjutant was summoned, and when asked what the trouble was about, through our interpreter she pleaded to be allowed to see him before they shot him. We were all horrified, and the adjutant explained that he had been very naughty, missing the curfew, and asked her to see that he was home earlier in the future, ending with 'He is now in the guard room having his breakfast. If you hurry up you can have some too, and then you can take him home.' This was worth a great deal of diplomatic negotiation in making our presence acceptable to the local people. Before moving on I was given two administrative tasks to perform. Firstly, an audit of the regimental accounts, the relevant transactions having been in Belgian francs, Dutch guilders and German marks, with a parallel column for sterling. Then I was asked to conduct the prosecution in the very rare and delicate case of a man charged with desertion in the face of the enemy. It was most interesting to me in view of its rarity. It might have been very difficult, the onus being on the prosecution to prove the firm intention of the accused not to return to his duty. Fortunately for me an enthusiastic and sympathetic defending officer made the mistake of putting his client's character in issue, which enabled me to throw the book at him, quoting past misdemeanours and peregrinations between leaving his unit and being picked up in Brussels by the Canadian Military Police. He was of course found guilty, subject to review of sentence by higher authority. Returning to normal activities, I was able to attend the Christmas performance of Handel's *Messiah* by the City Choir and Orchestra of Bielefeld in a magnificent concert hall rather like the Philharmonic Hall in Liverpool, which had escaped our blitz. A strange feature was that the audience did not stand for the Hallelujah Chorus – a tradition we owe to one of our German monarchs!

~ The Brass ~

From there I was transferred to Osnabrück, as second-in-command of the Royal Artillery Sub Unit. This was far more comfortable and less austere than the SS barracks, having a small theatre in what had been the riding school and a beer cellar incorporated into the officers' mess. As a member of the permanent staff I was entitled to drink genuine Scotch whisky, Gordon's Gin and, as a rare and expensive treat, Rose's Lime Juice. At worst we could be served with a palatable Friesian liquor called Doornknat or the popular and ubiquitous Steinhäger in its stone jar, a tipple not to be taken lightly as a kind of occupational disease known as Steinhäger twitch might be diagnosed. Officers passing through and visiting subalterns sometimes had to put up with lesser potions, more alcoholic but of doubtful provenance. Some of our Russian allies and nomadic displaced persons were known to be drinking petrol, occasionally filtered through bread, with dire consequences including blindness and mental disorders.

The day before Christmas I was sent for and given instructions to draw an ambulance from the transport pool and go armed to a small nursing home some kilometres away to collect a patient who was to be brought under guard to the court at Osnabrück as a key witness in a war crimes trial.

Some months before, an Allied plane had been shot down in an air raid. The crew baled out and two Canadian airmen hid in a barn, where they were found by two German home guards and killed. The Germans then went to a local inn and had several glasses of schnapps, which loosened their tongues so that they began to talk freely and boast about their exploit. The landlady overheard, and when the area was overrun by our troops, whether in the interests of justice or in order to ingratiate herself with the conquerors, reported the incident. The two men were arrested and in defence pleaded obedience to the orders of a superior officer. This failed because it had been established as a principle of law that the orders must have been reasonable. The order to take no prisoners was alleged to have been given by the area commander, a major in the Luftwaffe. He was charged jointly with the two home guards, but since no written evidence was available his denial of ever having issued such an order was accepted and he was discharged, leaving the men to fend for themselves. There were still a few enemy partisans in the area and not a few who disapproved of the landlady's part in the matter. In order to get her to the court a fictitious accident was arranged, necessitating her removal to a small hospital. There I called without warning in the ambulance, had her loaded onto a stretcher and drove off quickly. The driver and I both had .38 pistols in our pockets, in case anybody might notice the presence of an armed guard in a Red Cross vehicle. We delivered the woman to the court in the great hall of the Rathaus in Osnabrück, the scene of the signing of the Peace of Westphalia. I stayed in the court until the hearing of the case was concluded. All the speeches and questions were in English, translated immediately, sentence by sentence, into German. The accused were represented by counsel and given a very fair hearing, which was acknowledged by the German lawyers. The two men were found guilty and were sentenced to be hanged, which added a grim touch to the proceedings. The witness was then returned to my custody to be escorted back to her village. She did not seem as anxious to get home as I was to be rid of her.

Major Jones is in many ways what a civilian would imagine a pukka Army officer to be like. Crisp, efficient, no-nonsense, 'get on with the job'. The more unconventional type of officer with a streak of rebellion in him isn't so easy to find, but there are a few.

In the 1970s, Colonel Hugh Thomas, whom we have already met in the chapters on Berlin, served in Berlin and Northern Ireland. He remains far from typical of the career officer one might find in the ranks of the Royal Army Medical Corps. He took full advantage of his time in Berlin. He found his fellow officers in the main to be intolerable military sycophants and avaricious fools. He was an oddball. He spoke German and, living with his wife Joanne in Berlin's suburbs, refused to send his children to the BFES school, preferring them to have a German education. They have never regretted it. He tells of the way the military hierarchy milked the generosity of the Berlin authorities for all it was worth. Fresh flowers from all around the world were flown in every day just to decorate their tables. The British, he says, in Berlin, were definitely 'the last vestiges of the old Raj from India'.

He preferred to dine with the French Army – not out of a sense of snobbishness but because they had the best food. He's a funny, cultured and erudite man, a bestselling non-fiction author for whom Germany, despite the professional company he was forced to keep there, formed the most happy memories of his long career in medicine.

'Officers? I was in the Army for a reason. It was a passport for me to get into the Health Service as a consultant. So I can't talk of my experience as an officer as such; I was more like an outsider looking in. Apart from one orthopaedic surgeon who was very good – although he was a complete sycophant – I found the Royal Army Medical Corps to be mostly staffed by incompetents – and sycophants – and on the administrative side absolute buffoons.

'I can say that I met one general during my time in the Army who was impressive. He was a no-nonsense type, an intelligent man. As for the others, well . . . All I can say is that a lot of them were completely inane. In the RAMC, of the ones I met I would say in general only about one in four were competent. Many of them were idiots. Although I met one good one, there was a feeling in the Army that there certainly weren't enough. In the intelligence world, they were introverted and twisted. Peculiar people. Some of the officers when I was serving were laughable. I'll give you an example. There was one brigadier who, knowing I was a surgeon, approached me with the question: "Er . . .Thomas, is it? Thomas? Right. Now, Thomas, tell me – how much do you charge for a vasectomy?"

'I replied, "Well, sir, it depends on whether you have one side done or two. I'll charge £35 to £40 and for two, 20 per cent extra." Of course, I was being facetious.

'He mulled it over. "Ah, yes. Far better to get both done, what?"

'I was joking – but he was being serious. That summed up the tragedy of the Army hierarchy. As thick as two short planks.

'One of these officers, another brigadier, was a Catholic.

'He announced to me one day, "Now, none of your 'boys' here" – meaning the doctors – "are going to carry out any vasectomies. Is that clear?"

'I said, "But you're not a brigadier who is qualified in medicine at all. You're just an administrator."

' "Yes – but I am *your* brigadier!"

'I said, "Yes, you may be 'my' brigadier, but you have no moral authority in surgery. You have no practical authority in any surgery done by any of my juniors."

'I told of a case in question at the time, of a young married soldier who had six months to do and whose wife didn't want to have any more children. I told him that we didn't enter into these things lightly, that people came to us and we discussed such cases carefully. Anyway, the upshot of all this was that we had a shield made bearing the inscription "*Veni, Vidi, Vasectomy*" (I came, I saw, I vasectomised). It was erected above our door. When this brigadier left he looked at it, puzzled, and read it, saying, "I say, I've been seeing that sign for months now – what *does* that mean? I've often wondered . . ." So I told him.

'These people were unbelievable. I found a lot of these military goings-on laughable. One funny occasion was a parade I attended. It was a regular inspection of the French troops on the big parade ground. It was chucking it down with rain and these immaculate Frenchmen wore white spats over their boot-tops. Unfortunately, they'd been standing in ranks in an area on the field where the lower level of the ground was rapidly collecting the rain. It was a flash flood. By the time this general was walking up and down inspecting them, he was sloshing through mud and the soldiers were ankle-deep in dirty water.

'I was on the covered stand seated behind all the other top brass – generals, etc.

'When the procession of French Chausseur tanks drove towards us the man in the turret would salute the stand smartly, and the tank's gun would swing and face us in a kind of salute. It was all very smart, but this leading tank's gun swung towards us, and caught the supporting corner pole of the pavilion. I knew we were in danger with the collapse, but it was so damned funny I had to stuff my handkerchief in my mouth to stop laughing.

'But I liked the French. I ate with them in their superior equivalent of the NAAFI, the Economat. Their food was excellent. We had wonderful meals. All the British families received what was called "FRIS" rations – Families Ration Issue Service. These rations would come from all over the place – like superb pork from Denmark, for example. You could only buy FRIS rations from the NAAFI with special FRIS coupons. Well, talking of the officer class, on occasions I would have a couple of British generals stay at my house when they were visiting Berlin. They would actually try to cadge, from my wife and me, our FRIS coupons. I found it appalling that those senior ranks, ostensibly on a short visit to inspect our place of work, a senior general, no less – would go around asking *us* for our FRIS rations so that they could load up their official car and take their spoils back to BAOR in Germany. The stuff we could buy with FRIS coupons was priced so low – less than a quarter of what we'd normally pay. Yet that was what these people were like.

'Another event which stays in my mind is Operation Rocking Horse. This was usually announced at around two o'clock in the morning by a bloke in a van cruising down the street announcing, "Hoperashun' Rockin' 'orse! Hoperashun' Rockin' 'orse!" over a loudspeaker. What this meant was that you had to turn out, get fully kitted out in your combat gear and go over to the nuclear bunker, and prepare yourself, as medical officer, to receive "mock casualties". This was to be the operation which would set in once the Russians had invaded. The trouble with Operation Rocking Horse is that after the bloke had gone around with the loudspeaker, the tanks would start rolling down the Heerstrasse, and they'd come down from Gatow. It wasn't too popular with the local German residents. They genuinely thought this was the real thing. In the beginning there was a spate of suicides over this exercise. The memory of the Red Army's invasion of Berlin was still a very fearful reality for these people. Behind the heavy steel bomb-proof door of the nuclear bunker we had about 100-plus beds to receive casualties, blankets, bedding, gas masks, everything we needed to combat chemical warfare etc. There were huge packs of Fuller's Earth, and a decontamination unit. We were supposed to assemble there and wait with our commanding officer, who would be fussing around in a very officious manner asking the obvious like "OK, chaps, are we ready to receive casualties?" and we'd be standing around bemused by all this. This was a time in the Army when these officer morons would turn up all kitted out in their combat fatigues yet with their boots all polished and sparkling. We called them "twinkletoes". I recall one very naughty occasion where we locked the doors on this hierarchy and all went home and back to bed. They were all discovered by the guard the following morning – the all-clear had been declared – and there was an investigation as to who had locked them in but they never found out who did it. Still, it gave them the opportunity to look "important" all night.

'There were other annoying things about officers when I was in Berlin. For instance, when we went into the Eastern sector, we were supposed to change our money on a one Eastmark equals one

Westmark basis. Of course few did; you could get a rate in Spandau of about eight to one or four to one in the West Bahnhof. There was an official place to change your money in the East but I was surprised to find that I was the only officer to ever enter it. The people in there were amazed to see me. Even though that one to one system was the law, even the Military Police chief stopped me one day and said, "Hugh, what the bloody hell are you doing changing your money that way for?"

'I said, "Well, that's the rule!" One general – and he was an earl – even ran a bank and was cashing a cheque in the Brigade shop every week to profit from the change. Then there was Sir Ronald Tree, who had an RMP sergeant collect a brown paper bag for him in the East – it was stuffed full of uncut diamonds. That sergeant must have been an honest bloke because Tree was acting as a diamond merchant. The diamonds were safely delivered – they must have been worth an absolute fortune – and Tree later contributed a measly $100 to the Save the Children fund. The avaricious way they went about things was pitiful. The intelligence boys didn't like me buying Meissen glassware from the Meissen shop in the East either. I was too open about it. Of course, they all bought it and had it crated up and sent home, yet in some way they seemed to treat that as their covert privilege. Yes, the majority of the officer class I met in Germany were awful.'

I often used to wonder what drove real career soldiers to study their art, what made intelligent, educated and sophisticated people from the higher echelons of society take to the science of fighting large-scale battles. Sadly, we will always need those who are prepared to fight our wars, to stand in the way of maniacs and aggressors.

For an example of how much the high command of the Army has improved over the years since the Second World War, you need look no further than Lieutenant-General Sir Mike Jackson, KCB CBE. I was privileged to interview him following his return from the Balkans conflict in 2000.[2] What he said then displayed a shrewd sense of prediction when considered in the context of the military activity around the world since 11 September 2001.

No stranger to Germany, he spent a good deal of his career based at Rheindahlen. His rise through the ranks during the past four decades is packed with achievement.

After Sandhurst Royal Military Academy, he was commissioned into the Intelligence Corps in December 1963, and studied for an in-service degree in Russian Studies between 1964 and '67. In the early '70s, as the Troubles began to gather momentum, he was sent to Northern Ireland. This was followed by a two-year spell as brigade major with the Berlin Infantry Brigade, after which he was back in Ulster, this time commanding a parachute company for a further two years.

I did not speak to him about his time in Germany. However, many ex-soldiers who served in Rheindahlen will recall Lieutenant-General Mike Jackson, and his thoughts about the Army's modern deployment, his views on national service and the future of warfare offer an example of the kind of leadership today's Army enjoys. When you consider that the following comments were made in 2000, then despite his opening remark, his grasp of future international affairs seemed spot on.

'There's one thing I've learned in 40 years and that is that whatever you predict you'll probably be proved wrong. If you were Saddam Hussein, and for example, you wanted to hurt the United States, you would have learned from the Gulf that it's not sensible to take on the West and the US at its strongest point – i.e. conventional capability. Therefore you'd go for an unconventional approach. The next threat? Well, it doesn't take an Einstein to recognise that the Middle East is far from stable, then there's the Far East, Indonesia, which becomes more unsure, the problem of East Timor, Taiwan, and Africa is a great sadness.'

On national service, that popular hobby horse for all those who believe that two years in the Army will cure all our social ills, his views are not what one might expect:

'Nations must, for whatever reason, decide for themselves. The reasons for conscription can be political, or social. France, for instance, took the decision four years ago to move to more regular forces. Germany is having a defence review; I don't know which way that will go. Britain was one of the early nations to abolish conscription. The last national servicemen were just spending their final few months 40 years ago when I joined up.

'I don't think any of us can conceive now of a conscripted British Army. There are those who say that this generation doesn't match up to past ones, but I don't find that to be the case. When we're out there doing the job and we've a problem to solve and I go and see my soldiers, they get on with it. I come back and I think, "This is good – they're OK." So I'm proud of my soldiers.'

11

New Century, New Army

> Some senior officers, in expansive mood, love to
> philosophise on the subject of the Army and politics.
> 'Democracy is like a raft,' said a brigadier in the Rhine Army.
> 'It never sinks but you've always got your feet wet.'
>
> Antony Beevor, *Inside The British Army*

I wondered how many Colonel Blimps, Chinstraps and Major
Bloodnoks I would encounter once I set foot at my first call in
Herford at the 1st Armoured Division's HQ, Wentworth Barracks.

I was in for some serious enlightenment.

To begin with, I was surprised when I organised my German tour
that in the main all my Army contacts had been women. It was a
grey, cold winter afternoon at the end of a long drive from
Rotterdam when, following the clear and reliable faxed instructions
from Germany, I pulled up at the sentry box in Herford. After
passing through two countries, where town and village names such
as Appeldoorn, Enschede, Huffen Steinbeck and Harsewinkel
provided regular reminders that, despite being designated a 'home
posting', this was a foreign land, I suddenly felt as if this was
England again. I noticed the comforting sight of parked vehicles,
Fords, Vauxhalls and Rovers, with their UK number plates. The
armed guard was efficient and polite. I parked the car and reported
to the Guard House, where a chatty young sergeant from Whitby
immediately made me feel at home. The barracks, huge, solid
buildings built for Hitler's Wehrmacht, looked Teutonic enough,
but right in the middle stood a British post office, complete with its
red sign and post box. Yet despite this, the pub, the Sports Club and
the NAAFI supermarket with its familiar Typhoo teabags, HP Sauce

and Robertson's jam, this is not Britain. English within these fences may be the lingua franca, but this is still a very German place. I was met by Carolyn Battey, the Army's media operations information officer. In her civilian clothes, this attractive young woman seemed a world away from the female soldier I'd expected.

Over coffee in the Media Operations office I was introduced to Mike Whitehurst, Herford's information officer. The whole experience seemed more like a visit to an editorial office or an advertising agency, until into the press office, clad in camouflage fatigues with boots sparkling, stepped Warrant Officer Sergeant-Major Will Betts. Will, 42, has spent 24 years in the Army, and his open, friendly manner seemed immediately well-removed from the sergeant-majors of my father's generation. Like all the soldiers I met on this trip, his handshake was firm and meaningful, and I could tell by the honest, confident smile that here was a man I could get along with. Somehow, though, with his rank in mind, I couldn't imagine him bellowing into a raw recruit's ear that hoary old yell: 'You 'orrible little man!' Yet soon I realised that such behaviour in the modern Army is now nothing more than an outworn cliché.

'No, we can't shout at people anymore. In fact, we have to be careful these days. Things have altered. The old Army was run on bull – spit and polish, repetitive routines. The bull has, in the main, gone. But we can still turn out smart without it. You have to find other ways of getting lads to do something. Since I joined up nearly 25 years ago everything has changed. Society at home has altered radically and the Army has had to reflect this.'

As a warrant officer, how concerned was he with the situation?

'You adjust, get on with the job. The old way was one way of running the show – now we have a different way. As long as the training's up to scratch and we can get the lads drilled to the level of performance we're looking for, fair enough.'

Will Betts' twenty-first-century Army is a vastly different one to the one at the beginning of this book. Was he looking forward to leaving it?

'With a bit of luck I'll get another ten years in. I don't regret one minute of my service. To be honest, it's been great.'

But what will a man like this do back on British soil, in a totally different social environment?

'I doubt I'll be going home. Sure, I go back to see my parents now and again. But I live here. I married a German girl, live in a German house, and have German neighbours. To me, Britain has become a foreign country. When I'm there, it feels almost like visiting Turkey or some other place . . . So I might well stay here. I like the Germans. They seem to like us, and I feel more at home here than anywhere.'

Outside twilight was falling but Carolyn had another port of call for me on her itinerary. The Army's Public Relations machine is nothing if not efficient. We walked from the camp through the leafy suburbs of Herford with its pristine roads and pavements, flanked by immaculate German gardens. In a large white house I was introduced to Colin Gordon, a warm, imposing man who acts as the Army's liaison officer.

He told me how far relationships with the Germans had changed over the years he had spent here.

'For instance, the British Army and the new German Army, the Bundeswehr, today share a very healthy mutual respect. We work together on exercises and manoeuvres. As for Anglo-German relations, the civilians here hold us in high regard. After the 1960s and through to the '80s a lot more soldiers and their families learned to speak the language. Colloquial German is far more common among Army personnel now than it was years ago, and the standard of behaviour today among our soldiers has improved a lot. All the buildings we occupy still belong to the German government, but we employ local firms to carry out all maintenance and repair work, which is all paid for by the British Army. In fact, our very presence here puts about eight million euros into the local economy. There are some towns in Germany, such as Sennelager, which revolve totally around the British Army's presence. If we left, the effect would soon be noticed.'

Twelve years previously, he'd been Major Gordon. I asked him if he missed the old tensions of the Cold War. Was it true, as some squaddies had intimated, that we weren't always as 'ready for action' on the East–West border as the folks back home imagined?

'The Soviets certainly were. Perhaps in our case we sometimes had a more relaxed attitude – especially after 1 p.m. on a Friday afternoon. If it was a Bank Holiday then things were certainly very quiet. I recall in Berlin some years ago being left in charge of our operation, more or less on my own, as duty officer. I was sitting in my office on a warm summer afternoon one Friday and the phone rang. It was a young chap – not any senior rank – calling from our RAF base. He said he was seeking my guidance as he had a "situation" on his hands, and, like me, he was on his own. Apparently, an East German jet – a trainer – had landed on the runway. The pilot, and a passenger, had come to him claiming that they were seeking political asylum. He asked me what he should do. I told him to make them a cup of tea and sort it out on Monday. But in general, the Soviets always had up to 80 per cent of their troops employed in readiness at the border. Even after the Berlin Wall came down and we went in, we discovered that all their tanks were "bombed up" and ready to roll.'

Colin Gordon was another of the many Army personnel who seemed to love Germany. Looking at his surroundings, the superb building he works in and the relaxed ambience of Herford, it was hardly surprising.

By now it was dark and very cold, and having missed lunch it seemed a long time since the fine English breakfast I had eaten on the ferry at Rotterdam. In their thoroughness, the Army had even booked my hotel for me, and Carolyn guided me into the centre of Herford to find my billet for the night. The Stadt Berlin Hotel, opposite Herford's neat railway station, proved yet again what an open, cosmopolitan country modern Germany is. The hotel was manned and run by Hong Kong Chinese. They all spoke fluent German, but Cantonese to one another, and, to me, perfect English. After a fine dinner of roast duck I decided to have a wander around Herford and try the local beer. As I walked through the main shopping centre, all was quiet. Floodlit churches rubbed shoulders with quiet Italian restaurants and kebab houses. The shops were ablaze with Christmas decorations, something the Germans are particularly good at. Yet one thing caught my eye as I turned a corner. There before me, in a small square, stood a red British General Post Office (GPO) telephone box. It seemed to represent our presence more than anything else.

I found a cosy bar, and over some fine Herforder Pils began to utilise my faltering tourist German in a conversation with the locals.

What did they think to the British Army? The old man on the stool next to me lit up a cheroot and smiled. It was a familiar response.

'At least they're not the Americans,' he said, his command of English putting my ersatz Deutsch to shame. The barman laughed. Several other drinkers cast a knowing glance at the old man then winked at me, as if warning me of some imminent, well-trodden local 'wisdom'. My new-found drinking buddy did not disappoint.

'I'll tell you what the British are – the British are almost the same as us. That's why we get on with them. Respect. Now, the French – they hate you because they think they used to run the world, when all the time you did. Us Germans? Well, we tried to but maybe we tried a bit too much. Now we're all Europeans all that is finished. So it's good to have you and your soldiers here. As for the Americans – well, I like their rock 'n' roll music and their country and western. But they don't mix in with us like the British do.'

The following day Media Operations had arranged for me to visit our bases at Gütersloh and Sennelager. Driving out to Gütersloh in the early morning frost, I passed through dark woodland, then alongside broad fields and neat farms, and pondered over what this countryside had seen and what these attractive villages had experienced during the past 60 years. The Germans of the twenty-first century are indeed a totally different people to those who fell for National Socialism all those years ago. But I doubt if, even in Gütersloh, you chose to remind any elderly residents of what took place in this smart, modern town in November 1938, when the SS entertained a large crowd of onlookers as they set fire to the Gütersloh Synagogue and other Jewish premises, they would welcome the memory.[1] Yet as Bosnia, Kosovo and Rwanda have proved in recent years, across the board, in general, humanity hasn't improved all that much.

A HISTORY OF GÜTERSLOH FROM LUFTWAFFE TO LAND COMMAND

Gütersloh was for many years, until 1994, the major RAF base in Germany. When the RAF moved out, the Army moved in. Today it still has flyers, but now they leave the runway in Army Air Corps helicopters. This is the headquarters of 102 Logistic Brigade, under direct command of HQ Land Command in the UK. It comprises five regular units, based in Germany and in the UK, including two transport regiments, one supply regiment, one field hospital, and one Military Police regiment. The brigade, which has operational experience in the Balkans, is here to receive troops and equipment into an operational theatre and organise their movement into the battle area. The Gütersloh base is perfectly situated for its task. Well served by road, it has its own rail spur that runs straight to the centre of the camp. This brigade can set up hospitals, evacuate casualties and transport everything from foodstuffs to Challenger tanks. Nowhere do modern military logistics figure so largely as they do in Gütersloh. The job here encompasses an in-depth understanding of transport systems, fuel and ammunition.

I was met at the Gütersloh Senior Liaison Officer's office by Madeline Donelly, a civilian who has lived in Germany since 1971. She told me the history of the barracks here. They were built, in breach of the Treaty of Versailles, for the Luftwaffe in 1936. As with many bases occupied by the British in Germany, the story behind these solid buildings and impressive parade grounds, the home for so many British servicemen and their families for almost 50 years, is a fascinating one.

On 2 November 2000 Stephan Grimm, the curator of the archives in the town of Gütersloh, gave a pre-dinner speech in the Officers' Mess at the Princess Royal Barracks.[2] His theme was the Second World War in Gütersloh. The transcript of that speech offers an interesting insight into the attitudes of modern Germans and their relationship with the rest of Europe in the new century.

At the start of the Second World War, the town had a population of 32,841. Herr Grimm went on to explain the atmosphere of total enforced commitment to the National Socialist cause:

> German society became subject to strict military control. The forced membership into the NSDAP (the National Socialist Workers Party) and into the Hitler Youth Movement, and the obligatory attendance at Party functions, all served to unite the country for war [. . .] it was believed that the idea of belonging to an Aryan super-race would spur the peoples' will to conquer. For Hitler and the Nazis, 'History is the presentation of a nation's struggle to survive . . . therefore, whoever wants to live, has to fight – and whoever will not fight in this world of eternal struggle, does not deserve to live'.

Sadly, the last part of *Der Führer*'s quotation would still seem to be the philosophy of quite a few of today's less-reflective politicians.

The idea of building an airfield on the western side of Gütersloh had first been discussed as early as 1913. With the Nazi takeover in

1933, and the subsequent rebuilding of the Wehrmacht, military units began to build in East Westphalia with bases in both Herford and Bielefeld. On 10 December 1935, Gütersloh's new Nazi Bürgermeister, Herr Bauer, made a request to the Reich Defence Ministry in Berlin to establish a military garrison. It was to be almost a year before his wish was granted, when the Ministry of Aviation in October 1936 approved the acquisition of land and granted contracts for the building of barracks. To the east of the town, land was set aside for the training of troops, whilst to the west, bordering on Marienfeld, more land was acquired. Despite the ostensible commitment to the Nazi cause, the Burgermeister's rapacious requisition of land, in his eagerness to impress the Party, must no doubt have caused some well-guarded consternation in the town. Herr Bauer moved fast, with all the arrogance one would expect of the Nazi regime, as even before the contracts were signed, the fifteenth-century Osthus farm, the oldest in the region, was flattened, along with many acres of ancient surrounding woodland. To build the airport on Marienfelder Strasse, yet another ancient farm faced the bulldozer. Teams of craftsmen and labourers worked day and night to build the Barracks on the Verler Strasse, and many of the other buildings were completed in record time. Of the 302 acres of land the scheme required, 195.34 were leased to the Kreis Air Command, with the Luftwaffe being the beneficiaries of the remaining 107 which were presented as a 'gift'. The new Mansergh Barracks were soon occupied by the Air Intelligence Company. By 1941 the Luftwaffe Women's Auxiliary Force were putting new signallers, many of them women, through a 15-week training course, followed by an additional 15-week infantry course. This training establishment soon became the largest of its kind in wartime Germany. In 1987, a book was published to commemorate 50 years of military operations in Gütersloh.[3] Herr Grimm, in his speech, quotes a passage from this that indicates how the long-held agricultural traditions of the area became hostage to military progress. The Officers' Mess at Gütersloh is actually built on the site of yet another ancient farm:

> An item of particular interest is the stained-glass window which gives its name to the 'Window Room' of the Officers' Mess. The window contains a potted history of the building from 1150. The first pane shows the old farmhouse with the

inscription that the house belonged to the family of Wixfort from 1150 to 1937. This is completed by the badges of Westphalia and Gütersloh. A double-headed horse is in recognition of the fact that the airfield is situated near the border of two lands, through which wild horses once roamed – Westphalia and Lower Saxony. Other panes record the beginning of the present building in 1935 and the *Richtfest* in 1937, to celebrate the completion of the walls and roof beams.[4] The story of the farmhouse is concluded in the last pane, in which a key symbolises the hand-over of the building to the Luftwaffe in April 1937. The historical links are sustained further in the 'Blue Room', a small ante-room in the mess, which occupies much of the area of the old farmhouse. The Blue Room contains a large fireplace with beams surrounding it, in replica of the old farmhouse's front gateway [. . .] the inscription on the fireplace records in German 'Formerly I was the House of Wixfort, then came the fire and through the master builder, I now stand here newly built 1735–1964'. This inscription is a reference to the gutting of the room by fire in 1964, in which the original beams dating back to 1735 were destroyed.

On 24 April 1937 the IV/254 Fighter Squadron of the Luftwaffe moved in, and the Air Intelligence personnel joined with the newly arrived flyers and the local population to celebrate this fresh military status for the town. Bürgermeister Bauer made no bones about Gütersloh's new military prowess in his speech: 'As in all German states, we recognise and feel the great changes and are acutely aware of having once again become a nation of fighters.'

It must have seemed, therefore, a bitter twist of fate just a few decades later, that these very same buildings should become the domain of first the RAF and later the British Army. As with so many similar sites in Germany, an air of tragedy dulls the sheen of their historical glory. Between 1943 and '44 Allied air attacks on Gütersloh, increased so that a new, 20-metre-wide runway was constructed at a length of 2.25 kilometres. The work was done by Russian and Polish slave-labour gangs, many of whom died on the site from typhus and malnutrition. Of these workers, 17 are actually buried on the airfield, and just 20 kilometres from Gütersloh, at

Stückenbrock, the site of a POW internment camp, 65,000 Polish and Russian prisoners are buried in a mass grave.

In 1944 Gütersloh suffered no less than 302 air raids, and like their nearby neighbours, Paderborn and Bielefeld, the resulting damage was immense. On the day before Hitler's 55th birthday, 19 April 1944, 62 USAAF bombers dropped 179 tons of bombs on the airbase, most of which missed their target. It has been suggested that this may well have been a deliberate ploy to preserve the base for the Allies – the bombing perhaps having more of a demoralising intent rather than a destructive one. Yet despite further bombings, right up until the eve of Allied victory, the barracks were still standing.

On Easter Sunday 1945, 1 April, Gütersloh's Vicar, Paul Gronemeyer, carried a white flag along the Verler Strasse to the exit for the autobahn. There he met the advancing Americans and offered unconditional surrender. Bürgermeister Bauer, prior to his forthcoming 18 months internment by the Americans, during which he would undergo 'de-Nazification', managed to perform one last act for which today's occupants on the base came to be thankful. He negotiated with the commandant of the airfield and convinced him that the site should not fall victim to the then prevalent 'scorched earth' policy. Thus the buildings, barracks and airfield of the Gütersloh garrison were preserved.

The Americans took possession of the base on 6 April 1945, and the day after Germany's capitulation, 9 May 1945, the first British aircraft landed here. When Air Vice Marshal Maintland addressed the first parade of the new occupants on the airfield, he reminded them that they were not to behave as 'military overseers', and that they were primarily ambassadors of their country.

Those ambassadors are still there over five decades later. During that time the local population and the British troops have formed a good relationship. Much of this has its roots in the sensible policy adopted in those immediate post-war years that decreed that one of the main principles of occupation was that the Germans should be helped to help themselves.

Of the bases in Germany, Gütersloh seemed to be one of the busiest. Trucks and cars came and went as I waited for instructions in the guardroom, in which around ten young soldiers were busy handling phone calls and paperwork. It was nice to know that at least one of their number could take time off to talk to a visiting writer.

~ New Century, New Army ~

Warrant Officer Dave Walkley of the Army Air Corps has been in service since 1977.

Like his counterparts on other bases, he seems totally at home in Germany. He'd married a German girl, Michaela, who had at one time served him beer as a barmaid. One thing I soon learned was that you don't have to mention the RAF too often to a 'soldier pilot'. Dave soon put me right:

'Soldier pilots are nothing to do with the RAF. We fly helicopters, fixed-wing craft, Chipmunks and Fireflies.'

As with my conversations at Herford, I was left with no doubt after talking to Dave Walkley as to the total immersion into German life many of these long-service soldiers had undertaken. He also appeared to find his country of origin a slightly strange place these days.

'I've become used to Germany. Britain seems more foreign. I live away from the base and have German neighbours, and when off-duty I'm even a member of the *Schützverein* – the local German militia. It's not particularly military – we go out shooting and stuff like that, but yes, as a British soldier I'm honoured to be a member. I like this life; I like Germany, and it's a grand job being here. A lot of soldiers feel the same. We've learned the language – or at least can get along in it – and this is a totally different way of life to any you could have back in Britain. Since being out here I've seen a lot of changes, and relationships between us and the civilians have improved remarkably over the years. I've experienced most of the changes from the old Cold War years to the present. Back then the threat of something "going off" was always there. Some things that happened were a bit odd – I remember us back in the early '90s one very foggy night tracking an aircraft which we thought was one of ours and it turned out to be a Russian Hip helicopter – way off course and in our airspace. Back then I spent some time with NATO – very boring it was, too, but we were always ready in case something happened.

'Soldiers have changed a lot since I've been in. There used to be an element of the "thinking thug" with some of them, but it's different today. And training has changed so much. For instance, when we used to carry out really large exercises a few years ago, we could cause all sorts of damage to the German landscape. Hardly surprising with about 40,000 soldiers and about 5,000 tanks rolling over it. The Deutsche Claim Commission – that's the body farmers could complain to if we damaged roads, fields or hedges – would be awash with claims and complaints from angry farmers. Mind you, quite often, a farmer wouldn't mind a bit of demolition in the right place – an old barn he wanted knocking down or a hedgerow that needed removing. He'd be compensated, but after a while we needed a larger area to carry out these exercises and that's how BAOR found itself in Canada. We had all the space we needed there in a similar terrain, about 200 miles east of Calgary. Of course, since perestroika and the Wall coming down, there's not nearly as many of us here as there were back in the '70s and '80s, and we've found new ways of training since technology improved – as you'll find out when you get to Sennelager.'

The mention of the change in the standard of recruits and soldiers' behaviour led me on to a question about officers. To the outsider, it has always appeared that the 'officer class' was just that – men from a different echelon of society, passing through the quality control of Sandhurst and into instant leadership. Once again, Dave put me right. It isn't like that anymore.

One important name came up during this part of the conversation: Major Eric Joyce. Madeline Donelly recommended that I look up Joyce's story. In terms of changing the way the Army is perceived, it is a very important one.

Major Eric Joyce joined the British Army in 1987. A former Scottish Judo champion and 'Sportsperson of the Year' at Stirling University, he had served in Germany. Whilst with the Adjutant General's Corps in 1997, he took a great risk for a serving officer – he made public his misgivings about what he saw as the outmoded shortcomings in the structure of the Army's higher echelon. That he chose to do so in a journal loosely associated with the left-of-centre field of politics only seemed to add to his transgression.

He published a Fabian Society leaflet under the heading 'Labour In Action', entitled *Arms and The Man: Renewing the Armed Services.*[5] He did so without first seeking permission from the Ministry of Defence, a clear requirement under the Queen's Regulations for a serving officer. However, Major Joyce knew what he was about. In an interview in *The Times* on 4 August 1997, he said, 'You can't get radical ideas like this into the public domain if you go through the chain of command.'

The MOD was not pleased. Going 'through the chain of

command' is what soldiers are supposed to do. More media attention followed. The general thrust of his argument was that many of his fellow officers and their seniors in the Army were, in the main, class-ridden products of the public-school system. Yet beyond this controversial element, much of what he had to say made sense – to some. On 9 December 1998, the Member of Parliament for Mid Norfolk, Keith Simpson, raising the case of Major Joyce in the House, commented:

> I read his pamphlet with great interest. He touched on many issues, including recruitment, training, ethnic minorities and civil liberties. Much of what he said was controversial; some of it was interesting; some of it was obviously plain wrong and some of it was eccentric. It was really a political polemic.[6]

By this time Major Joyce was in deep trouble. He had been warned by the MOD repeatedly that he should not speak to the media, yet he had continued to do so. His wife spoke to the press in October 1997 and said that in the event that her husband faced a court martial, he would respond by taking the Army to the European Court of Human Rights.[7] He was indeed facing the prospect of disciplinary charges and if MPs such as Keith Simpson were to have their way, he might lose his job:

> Major Joyce continued to criticise senior officers and expected to have the right to do so. I put it to the House that most organisations, after giving warnings, would tell an employee that, if he continued his actions, they would reluctantly have to 'let him go', to use the current management jargon.[8]

But political exigency is a stern master. The Honourable Member for Mid Norfolk had smelled a spin-doctoring rat after it had come to light that, far from any disciplinary measures, Major Joyce had been granted permission to publish in a journal called *The Armed Services Forum*.

> Why did the Army and the Ministry of Defence make that decision? We learned, once again through the press, that the

Lord Chancellor had written to the Secretary of State for
Defence advising him not to take action against Major Joyce
because of the fear that, if the officer took his case to the
European Court of Human Rights, any ruling would come up
in the run-up to the next election, which 'would not be good
timing'.[9]

Mr Simpson was like a dog with a bone. However, a rapid-fire
exchange regarding Major Joyce's *Armed Services Forum* between
the MP and the Secretary of State for Defence, failed to ignite any
retribution.[10] In reply to his questions, Mr Simpson was told that
there were no constraints against Major Joyce's publication, other
than those in the Queen's Regulations, that all Army personnel are
entitled to publish any magazine within the bounds of those
Regulations, that it was a private venture, with no cost to the MOD.

In the end, the Army's loss was Parliament's gain. After leaving
the Army in 1999, Major Joyce took up a post as Public Affairs
Officer for Racial Equality. In December 2000 he was elected to
Parliament as the New Labour MP for Falkirk West. Currently, in
addition to his MA and BA, he's studying part-time towards a PhD
in Education Policy through Bath University. Soldiers who become
Executive Members of the Fabian Society, Secretary of their local
Labour Club and members of the Transport and General Workers'
Union could be regarded as a rare breed. It is difficult to discern
what the ultimate effect Major Joyce's spat with the MOD may have
had on Army life, but to a civilian observer it would appear that the
Army is indeed changing. Some of the older, longer-serving officers
may well give off an expected public-school ambience, and for all
we know may still take tiffin at midday on the veranda, but not the
ones I met in Germany.

SENNELAGER: GERMANY'S LITTLE ENGLAND

Sennelager, near Paderborn, is the training centre for the British
Forces in Germany. All along the long, straight main road through
the town the various shops, businesses and bars rely heavily on the
British presence. The suburbs are quiet, neat, green and pleasant.
The first man I met at the Land Warfare Collective Training Group
(Germany) (LWCTG[G]) was Martin Waters at the base liaison office.
Once a major with the Queen's Own Hussars, he's no longer in
uniform, but back in the days of national service he was one of the

first British soldiers to go out on a patrol along the East–West German border. His length of service – 38 years, during which time he spent a total of only 18 months in the UK, meant that he was also on the last patrol. Few people know more about this fascinating piece of Army territory.

'Sennelager is unique in Germany, because we have 120 square kilometres here which is looked after by the British – since 1945 the main British-administered area in Europe. This is where we do all our training with the 20th Armoured Brigade. We have a wide range of courses and exercises here, including combined arms collective training at battlegroup level, training of individuals, even dog handling and environmental hygiene.

'We all know it as "STC" – Sennelager Training Centre – but its history as a German military landscape goes back well over a century. The land, 20,000 acres, was purchased as the Sennelager Ranges back in 1892 and the first units arrived here that summer. The officers lived in huts, whilst the men lived in tents. The following year proper buildings went up and in 1895 Kaiser Wilhelm III came here to lead a large cavalry exercise. He was back again in 1905 and it was quite an occasion. In those days the town had an electric tram service but the number of visitors was so great that they had to lay special trains on from Paderborn. The place has never been out of use, because even after the Army was reduced after the First World War, this became a holiday camp.'

During that war it had housed POWs. Between 1925 and 1927, 6,500 poor German children enjoyed a holiday here at the Staumühle camp. This was the same camp that was later used to house the many refugees who arrived at Sennelager railway station from East Germany following the fall of the Wall. In 1928 a swimming pool was built at the Normandy Barracks. When Hitler's Wehrmacht began to build up in the 1930s, the land used for ranges at Hovelsenne, Hastenbeck and Schlangen was compulsorily purchased and the camp laundry was moved to the castle at Schloss Neuhaus, with new barracks blocks erected at Augustdorf. During the Second World War, Allied POW's shared the base with German Military units who were sent there to recuperate before returning to the front. Apart from the ammunition depot, the rest of the base was undamaged by the last war and when the British arrived in 1945 they took over, and have been there ever since.

The Sennelager Range is an area of outstanding natural beauty. In the modern age of environmental concern, the British Army, as its tenant, is obligated to care for this stretch of countryside. Because of its military history, it contains some unusual horticultural oddities unique to Germany. There are foreign plants growing here that don't even belong in Europe. Canadian wild cherry, for instance, acts as a firebreak but demands a lot of environmental husbandry. One legend is that throughout its history, Sennelager has housed soldiers whose postings have taken them around the world, and some plants, such as rare orchids, may have grown there from seeds dropped from boots or clothing. Over this wild, wide area, where time sometimes seems to have stood still, the British soldier in his Challenger tank gets about as close to a real battle scenario as possible. Well away from the population, hidden in the heart of this 120 square kilometres stands an abandoned village, Haustenbeck. This once-idyllic rural settlement was destroyed by Hitler in the 1930s, but still holds a special place in the hearts of Germans. There are up to 100 websites around the world where emigrants of German origin can trace their genealogy back to this one small site, now almost hallowed ground in the middle of what has become 'tank country'. The church foundations still stand, and the graveyard is still respected. This is now the domain of British tanks. The development of the Third Reich's famous Panzer tanks has many connections with Haustenbeck. This was the Wehrmacht's proving ground, and tank buffs around the world still celebrate that this little village provided a 'missing link' in their researches when the British Army discovered the only existing prototype of the massive, 140-ton E100 tank here in 1945 at the Henschel test plant in Haustenbeck.

But these days, long before soldiers get the chance to roll out a real tank through the woods, fields and hedgerows of this piece of Germany's National Park heritage, they'll be relying on Sennelager's vast array of computers to prepare them for any 'hands-on' experience.

Being a 'tankie' is a very special kind of soldiering. Tanks are essentially big mobile guns. The fact that they have human beings inside them seems almost incidental. There's a sinister robotic blankness, an inhuman anonymity when a tank lumbers into view. It's a strange, metal military beast, with one aim – to smash over everything and wreak maximum destruction. When it comes to training for tank warfare, Sennelager leads the way. Of all the NATO forces stationed in Germany, STC is regarded as the apex of military training, and has been used by forces other than the British, such as Germany's own Bundeswehr.

A Battle Group is based on either a regiment or a battalion, and can be defined as a force which is comprised of a mix of infantry in armoured vehicles together with tanks. For support it has field artillery, and the whole show is usually commanded by a Lieutenant-Colonel.

At Sennelager, armed with some amazingly versatile technology, Lieutenant Colonel Martin Bacon commands a virtual environment where soldiers can be taken through every kind of tank and artillery exercise without leaving the huge virtual battle group building. In the age of games consoles, this is electronic heaven.

Martin Bacon is a lively, compact man and, as one would expect, very articulate when presenting the details of his command. He's come a long way through the ranks – with a six-month spell at Sandhurst en route – since joining up at the age of 19 in 1973 as a mere private. He's a busy man and can't spare too much time, yet he packs a lot in.

'I'm running a system that is a networked grouping of simulators that represents the weapons systems that a Battle Group would find in the field. I have tank simulators, armoured vehicle simulators, Royal Artillery simulators which represent the command and control vehicles they use and what we call generic vehicle simulators, which represent the whole range of weapons systems or support systems such as bridge layers, armoured reconnaissance vehicles, attack helicopters and general-purpose helicopters. I can create an environment where a Battle Group trains with all the support they could expect for real in the field. This training takes place in a virtual environment, into which I can pull up databases which are based on towns in Germany. So we have people here who are "driving" tanks towards "enemies" around the Paderborn area. It's not a "game" as such, but it is a very sophisticated computer exercise. It's based on an American system called Close Combat Tactical Training. However, it must be realised that although simulation is very effective, it can never replace live training. You cannot recreate the friction of driving in the dark, being lost with 40 vehicles behind you, trying to turn around in an enclosed space; you can't replicate the danger, or having to get out of your armoured vehicle to replenish it – put petrol in – at two in the morning, and if you don't shut the hatch properly when you get back in you could cut your fingers off. The sheer danger of firing live ammunition can't be replicated in a simulator because it's not real. But you can improve your drills and procedures so that the next time you go into the field you can be more effective in exercises. But given the fact that training today in a live environment is difficult, we need to use simulation more carefully. There have been changes since the 1980s. I can remember, along with my colleagues, coming over to Germany to be based here and going out on large exercises where we would leave our barracks at short notice and go into the field for many weeks. We would train over the German countryside and would dig in and create defensive positions, in woods and ancient villages. We would practise attacks, damaging crops and generally quite upsetting the German people. We were able to do live training up to a quite high level where generals could practise moving their formations around the German countryside. But since the Wall has fallen and the Russian Army has departed, that type of training is no longer possible in Germany.'

Lieutenant-Colonel Bacon is an infantry officer and, surprisingly, he claims not to have had any particular computer technology experience before taking on this all-new facility. He sees his military experience, his work in the Army's project-management planning and his lack of previous technical duties as advantages which have assisted him in tackling this technical environment.

'It's helped me to focus on the issues, and not get distracted by some of the hype which goes on surrounding technology. I wasn't worried about the technical intricacies – I wanted to know how all the elements here could be brought together to make this system work. I'm basically supplying a product. If a component breaks down I have to be able to grasp what the problem is. I've achieved this, and as I hope you'll see, the system works . . . last week we had the Americans in here, this week it's the Germans and the Dutch. That's the great thing about being here in Europe – we're a truly international operation.'

Before being led on my fascinating tour of this military wonderland, I decided to get Lieutenant-Colonel Bacon's views on the way this new Army environment compares to that which he entered in 1973.

'I think when people today talk about equal opportunities then yes – we can do it. The opportunities are there. They may have been there in my early days, but perhaps I wasn't particularly aware of them. The year of officer training I underwent was made easier after that six-month grounding I got at Sandhurst.

'It was tough at Sandhurst – physically and otherwise. I think today's Army is more relaxed, more open, but you have to remember that back in the '70s it was twice the size. I haven't been near recruit training for quite a while, but I can answer for collective training and say that although training might not be as robust as it once was, today's Army requires a good degree of self-motivation and self-discipline and if you don't have this you're not going to fit in. If you're not going to turn up for work on time then you shouldn't be in the job in the first place. If you consider the level of sophistication which you'll see in this building you'll see that we expect our soldiers to operate with significantly complicated kit, more advanced than anything our forebears had to handle. They were often given appalling equipment – for instance, the British soldier's helmet design in the Second World War had hardly altered since Agincourt – but now we have proper, decent equipment which fits. I can remember when I joined we still had that Second World War helmet, slightly amended – but once you started moving around it used to jiggle up and down. A lot of people have gone into these problems and we've had improvements. Of course, today we're an expensive army, but perhaps that's why we've gone from a quarter of a million in my time to 100,000.'

Simon Tanner has been in the Army for 25 years. He's a pilot by trade, tall, no-nonsense, articulate, and extremely proud to be serving under Lieutenant-Colonel Bacon in the Battle Group Simulator unit. He was probably the best man at Sennelager to give me a guided tour around this fascinating complex. Entering the nerve centre, the main computer room, immediately brought to mind Stanley Kubrick's film, *Dr. Strangelove*, and those hilarious lengthy scenes in the US president's centre of operations, the 'War Room'. In particular I thought of that classic line in the movie where Peter Sellers tells the squabbling diplomats and military hawks: 'Gentlemen! This is the War Room – you can't fight in here!' The truth is, in Sennelager's version of the War Room, you can fight, and on a grand scale. I was shown an almost CinemaScope-sized bank of linked TV monitors upon which the rolling landscape of the Sennelager range was laid out before us in vibrant colour. Serious young camouflage-clad soldiers were sitting at their control stations behind keyboards and joysticks, guiding various realistic tanks through swathes of forest, hiding them behind hills and ambushing imaginary cyberspace enemies. All that seemed to be missing here was Captain Kirk and some pointy-eared Vulcans. Anything can be brought up on these screens. There is even a desert database for training 'tankies' for a hotter, dustier battle than the fresh green German vista on today's menu. The amount of information I received in the 20 or so minutes I spent in this huge room was mind-boggling, and would be to the reader if I tried to reinterpret it all here. Suffice it to say that every possible heavy armoured battle scenario you could face in reality can be simulated behind closed doors in Sennelager. Offence, defence, delay, advance to contact, obstacle crossing, attack on enemy position – all these can be refined to the point where, once seated in his multi-million-pound *real* tank, the soldier on exercise will feel that he's already had months of experience behind the wheel and the gun sight long before donning his helmet. In financial terms, as my guide explained, for the taxpayer, the £330 million-plus spent on this complex is money well spent. If we spent £330 million on tanks alone we wouldn't get too many for our money. So rather than wear out or damage the fleet we do have on actual exercises in the field, it makes more sense for soldiers to spend much of their tank training in this building before being let loose on the land in expensive hardware.

We moved from this flickering cinema of battle technology into the actual simulator hangar. In this vast, cavernous, ultra-modern building with its clean concrete floors and miles of air conditioning ducts, I had imagined I would see mock-ups of tanks and armoured vehicles. So I was a little taken aback when there stretched before me a series of uniformly sized buff-coloured windowless steel boxes, each about the size of a generously proportioned garden shed.

Once inside one of these, however, all the claustrophobic reality of real tank warfare takes your breath away, and makes a man far past his prime joyful that he's never had to fight a war and will never be called upon to do so. The interiors of these boxes are exact replicas of the insides of Challenger tanks and Warrior Armoured fighting vehicles. Everything in the computer centre is relayed into these machines so that battles can be fought and manoeuvres experienced visually through screens and through the sights of these vehicles, all coordinated from that central room I had just left.

I'm not the thinnest of men and was amazed at the small, restrictive driving seat a tankie has to put up with. According to my guide, Simon, 'That's why tank drivers are generally smaller guys. I couldn't fit into one, either.'

The reality factors include climate changes – so if it's raining, you can hear the rain splashing down on the metal hull around you. All the engine noises and vibrations are here: put your foot down and you'll feel and hear all the gear changes. If an enemy opens up with a machine gun, you'll feel the rapid 'ping-ping' of bullets as they ricochet off your turret. Firing off 300 rounds of live ammo, even on an exercise, is very expensive. In one of these simulators, with its replica 120-mm armament, you can achieve the same effect without wounding the taxpayer. Apart from the tank and Warrior simulators, there were 16 'Generic Vehicle Simulators' which could undergo 14 variations of conversion for training purposes, turning them into anything from attack helicopters to bridge-layers. I imagined what it must be like for a modern lad in his late teens, brought up on video games and *Terminator* movies, who might join up and be posted here. This would be heaven – and they pay, clothe and feed you. Sure enough, you might be asked to do all this for real at any time, but at least you'll have had some fun in preparing to face the true dangers of combat.

When I left Sennelager it was dark. The camp pub was open, the sports club was busy and a large detachment of Dutch soldiers was just arriving, probably for their own few weeks of virtual battle. As I drove past the ranks of trees and out through the gates into civilian German life again, the past couple of hours seemed imagined rather than real. All the visions I'd had of square-bashing, bellowing RSMs and repetitious bull had faded away.

In need of refreshment, I pulled up at a bar in Paderborn. Inside it was quiet, apart from three British privates who were chatting over a beer close by. It was obvious to them that I was British, but assessing me physically and in terms of age they soon realised I wasn't off-duty brass, so we struck up a conversation. I discovered that they were all 'singlies' – unmarried soldiers. Once they'd learned what I was up to, they were very guarded at first. They didn't want 'any of this getting back' and it was easy to see that their spokesman was choosing his words carefully. Tom was from Cheshire, he'd been in for three years and, like his comrades, had few reservations about Army life.

'I had a chance to go into my uncle's plumbing business, but I thought, yeah, good trade and all that, but do I really want to be driving a white van to Birkenhead and back every day for the rest of my life to clean some old biddy's S-bend out? Not much. A couple of guys I'd been to school with had joined up and when they came home on leave they seemed more confident and more "grown up" than the nerds I was knocking about with. So I thought I'd give it a try, and I don't regret it. The way I see it you have a choice. You can just do as you're told – and that's what soldiering's about – and keep your head down, or you can throw yourself into the job and make something of it. So, if there's a course or some way of improving myself, I go on it. Being a singlie based out here can be a bit frustrating at times because at least the married guys have a bit of a domestic life outside of soldiering. There's a limit to how much boozing and leg-over you can get up to –'

At this point the other two burst out laughing. Kevin, from St Albans, shook his head. 'Bollocks – you can't get enough of that!'

Tom nodded and continued. 'And you can't really make lots of plans for the future because in Army life anything can happen – for instance, there's a good chance we could be off to the Gulf any time. But if you look at some of the guys who've joined up and stuck at it for ten, twenty years, they're basically happy or they'd have got out.'

It seemed a facile thing to say, but I had to mention the fact that being in the forces meant that you could well get killed.

Rob, from Andover, shrugged his shoulders. 'So? We're basically trained to stay alive – and I've got no intention of letting some towelhead pick me off. You're just as likely to cop it on the M25, or from some mad bastard blowing your plane up when you're off on holiday. At least we've got guns and we get to use 'em.'

Terms like 'towelhead' for Arabs immediately take you back to the Second World War and the American slang for German people: 'krauts'. The rough and ready lingua franca of the soldier still smacks of the old days of empire. We may not hear the terms 'wog', 'wop' or 'dago' any longer, but it seems that every generation of warrior will find a new name for his faceless enemy.

I wondered how the lives of these men back home might have panned out had they not become soldiers.

Kevin's response seemed to make it clear that he'd made the right decision. 'I had three good mates at school and we were right old tearaways. But we never had much money and only two of us got proper jobs. I'd thought of working in McDonald's at one time, but although I don't mind eating their burgers, the thought of having to serve them to people I'd been at school with soon made a difference. I went on a couple of IT courses run by the Job Centre – what a joke. Two of my mates got into drugs. One's doing time and the other's a junkie. The other got three good A-levels and you know where he is? Stacking shelves at Tesco's. Well, fuck that. I've got a uniform, three square meals, good mates, and I'm doing something worthwhile, and if somebody in Baghdad or Kosovo or somewhere else gets stroppy, then I'll be one of the lads sent to sort them out.'

As I drove back to Herford the gung-ho confidence of those three young men stayed with me. Perhaps that's what they call the British soldier's 'fighting spirit'. It made me realise just what a different culture I inhabited as a civilian.

It was a brilliant, sunlit morning as I pulled out of Herford to head for the E30 autobahn and my ultimate destination, Berlin. It was still very early, not yet 7 a.m., and the rolling fields and woods of Bückerberg in the Wesbergland Naturpark were dusted with an icing-sugar coating of sharp frost. Over lush valleys the orange sun glinted through banks of rolling mist onto the fast-moving BMWs, Volkswagens and Mercedes which sped past me, even though I had my foot to the Vauxhall Vectra's floor. I tried to imagine the struggle and horror this pristine panorama had undergone as the Third Reich began to fall apart. Along these roads the convoy of military history had always rolled, first east, then west. This was still a dreamscape of extremes, of dark memories behind beautiful towns and villages, picturesque houses, busy farms. It still felt rather odd that over there, perhaps behind that wood, or beyond bustling towns with names such as Minden and Bad Oeyenhausen, or in the urban sprawl of Hanover, little enclaves of military Britain had existed, complete with their pub, school, church and post office. In the 60 years since the last black SS uniform was mothballed or thrown onto history's bonfire, both Britain and Germany have changed so much. Yet it has been here, over those six decades, throughout the uneasy peace of Cold War, just a few hours away from home, that many thousands of ordinary British men and women, either voluntarily or through conscription, have had their limited vista of the world broadened and embellished. To those men at the start of this book, whose acute memories have so helped to demonstrate how far Germany has come, and how important our part has been in that transformation, I offer my heartfelt thanks.

There ought to be some lucid quotation from Shakespeare to encapsulate all this, yet there is a simpler philosophy from other men, like the British and the Germans – warriors in their time. There is an old Sioux proverb: 'Before I judge my neighbour, let me walk a mile in his moccasins.'

The Allies were right to be magnanimous in their victory in 1945. Walking that mile in Germany has been all the better for it. From enemies to friends isn't a bad journey to make, and in Germany, we've made it in style.

Notes

INTRODUCTION

[1] Thayer, George, *The Arms Business*, Simon & Schuster, New York, 1970
[2] Warren Howe, Russell, *Weapons*, Abacus, London, 1981
[3] *Ibid.*
[4] Clipping from an unspecified UK newspaper available at www.brixmis.co.uk/images/incident.jpg
[5] The Territorial Army, which was previously a collection of volunteer militias to protect the mainland against invasion, was formed as a result of the Haldane reforms of 1907 (Richard Haldane, 1st Viscount Haldane, 1856–1928). By 1939 the TA numbered 204,000 officers and men, and more than doubled by August that year to 480,000. In 1967, still a volunteer force, it was drastically reduced to an internal security force to become the Territorial and Army Volunteer Reserve (TAVR) numbering some 50,000 men (Barnett, Corelli, *Britain and Her Army 1509–1970*, Penguin, London, 1974). Today it forms a very important part of the British Army's overall manpower.
[6] *Stars & Stripes*, 24 March 1985

CHAPTER 1

[1] Elliott, B.J., *Western Europe After Hitler*, Longman, London, 1970
[2] 'Words like "nation" and "Fatherland" are still suffering from the encumbrance of National Socialism.' Marsh, David, *The Germans: Rich, Bothered and Divided*, Century Hutchinson, London, 1989
[3] Royle, Trevor, *National Service: The Best Years of Their Lives*, Andre Deutsch, London, 2002
[4] Saville, John, *The Labour Movement in Britain*, Faber & Faber, London, 1988
[5] *Ibid.*
[6] Lale Andersen, 1910–72. Her story, plus that of *Lili Marlene* is included in my chapter on entertainment.
[7] Donnison, D.V., *Housing Policy Since The War*, Codicote Press, London, 1960
[8] Foot, Michael, *Aneurin Bevan, A Biography Vol. II 1945–1960*, Davis Poynter, 1973 (quoted also in Hennessy, Peter, *Never Again, Britain 1945–51*, Jonathan Cape, London, 1992). 'Nye' was Aneurin Bevan's popular nickname in both the Commons and the press.
[9] Lewis, Michael, *The Navy of Britain*, Allen & Unwin, London, 1948
[10] Gardner, Juliet & Wenborn, Neil (eds), *The History Today Companion to British History*, Collins & Brown, London, 1995

CHAPTER 2

[1] Anon (Foreword by Field Marshal Viscount Montgomery of Alamein, KG, GSB, DSO), *6*, Ward Lock, London, 1954
[2] Morris, Terry and Murphy, Derrick, *Europe 1870–1991*, Flagship History Series, Collins Educational, London, 2000

CHAPTER 3

[1] Beevor, Antony, *Inside The British Army*, Chatto & Windus, London, 1990

CHAPTER 4

[1] *The Mendener,* newsletter of 50 Missile Club, issue 4, volume 4, December 2002
[2] *British Forces Germany: Fact Finder,* MOD leaflet, 2002
[3] *Daily Telegraph,* 9 February 2003
[4] *Guardian,* 23 May 2002, 'Women Still Barred from Frontline Military Duties'
[5] 'UK Military to Offer Equal Benefits to Same-Sex Spouses', *Observer,* 14 August, 2001
[6] Timofei Byelo, *Pravda,* 30 April 2001
[7] Frey, Sylvia, *The British Soldier in America,* University of Texas, 1981
[8] *Sunday Telegraph,* 1 February 2002

CHAPTER 5

[1] Berlin was isolated during the cold war as an Allied island in the midst of Soviet territory. An agreement was reached that, for the Allies to have access to Berlin, a 'corridor' would run from the border of the British sector of West Germany to Berlin. This basically followed the railway line from Helmstedt, east of Braunschweig, direct into Charlottenburg in Berlin. Air traffic followed this route, and it was forbidden for any Allied traveller to leave the military trains along it.

CHAPTER 6

[1] Read, Anthony and Fisher, David, *Berlin Rising: The Biography of A City*, Norton, New York, 1994
[2] *Der Tagesspiegel,* 18 August 1961
[3] *Ibid.*
[4] Hildebrandt, Rainer, *German Post War History in Selected Articles 1949–1993,* Verlag Haus am Checkpoint Charlie, 2002
[5] Hilton, Christopher, *The Wall: The People's Story*, Sutton Publishing, Stroud, 2001
[6] *Der Tagesspiegel,* 12 September 1961
[7] Hildebrandt, Alexandra, *The Wall: Figures & Facts,* Verlag Haus am Checkpoint Charlie, 2002
[8] *Ibid.*
[9] Andrew, Christopher, and Gordievsky, Oleg, *KGB: The Inside Story,* Harper Collins, London, 1990

CHAPTER 7

[1] Speer, Albert *Spandau: The Secret Diaries,* Weidenfeld & Nicolson, London, 2000
[2] Sentences/dates: *Encyclopaedia Britannica* and Snyder, Louis L., *Encyclopaedia of the Third Reich,* McGraw-Hill, London, 1976

~ Notes ~

3   Wright, Michael (ed), *The World At Arms*, Readers Digest, London, 1989
4   Speer, Albert *Spandau: The Secret Diaries*
5   Thomas, Hugh *SS-1: The Unlikely Death of Heinrich Himmler*, Fourth Estate London, 2001. Other titles by Dr Thomas include *The Murder of Rudolf Hess*, *Hess: A Tale of Two Murders* and *Doppelgangers*.

CHAPTER 8

1   Miller, Harry, *Service to The Services,* Newman Neame, London, 1971
2   Not everyone regarded Gracie Fields as entertainment. Refer to any of Spike Milligan's war memoirs, such as *Mussolini: His Part in My Downfall* (Penguin, London, 1980) for further enlightenment.
3   Reimann, Viktor, *Josef Goebbels: The Man Who Created Hitler*, Sphere Books, London, 1979
4   Hardy, Phil, and Laing, Dave, *The Faber Companion to 20th Century Popular Music*, Faber and Faber, London, 1990
5   AFN Europe – History: www.usarmygermany.com
     see also www.afnurope.army.mil
6   Grace, Alan, *The Link With Home – And The Germans Listened In,* Allied Museum, Berlin, 2001
7   *Ibid.*
8   The British in Berlin would not reap the full benefits of British Forces Broadcasting via their own independent transmitter until 1961.
9   Grace, Alan, *This Is The British Forces Network: The Story of Forces Broadcasting in Germany*, Sutton Publishing/Services Sound & Vision Corporation, Stroud, 1996.
10   *Ibid.*
11   www.usarmygermany.com
12   Rees, Dafydd, Lazell, Barry & Osborne, Roger (eds.), *The Complete New Musical Express Singles Charts*, Boxtree, London, 1995

CHAPTER 9

1   Sutler: the word is derived from the Dutch term '*soetelen*' (to befoul).
2   Barnett, Corelli, *Britain and Her Army*, Penguin Books, London, 1974
3   Gardiner, Juliet and Wenborn, Neil, T*he History Today Companion to British History*, Collins, Brown, London, 1995
4   Miller, Harry, *Service to The Services – The Story of the NAAFI*, Newman Neame, London, 1971
5   Ibid.
6   'Go and Get It Season at HQ', *Keynotes*, 13 September 1958

CHAPTER 10

1   *Times*, 24 January 2003
2   Bainton, Roy, *The Soldier's Soldier*, cover feature, *Saga* Magazine, June 2000

CHAPTER 11

1   Hesse, Klaus and Springer, Phillip, *Vor aller Augen*, Klartext Verlag, Essen, 2002
2   Grimm, Stephan, *Zweiter Weltkrieg in Gütersloh,* Stadtarchiv, Gütersloh, 2000
3   Lewis, Gerry *Flugplatz Gütersloh* 1937–87, publisher unknown and currently out of print, but see Annotated Aviation Bibliography at www.geocities.com/sturmvogel_66/ItalyBib.html
4   A *Richtfest* can be compared to the British builder's 'topping out' ceremony once the major framework of a building has been achieved, or the top storey

completed. In Germany this rather happy tradition, with its beer and food, is still adhered to throughout the building industry.

5   Joyce, Eric, *Arms And The Man: Renewing the Armed Services,* Fabian Society, London, August 1997.
6   *Hansard,* 9 December 1998, Column 296, available at UK Parliament at www.parliament.the-stationery-office.co.uk
7   *Sunday Telegraph,* 12 December 1997
8   *Hansard,* 9 December 1998, column 296
9   *Ibid.,* column 297
10   *Ibid.,* column 475

Bibliography

Armstrong, David and Goldstein, Erik, *The End of The Cold War,* Frank Cass, London, 1990

Barnett, Corelli, *Britain and Her Army 1509–1970*, Pelican, London, 1974

Beevor, Antony, *Inside The British Army,* Chatto & Windus, London, 1990

Briggs, As and Clavin, Patrick, *Modern Europe – A History 1789-1989,* Longman, Harlow, 1997

Davis, Brian L., *NATO Forces,* Blandford, 1998

Dockrill, Michael, *British Defence Since 1945,* Blackwell, Oxford, 1988

Freedman, Lawrence, *The Cold War,* Cassell, London, 2001

Gibbons, S.R., *A Handbook of Modern History,* Longman, London, 1986

Grace, Alan, *This Is The British Forces Network: The Story of Forces Broadcasting in Germany,* Sutton Publishing, Stroud, 1996

Hawkes, Nigel (ed.), *Tearing Down The Curtain: The People's Revolution in Eastern Europe,* The Observer /Hodder & Stoughton, London, 1990

Hesse, Klaus and Springer, Phillip *Vor aller Augen,* Klartext Verlag Essen, 2002

Hildebrandt, Alexandra, *The Wall: Figures, Facts,* Verlag Haus am Checkpoint Charlie, 2002

Hildebrandt, Rainer, *German Post-War History in Selected Articles 1949–93,* Verlag Haus am Checkpoint Charlie, 2002

Hildebrandt, Rainer, *It Happened At The Wall,* Verlag Haus am Checkpoint Charlie, 2000

Hill, Christopher, *The Wall: The People's Story,* Sutton Publishing, Stroud, 2001

James, Peter (ed.), *Modern Germany, Politics, Society & Culture,* Routledge, London, 1998

Marsh, David, *The Germans: Rich, Bothered and Divided,* Century Hutchinson, London, 1989

Miller, Harry *Service To The Services: The Story of NAAFI,* Newman Neame, London, 1971

Morris, Terry and Murphy, Derrick (eds), *Europe 1870–1991,* Flagship History Series, HarperCollins, London, 2000

Prittie, Terence, *My Germans 1933-1983,* Wolff, London, 1983

Royle, Trevor, *National service: The Best Years of Their Lives,* Andre Deutsch, London, 2002

Rürop, Reinhard, *Berlin 1945,* Verlag Willmuth Arenhövel, Berlin, 1995

Rürop, Reinhard, *Topography of Terror,* Verlag Willmuth Arenhövel, Berlin 12th Edition, 2002

Schültz, Carl, *The British Army of the Rhine*, Widrowe & Greene, London, 1995

Stern, James, *The Hidden Damage*, Chelsea Press, London, 1990

Thomas, Hugh, *SS-1 The Unlikely Death of Heinrich Himmler,* Fourth Estate London, 2001

Trotnow, Dr Helmut, *Every Object Tells A Story*, The Allied Museum, Berlin, 1996

Trotnow, Dr Helmut, *Past and Present: 50 Mementoes recall The Western Allied Presence in Berlin 1945–1994,* The Allied Museum, Berlin, 1996

Trotnow, Dr Helmut, *An Allied Museum for Berlin*, The Allied Museum, Berlin, 1995

Weiss, Florian (ed.), *The Link With Home: And The Germans Listened In,* Allied Museum, Berlin, 2001

Wood, Anthony, *Europe 1815–1960,* Longman, Harlow, 1996

Timeline

1945

Soviet and US forces meet at the River Elbe. The Russians take Berlin.

Admiral Doenitz briefly becomes leader of the Third Reich after Adolf Hitler commits suicide. Germany surrenders. Austria and Germany become zones occupied by the Allies. The Potsdam Conference imposes strict controls on post war Germany. The UN (United Nations) is established.

In Britain, Clement Attlee is elected prime minister in the Labour election victory.

1946

Troops remain in Germany as the four Allied zones become established, British, French, Russian and American. British government lays plans for the welfare state and nationalises the coal industry.

1947

The National Service Act is passed making 12 months' military service compulsory for all males over 18.

1948

The Russians blockade Berlin, leading to the Berlin Airlift which keeps the city supplied with food and essential materials.

1949

Federal Republic of Germany is established, with its capital in Bonn. In the east, the Soviets establish the German Democratic Republic.

The USSR tests an atomic bomb. NATO (North Atlantic Treaty Organisation) is established.

1950

National Service increased to two years. In Britain, soap and petrol rationing ends.

1951

West Germany is admitted to the Council of Europe. Britain tests an atom bomb in the Pacific. In Britain, the Conservatives win the election; Winston Churchill becomes prime minister.

1952

George VI dies of cancer aged 56. Elizabeth II becomes queen. The first pop charts for single records appear in the *New Musical Express*.

1953

Konrad Adenaur is re-elected as chancellor of West Germany.
   The Coronation of Elizabeth II. Churchill suffers a stroke; later in the year he receives the Nobel Prize for Literature. After 14 years, sugar rationing ends in the UK. Joseph Stalin dies. Nikita Khrushchev takes over as first secretary of the Communist Party of the Soviet Union.

1954

Food rationing comes to an end in Britain. President Nasser of Egypt asks for British troops to pull out of Suez: Britain agrees.

1955

West Germany joins NATO and Allied occupation troops begin to withdraw from the country, but leaving established bases throughout Germany as part of their commitment to NATO. The communist countries of Eastern Europe form the Warsaw Pact with the Soviet Union.

1956

An anti-communist uprising in Hungary is crushed by Soviet troops. The Egyptians nationalise the Suez Canal, resulting in a full-scale intervention by 8,000 British and French troops.

~ Timeline ~

1957 West Germany joins France, Italy, Belgium and the Netherlands to sign the Treaty of Rome, establishing the EEC (European Economic Community) or 'common market'. Harold Macmillan becomes British prime minister.

1958
Nikita Khrushchev becomes Soviet Premier. In Britain, rock 'n' roll and the Teddy Boy culture begin to spread.

1959
Macmillan visits Khrushchev in Russia. Macmillan's Tory party sweep back to power under the slogan 'You've never had it so good'.

1960
The USSR shoots down an American U2 spy plane and capture the pilot.

1961
The Soviets build a wall across the divided city of Berlin. John F. Kennedy becomes president of the USA.

1962
Disarmament conference starts in Geneva. Britain explodes a nuclear bomb.

1963
France vetoes Britain's entry into the Common Market. Britain, the USA and USSR sign a nuclear test ban treaty restricting tests to underground only.

1964
Khrushchev is deposed in the USSR. Leonid Brezhnev becomes first secretary with Alexei Kosygin as prime minister. In Britain, Harold Wilson is elected prime minister.

1965
Winston Churchill dies.

1966
France withdraws from NATO.

1967

EEC becomes the Economic Community (EC). Britain applies to join: again, France vetoes the application.

1968

Soviets put down the Prague uprising in Czechoslovakia. Massive student unrest throughout West Germany and France.

1969

Willy Brandt becomes chancellor of West Germany.

1970

Strategic Arms Limitation Treaty (SALT) talks take place in Helsinki.

1971

Austria's Kurt Waldheim becomes secretary general of the United Nations.

1972

Britain joins the EEC.

1973

British prime minister Edward Heath declares a state of emergency and a three-day week is established due to continuing industrial unrest.

1974

Labour wins the election with a small majority.

1975

Discussions between NATO and Warsaw pact – the Helsinki accords on peace and human rights. Britain becomes an oil-producing country.

1976

Members of the EC sign an agreement to set up a European Parliament.

Harold Wilson resigns as prime minister, succeeded by James Callaghan.

~ Timeline ~

1977

Roy Jenkins becomes first president of the EEC Commission.

1978

In Britain, a series of strikes results in 'the winter of discontent'.

1979

Margaret Thatcher elected as first woman prime minister.

1980

Polish shipyard workers led by Lech Walesa form Solidarity union.

1981

Martial law declared in Poland.

1982

Helmut Kohl becomes chancellor of West Germany. The Falklands War breaks out between Britain and Argentina.

1983

Yuri Andropov becomes president of the USSR.

1984

Konstantin Chernenko becomes Soviet president.

1985

Mikhail Gorbachov becomes general secretary of the Communist Party

1986

Nuclear accident at Chernobyl in the Ukraine produces radioactive cloud over Europe.

1987

Gorbachov announces his policies of glasnost (openness) and perestroika (restructuring)

1988

USA and USSR agree to a limitation of missile numbers in Europe under the Intermediate Range Nuclear Forces Treaty

1989

Following huge protests in East Germany the Berlin Wall is dismantled.

The Cold War is over.

Websites

Just about every regiment that served in Germany has a regimental association and most of these have their own website. However, for a good overview of these and as a suitable starting point for links to sites, try:
www.militaryworld.com/Armedforces

For British forces in Germany:
www.bfgnet.de/sceweb
Berlin:
www.brixmis.co.uk

Other general websites referring to British forces in Germany:
www.dailysoft.com/berlinwall/memories/
www.cnn.com/SPECIALS/coldwar/
www.britains-smallwars.com/coldwar/BAOR.com
www.naafi.co.uk
www.sixth-sense.co.uk
www.soldiermagazine.co.uk
www.ssvc.com
www.50missileclubra.com
Public Records Office, Kew: www.pro.gov.uk
Imperial War Museum: www.iwm.org.uk